HABERMAS AND THEOLOGY

How can the world's religious traditions debate within the public sphere? In this book Nicholas Adams shows the importance of Habermas' approaches to this question. The full range of Habermas' work is considered, with detailed commentary on the more difficult texts. Adams energetically rebuts some of Habermas' arguments, particularly those which postulate the irrationality or stability of religious thought. Members of different religious traditions need to understand their own ethical positions as part of a process of development involving continuing disagreements rather than as a stable unchanging morality. Public debate additionally requires learning each other's patterns of disagreement. Adams argues that instead of suspending their deep reasoning to facilitate debate, as Habermas suggests, religious traditions must make their reasoning public, and that 'scriptural reasoning' is a possible model for this. Habermas overestimates the stability of religious traditions. This book offers a more realistic assessment of the difficulties and opportunities they face.

NICHOLAS ADAMS is Lecturer in Theology and Ethics at the University of Edinburgh. He has contributed to *Fields of Faith* (2005) and *The Cambridge Companion to Karl Rahner* (2005). This is his first book.

HABERMAS AND THEOLOGY

NICHOLAS ADAMS

CAMBRIDGE
UNIVERSITY PRESS

CAMBRIDGE UNIVERSITY PRESS
Cambridge, New York, Melbourne, Madrid, Cape Town, Singapore, São Paulo

Cambridge University Press
The Edinburgh Building, Cambridge CB2 2RU, UK
Published in the United States of America by Cambridge University Press, New York

www.cambridge.org
Information on this title: www.cambridge.org/9780521681148

First published 2006

Printed in the United Kingdom at the University Press, Cambridge

A catalogue record for this book is available from the British Library

ISBN-13 978-0-521-86266-0 hardback
ISBN-10 0-521-86266-3 hardback
ISBN-13 978-0-521-68114-8 paperback
ISBN-10 0-521-68114-6 paperback

To N.L.A.L.

It is not reason that is against us, but imagination.
(John Henry Newman)

Contents

vii

Preface

My thanks to Andrew Bowie, Charles Elliott, Nicholas Lash and Julian Roberts for encouraging this study in its early days. Colleagues and students at the Universities of Cambridge and Edinburgh read drafts of chapters, and I have benefited greatly from their critical comments. The research for this book was made possible by a research fellowship at Trinity Hall, Cambridge, research leave from the University of Edinburgh, the Arts and Humanities Research Board research leave scheme and a British Academy small project grant, the latter of which facilitated periods of study in Tübingen and Heidelberg. I am particularly indebted to the staff and students at the Evangelisches Stift, Tübingen, for their kind hospitality and friendship during my stay. Finally, I must express my thanks to members of the Society for Scriptural Reasoning, especially Peter Ochs, who read and commented on the final chapter.

CHAPTER I

Religion in public

How can there be argument between members of different traditions? This is arguably the most important question in contemporary moral philosophy and theology. To be a modern person is to participate in a public sphere characterised by rival voices, dissonant worldviews and forms of life that are baffling to each other. How are they to be coordinated? Many moral questions are bound up with religious affiliation. The major traditions have different narratives rehearsing God's care for the vulnerable: the young, the old, the abandoned, the poor, the imprisoned, the enslaved, the sick, the disabled. How do these narratives inform and hinder public argumentation? This study engages with Jürgen Habermas' views on religion and theology in the context of his understanding of the modern public sphere. Habermas is an unusual atheistic and secular philosopher: he makes positive claims about religion in modern society at the same time as insisting that moral theory must be post-religious or post-traditional. He has developed a well-known theory of communicative action and a discourse ethics whose purpose is to address the question of argumentation in the public sphere. His work over fifty years can be viewed as an attempt to articulate the unity that makes it possible to hear cultural differences as a diversity of voices rather than merely as a mass of dissociated utterances that are unintelligible to each other.

Religion plays a curious role in this theory. Habermas both values it and distances himself from it. He values it as the bearer of cultural life; he distances himself from it because it claims its members with an authority that undermines human autonomy. Religion, for Habermas, is what gives members of modern societies the vital material over which they argue. Without religion there would be no values and no forms of life about which to disagree. Yet at the same time the public sphere where such argumentation takes place cannot, and must not, be claimed as territory by any one tradition. The public sphere needs to be the locus of peaceable unity, within which there can be heated conflict, rival claims and unresolved differences. For Habermas the public sphere thus cannot be 'religious' or 'traditioned', because its task is to coordinate and host all religions and traditions. Habermas sees religious thought as 'mythic' and 'metaphysical', whereas modern thought is 'rational' and 'post-metaphysical'. He has argued that only a secular forum can adequately host a diversity of sacred and post-sacred spaces.

This study is neither a defence of Habermas nor yet another critique. There are voices in theology which defend and applaud Habermas' discourse ethics, or which try to put his theory of communicative action to work as a basis for theology, but these are plainly in the minority, and have not shown themselves to be convincing beyond a narrow circle. At the same time, there are critiques from many different perspectives which cause insurmountable problems for Habermas' project. This study takes seriously Habermas' claims about the public sphere and the need for genuine argumentation (and not merely rival voices) across traditions, and tries to repair his theory where it most obviously fails. The major problem for philosophers and theologians who wish to engage Habermas' views on religion is that they are embedded in complex arguments whose principal focus is often something other than religious life and thought. The main task here is thus to reconstruct what he says about theology and religion, and to situate it in the context of his wider claims about societal development and the nature of reason. At the same time, Habermas shows no knowledge of post-liberal theology, and I try to show not merely that his approach fails to do justice to contemporary theology, but that some of his own problems can be worked through more fruitfully when investigated in a post-liberal theological context. Post-liberal theology is a relatively new phenomenon, and has lacunae of its own. The most important from the perspective of this study is its uncertainty as to how to conceive the plural public sphere while doing justice to the specificities of traditions and their patterns of worship.[1] I do not solve that problem, but attempt to develop some useful tools for addressing these concerns. My argument will be that Habermas is too positive about religion because he is too ignorant of theology, and that being more circumspect about the difference between 'mythic' and 'modern' thought removes the need for moral theory to be post-religious.

Habermas' bibliography is large, and the secondary literature is substantial even within theology. Comprehensiveness is impossible. A limited spread of essays from across Habermas' whole career is considered here, in order to show both where Habermas has remained constant and where he has changed his mind, but no attempt has been made to include all his relevant writings. Texts from his early *Theory and Practice* up to his recent *The Future of Human Nature* and *Truth and Justification* are considered. For the most part the secondary literature does not receive detailed commentary; theological engagements are generally set to one side for reasons to be rehearsed below. Some of the secondary literature is very important, however. The challenges to Habermas that are most instructive for theology come from philosophers who reconstruct Hegel's philosophy of 'ethical life' as a critique of Habermas' heavy indebtedness to Kant. These challenges are rehearsed in more detail. Habermas is read in this study as a German philosopher contributing to, and reasoning reparatively within, the German tradition from Kant to Gadamer and Adorno. Habermas famously tries to make connections between the German tradition and Anglo-American philosophy, and where this bears upon questions of religion the relevant arguments are rehearsed. The German tradition is, however, not as widely known in theology as it was a generation or so ago, and where it seems appropriate the main topics are explained: detailed knowledge of the German Idealist tradition is not presupposed.

The work of Jürgen Habermas presents challenges to contemporary philosophers and theologians alike. It poses a simple question, and makes a simple acknowledgement. His simple question is: how can there be public moral debate between members of different

---

[1] There are exceptions. For three different attempts to describe spheres of public argumentation theologically, see Welker 1995; O'Donovan 1996; Fergusson 2004.

traditions? His simple acknowledgement is: all substantial ethical commitments have their roots in religious life. Christians are able to enter moral debate with each other, despite denominational or cultural differences, because they share a tradition. This tradition is admittedly contested, fractured and sometimes divisive, to the extent that members of some denominations are forbidden by those in authority to share holy communion with members of some other denominations. However, it is precisely the schisms that reveal the authority of tradition. To have such disagreements is to acknowledge common objects of debate: scripture, sacraments, priesthood, liturgy. The public sphere that arose in Europe in the wake of the reformations was a forum of discussion and argument within the tradition of Christian life and thought. Today things are more complex. The two most significant changes to the public sphere are difficult to reconcile: the rise of voices that reject their Christian heritage, and the participation of voices from other religious traditions. There is an anti-religious rhetoric that understands its tradition as 'secular' alongside a bewildering variety of religious voices that are often not bound together by common objects of debate.

Habermas' question about argumentation and his acknowledgement of modern life's religious roots goes to the heart of contemporary moral debate. If substantial ethical positions are rooted in religious life, and if the public sphere is a forum where different religions meet together, it is difficult to know how there can be argument over matters like law, education, medicine or art. It seems that modern people are doomed merely to repeat their own traditions' positions, perhaps in each other's hearing, but without agreed criteria for judging each other's reasonings. Habermas has produced a range of theoretical work aimed at transcending tradition, in order to solve this problem. This means systematically setting aside substantial ethical positions and common objects of debate. In their stead, he has argued for agreement on procedure. Habermas' conception of a public sphere is a forum where all participants agree on *how* argumentation is to take place, and he has various arguments to support his position which will be rehearsed in later chapters. Habermas' vision of the public sphere is a place where people willingly submit their substantial ethical commitments to criticism whenever these are contested by other parties. He thus needs some model for describing the process by which such criticisms can be raised, pursued and addressed. No one tradition can claim its common objects of debate or its ethical commitments as normative for all. This model is underpinned by Habermas' theory of communicative action, and its details (and aporias) are investigated in his discourse ethics project. Those who agree with Habermas have to explain how processes are related to substantial commitments. Those who disagree with him have to offer an alternative model for coordinating discussion in the public sphere. This study ends with an attempt at such an alternative.

'Public sphere' is here being used very loosely to mean the arena within which public debates take place. Habermas began his intellectual career with a more specific historical analysis, from a Marxist perspective (Habermas 1989a). *The Structural Transformation of the Public Sphere* charts the rise and development of 'public opinion' in bourgeois society: the world of letters, coffeehouses, *salons* and *Tischgesellchaften*. It is a story about the end of feudal monarchy and the cultural dominance of the court, and the increasing power of the bourgeois trading class, whose interests were debated in new kinds of 'public' life. What is most striking about Habermas' study, given his wider interest in universal reason, is its emphasis on cultural specificity. This nicely encapsulates the problems with which he struggles in all subsequent work. The notion of public opinion – something general – is shown to have arisen in situations whose history is unique – something particular. This acknowledgement is made right at the start of his book, right at the start of his intellectual career:

We conceive [the] bourgeois public sphere as a category that is typical of an epoch. It cannot be abstracted from the unique developmental history of that 'civil society' originating in the European High Middle Ages; nor can it be transferred, idealtypically generalised, to any number of historical situations that represent formally similar constellations.

(Habermas 1989a: xvii)

In other words, the public sphere was European; and that means it was, for the most part, Christian. Is there a Middle Eastern public sphere? Is there an East Asian public sphere? Is there a Muslim public sphere? Is there a Buddhist public sphere? Strictly speaking, no. This generates further problems. The ideas of civil and criminal law, of government, of taxation, are all to some extent products of the Christian European public sphere. They have analogues in other countries, not least because of cultural exchanges forged by trade, war and colonisation, and these cultural exchanges often predate the European High Middle Ages. At the same time, however, there are significant differences. What counts as an appeal to 'tradition' in Britain or the Netherlands is heard as an appeal to 'colonisation' in, say, India or South Africa. Democracy is arguably one of the effects not only of ancient Greek political practice but, more recently, of the rise of the Franciscan order in Italy in the thirteenth and four-teenth centuries. The Franciscans modelled a transformed relation between Church authority and *popolo*, at much the same time as the trading classes began to grow in power and towns started to become cities. The centuries in question are measured by a Christian calen-dar. Presumably it will not be a simple matter to hope for democ-racy in China, for example, whose traditions include neither Greeks nor Franciscans, and it would require enormous sensitivity and cultural-historical knowledge even to imagine the characteristics of a Chinese democracy. The point of this is that even the term 'public sphere' is a problem: it refers to an arena that is Christian through and through. This study will continue to use the term to describe the public arena in which different traditions might meet and debate, but only in default of a better term. I take it that there are no tradition-neutral terms; indeed, it is the guiding argument of this book that attempts to transcend tradition *in advance* in theory need to be replaced by more modest enterprises of making sense of instances in which different traditions actually and *already* meet together in practice.

If one best understands the rise of public spheres by attending to European Christian culture, it is obvious that one needs a greatly expanded set of intellectual tools to understand their contemporary forms. Habermas himself, in his earliest work, already noted the shift from cultural debate to cultural consumption together with a changed relation between public and private life in the world of work, and the advent of mass media in the form of newspapers and then radio and television (and now the internet). One can supplement and correct Habermas' account in various ways: by doing more precise historiography, by attending to theological transformations, by doing better ethnographies of contemporary everyday practices, and so forth. The real challenge to the very idea of a public sphere, however, comes from the twin advent of secular identities and religious variety in politics. If there is no Muslim public sphere, how can we best understand public argumentation between Muslims and Christians over matters of law? How are observant Jews or devout Hindus to enter debate with partners whose Christian cultural identity is masked by claims – the more difficult the more sincere they are – to be secular?

The rise of secular self-understandings, which are largely the product of shifts within *Christian* theology in Europe, has produced significant variations in how religious identity is related to political discussion in European universities and seats of government. The presence of Anglican (but not Roman Catholic) bishops in the House of Lords in Britain, the existence of a successful Christian Democratic Party in Germany, the relative absence of theology in the French university: these all call for specific attention to cultural histories and local theological debates if one is to make sense of their contemporary meanings. The historical accounts of law, of government, of economy and so forth are largely – though not exclusively – Christian. With the rise of secular self-understandings by politicians and political theorists there is a corresponding need to rethink all these categories, and in a context where the contemporary meanings of the secular are contested within philosophy. Appeals to scripture or received doctrines cannot be made in the same ways as in the past. But in any case these ways were the object of significant disagreement from the 1200s onwards in Europe, within the Christian tradition, and there was no ideal consensus to which one might return. Rethinking the Christian tradition in secular terms is a vast undertaking, and to be modern is to confront all the problems it entails. To attempt its rethinking in a public sphere where many other religious traditions are partners in dialogue, and thus where secularism is seen explicitly as a Western threat, seems problematic many times over.

Any account of political and moral debates in Europe and North America has to do justice to the significant role played by those whose identity has been formed in synagogues, mosques and temples as well as churches. Even this little recitation of religious houses betrays a Christian perspective: Jewish identity is arguably formed in the home more than in the synagogue; Muslim worship takes place just as significantly in the workplace as in the mosque (there is no Muslim 'Sabbath'). However one tries to describe such matters, it is certain that arguments in public debate cannot be settled by appealing either to Christian authorities *or their secularised forms.* Presbyterians and Roman Catholics may not celebrate Mass together, but they can debate with each other on how to interpret 1 Corinthians 11:23–34. Such fundamental agreements make disagreement possible. This is not the case when public debate includes members of other religious traditions. One cannot appeal to Paul's epistles. Perhaps one can cast one's net wide for shared commitments. What about democracy, or freedom or human rights? Our notions of democracy are rooted in developments in the European High Middle Ages; our ideas of freedom are stamped with the mark of the American and French Revolutions; the concept of human rights has its origin in the tradition of Christian natural law. It is difficult to think of any of our noble ideals whose genealogy does not unfold in this way.

The public sphere is no longer European, and it is no longer Christian. Christianity itself is no longer European. There are Europeans and Christians participating in the public sphere, but they are numerically inferior. It is in this confused situation that Habermas asks his question: how can there be moral debate between members of different traditions? His life's work is a long and complex response to this question. His answer is simple in conception. As I have already indicated, Habermas argues that one has to identify *rules* for argumentation that transcend tradition. Without such rules, there can be only the clash of competing views, or a succession of positions that do not engage with each other. The difficulty for Habermas is specifying those rules, and showing that they are binding on all participants in debate. Habermas' strategy has been to interrogate the tradition of modern thought, which admittedly is an often Christian and sometimes Jewish tradition. Habermas has never sought a view from nowhere, and he has never argued that one can occupy a position outside any tradition whatsoever. Instead, he has argued that there is a universal 'reason' that makes possible the diversity of traditions and forms of life. Habermas willingly admits that any substantial description of this reason, and indeed any substantial ethical position at all, will inevitably and rightly be located within a tradition. At the same time, he challenges anyone to deny that there is a *unity* that makes possible *diversity*. Without such a unity, he argues, there is no diversity: only unrelated objects and events. More than this, Habermas believes that it is possible to get a theoretical purchase on this unifying reason. This is not done via claiming a God's-eye view of things. This was, he says, the 'metaphysical' approach of the late Middle Ages which sought to establish an identity between thought and world, such that knowledge was the perfect correspondence between one's ideas and reality itself. Such a view has been made impossible, he believes, since Kant's *Critique of Pure Reason* of 1781. Kant set the agenda for subsequent philosophy by showing that there are conditions for knowledge. Kant may have been unpersuasive in his attempts to identify those conditions (sense data and concepts), but no-one has successfully retreated behind Kant to a position that denies there are conditions for knowledge. Instead, one's purchase on unifying reason has, for Habermas, to be 'post-metaphysical'. It acknowledges the situatedness of all human thinking, and has no access to an absolute perspective that can judge whether one's thoughts correspond to reality. To know that one's thoughts correspond to reality would require a viewpoint external to *both* reality *and* one's thoughts. To insist in the face of this that one's thinking nonetheless corresponds to reality is dogmatism; to insist that one has no way at all of linking thought and reality is scepticism. Kant's post-metaphysical transcendental idealism was a brilliant but flawed attempt to avoid both of these extremes. Whether one follows the details of Kant's philosophy or not, all philosophy, including all moral theory, must be post-metaphysical in this sense.

Habermas' attempt to produce a post-metaphysical account of the rules of public debate is riven with aporias, like all philosophy and theology. He himself has entered vigorously into debate with his critics, and like all great thinkers, he has generously risked positive claims while his opponents have had the luxury of identifying the problems in those claims. Habermas has shown himself tirelessly willing to produce theory, and to mount theses which can be tested, in an era which shows itself worryingly content with criticism and deconstruction. Any serious engagement with Habermas surely has to produce better theory, and theses which better withstand testing. The problems Habermas identifies, and the difficulty of the question he raises about argumentation in a plural public sphere, are acute, and he has few rivals who have produced a better answer to his question. The difficulties with his own theory are overwhelming, and his theses have not withstood testing: for this reason it makes no sense to be a Habermasian. Nonetheless, the question he poses is urgent. If the changing social composition of geographical regions requires a rethinking of the public sphere, taking account of secular self-understandings and a variety of religious identities, it cannot be sufficient merely to identify the shortcomings of Habermas' theory. Better theory, or perhaps something better than theory, is required.

It is the need for better theses that presents challenges for philosophers and theologians. Habermas has made many claims about religion in his work over the last half-century, and his views have changed over time. Discussions of religious life admittedly play almost no role in *The Structural Transformation of the Public Sphere*, but his amateur interest in theology extends well back into his earliest work, for example in essays in the first edition of *Theory and Practice* (1963).[2] His engagements with theologians, especially German Roman Catholics, have sharpened his views on contemporary religious life, while also furnishing him with an attentive (and perhaps overly enthusiastic) audience for his pronouncements on the persistence of religious attitudes in modernity. Habermas' work is shot through with claims about religious belief and practice: they are part of his theory of communicative action, they are integral to his political theory, and they characterise his more meditative judgements about post-metaphysical thinking. For Habermas modern moral theory is only intelligible as a development out of (and

---

[2] I do not investigate the different kinds of public sphere today; nor do I update David Zaret's criticisms that Habermas pays too little attention to religious life in the public sphere: David Zaret, 'Religion, Science, and Printing in the Public Spheres of England', in Calhoun 1992: 212–35. This is a topic for future work.

away from) Christian doctrine, and he famously insists in both earlier and later work that religious commitments will persist as long as modern forms of life are unable to generate within themselves the same richness of motivation and identity. The challenge to theologians is that while his accounts of religion and theology are unsatisfactory, often at a rather basic level, there seem not to be any significantly superior accounts within theology of how to think about public argumentation in the plural public sphere. To anticipate some of the arguments presented here in chapter 10, most theological writing in a post-liberal vein seems to be devoted to showing how Christians should think about doctrine and ethics rather than describing how Christians might enter into debate with other participants in the public sphere. At the other extreme, most theological writing in a 'public theology' vein seems to view post-liberal positions (such as those of Stanley Hauerwas or John Milbank) as dangerously insular. Chapter 10 of this study is an excursus on narrative and argumentation. Whereas the preceding chapters are interpretations of texts by Habermas, this chapter tries to work through some of the issues raised by Habermas' hostility to narrative, and by John Milbank's hostility to argumentation. I argue that Habermas' critics are wrong to think that he is too troubled by tradition: he has far too benign a view of it. Habermas writes as if making ethical claims is relatively unproblematic within traditions, and seems to claim that the serious problems only emerge when members of different traditions try to encounter each other in the public sphere. I argue that the serious problems are already present within traditions themselves, and that Habermas' search for a theory that grounds argumentation serves no useful purpose. I also insist that while narrative and argument are distinct, they are not separate.

Habermas' question presents challenges to both these polar opposites. Post-liberals are required to give a better account of the public sphere. Advocates of 'public theology' are required, by Habermas no less, to do better theology. Habermas has insisted, especially in more recent work, that the religious traditions are the principal sources of the passions, motivations and visions of the good life that allow modern persons to flourish (Habermas 2003a: 73). He himself received a secular intellectual formation which means that he views religious traditions with a kind of alienated detachment, and this sits awkwardly but honestly with his insight that a social life devoid of the gifts of the religions would be barren and without hope.

Habermas has inspired a number of books by theologians, and his theory of communicative action has been put to work in others. Habermas' approach to religion and theology has not provoked detailed commentary in English, however, and his work has often been used without asking whether his approach to reason brings him into fundamental conflict with Christian theology. In what follows I argue that he has so many theological blind spots that using his work as a constructive partner (let alone theoretical foundation) is problematic. If the arguments presented here are well formed, it will become obvious that theologians should use Habermas to sharpen their understanding of public argumentation, but not as a theoretical underpinning for their own modern theologies. I hope to explain some of Habermas' theological problems, so that those who wish to use Habermas can see clearly the main issues they need to address. I also try to repair some of his lapses and develop some of his generative insights along Christian theological lines. This will take us into engagements with scripture.

The most comprehensive study of Habermas' approach to theology in German is Hermann Düringer's *Universal Reason and Particular Faith: A Theological Evaluation of the Work of Jürgen Habermas* (Düringer 1999). Düringer takes seriously what Habermas says about religion in the modern world, and works through Habermas' explicit remarks about the relationship between theology and philosophy. Düringer evaluates Habermas' work using theological criteria. Düringer wittily uses the Chalcedonian formula to refer to the relationship between philosophy and theology in Habermas' thought as 'unmixed' and 'unseparated'. Unlike the two natures of Christ, however, they are unmixed because Habermas never takes the perspective of a participant, only of an observer; and they are unseparated because of the mystical roots of German philosophy, and Habermas' own close engagement with that tradition via his early work on Schelling (Düringer 1999: 19–25). I take a different approach. I argue that 'religion' and 'theology' are casual victims of Habermas' remarks about tradition, despite what he says about the need to acknowledge the value of religious traditions. To

understand what Habermas says about religion, one needs to interpret his remarks in the context of his arguments about rationalisation, secularisation and public argumentation. In other words, one
treats topics that are not peculiar to theology. This is not a novel
approach: most theological readings of Habermas approach him in
this way, at least to a degree. I claim, beyond this, that in much of
his work Habermas is not really interested in religion or theology
as practices or living traditions, but sees them as powerful, sometimes dangerous, sometimes inspiring ancestors to modern self-
consciousness. They are powerful because they unify worldviews
and bind members of communities to ethical life. They are dangerous because they see critical thinking as disloyalty and threat. They
are inspiring because they enact visions of the good life. They are
ancestors because they have been overcome and transformed by the
forces of reflection which arise when members of different cultures
encounter each other and try to understand each other. On the latter
point Habermas has equivocated, as we shall see. My thesis is that
Habermas wants the power and the inspiration without the danger.
I therefore do not treat him as a serious theological partner in
dialogue. This is not out of disrespect, but out of a recognition that
his theological readers need to reconstruct his arguments and so discover that he is not talking about their religious traditions, but about
the (idealised) ancestors of (idealised) modern self-consciousness.

Habermas understands that modern self-consciousness buys its
critical abilities at a high price: an increased 'distance' from its own
traditions, and a correspondingly increased 'motivational deficit'
with respect to ethical life. Habermas' view is that the power of
religions to bind members to ethical life somehow holds the key not
just to understanding morality in the past, but to making sense of
modern motivation. He wants to prise apart the worldview-unifying
forces from the ethically binding forces. Worldviews are not unified
under modern conditions: there simply are different cultures and
different traditions. The idea that they can be unified is a mask of
violent imperialism. This is a quite different question from the
acknowledgement of a unity that makes diversity possible. That
unity is very difficult to get at, and is not the same kind of thing
as a worldview. It is best thought of more abstractly as the condition
for difference. The notion of a worldview that unifies different

cultures is an utterly different kind of thing, and is decisively to be rejected. Habermas believes that despite the lack of such a unifying worldview, members of modern societies can be bound ethically. It is not only God's power that needs to be secularised into the modern form of human autonomy, which Habermas endorses and thinks has been achieved adequately in modern societies. It is also the power of the sacred that needs to be secularised into a modern form of commitment to what he calls 'communicatively achieved consensus'. Habermas' ideal modernity is characterised by autonomy, critique and commitment, and his descriptions of religion and theology serve this end. There is obviously room for significant and noisy disagreement between theologians and Habermas on these questions, but precisely where that disagreement should fall is not as obvious as one might think. I investigate these issues in later chapters.

Theologians who hope to persuade Habermas of the goods of modern religion will succeed all too easily. He readily admits that modern religious attitudes are part of the life blood of ethical life. For Habermas, however, this is merely to state the problem. The question for him is not whether religions are bearers of substantial ethical positions, but how to 'feed on' their normative power while 'keeping one's distance' from their authoritative air (Habermas 2003a: 108–13). For this to work, Habermas has to operate with a generalised notion of 'religion', and implicitly to claim that all religions are, equally, instances of religion. This further implies a narrow view of the function of religions which for him is, circularly, their ability to furnish ethical norms and motivate their members. This is a very 'positive' view of religious life: it emphasises the beliefs and practices which are peculiar to each tradition. It is one-sided. Habermas' view of religion inhibits proper attention to the 'negative' aspects. Christian worship, for example, *both* commends certain virtues *and* calls all human practice (even, and especially, the religious) fundamentally into question and places it under divine judgement. This is not merely to acknowledge the critique of bourgeois religion with which Habermas is in any case familiar from the work of Moltmann and Metz (Habermas 2001). It is to emphasise the prohibition on *all* forms of certainty and self-satisfaction. This self-corrective dimension of trinitarian theology, which threads incarnational intelligibility with pneumatological indeterminacy and the utter obscurity of *creatio ex nihilo*, is inaudible to Habermas. Perhaps his failure to engage with contemporary post-liberal theological thinking arises because much post-liberal theology fails to engage with the questions about 'publicity' that motivate his own work.

The following chapters thus combine two separate tasks. The first is to describe Habermas' approach to religion and theology. The second is to take the basic problem he poses in his theory of 'communicative action' regarding argumentation in the public sphere, examine some critiques of it, and propose an alternative to his theory. This alternative, 'scriptural reasoning', comes from the realm of religion and theology, and connects the two tasks.

Two tasks not undertaken here are worth mentioning. I only minimally rehearse Habermas' engagements with theologians (in chapter 9), and very little space is devoted to theologians' uses of Habermas. This might seem odd, given that the subject matter is centrally concerned with Habermas and theology. There are two reasons for this. First, this has already been undertaken well by Düringer, and for reasons of space I do not repeat his arguments. Second, Habermas is not a theologian, and although the questions he raises do have a significant bearing on theology, neither he nor his theological readers have developed them theologically. This distinguishes Habermas from other philosophers whose work has had a significant impact on theology. Kant's critique of metaphysics, for example, has a family resemblance to the Christian theological insistence that language cannot adequately correspond to God; Hegel's account of mediation grows explicitly out of incarnational theology; Wittgenstein's concern with grammar has helped theologians better articulate the significance of the ways in which theological claims are made. In the cases of Kant, Hegel and Wittgenstein there have been generative theological developments of post-metaphysical theology, theologies that emphasise the philosophical implications of Christology, and sharper attentiveness to the grammar of theological practices and claims. This is not true of Habermas. Habermas has not had this kind of influence on theology, and is unlikely to have it in the future. This is because his central concern is not about the content of particular practices and claims but about how different traditions can debate and cooperate in the public sphere. It is true that Habermas has claimed that the basis for such debate and cooperation lies in the nature of 'reason' or 'language', but this claim has not persuaded even friendly critics. If it has persuaded theologians, this is a problem: it means they accept Habermas' claim that reason and language are in some sense higher than understandings of God that are rooted in particular traditions. This study is motivated by a belief that Christian theologians do need to address Habermas' concerns about how different traditions meet each other in the public sphere, and in the final chapter I attempt to do so. However, the significant philosophical influences on contemporary Christian theology which give rise to post-metaphysical theology, to renewed emphasis on trinitarian patterns and to the significance of aesthetics are not best learned from Habermas, but – within the German-speaking tradition – from Kant and Kant's critics in the traditions of anti-Enlightenment (Hamann, Herder, Jacobi), Idealism (Fichte, Schelling, Hegel), Romanticism (Schlegel, Novalis, Schleiermacher), and their successors such as Kierkegaard, Heidegger, Benjamin, Bloch, Adorno, von Balthasar and Karl Barth.

To demonstrate the basic objections Habermas mounts against theology, chapter 9 is an account of Habermas' rebuttals of the approaches of Helmut Peukert and Michael Theunissen. This is provided by way of brief illustration of the problems theologians have had in engaging Habermas, but it also affords the opportunity to show how strong Habermas' arguments against such theologians are. Habermas not only finds his theological admirers and critics mistaken about what philosophy can offer theology, but judges them to be insufficiently theological. I raise the possibility that Habermas might not make the same objections to orthodox post-liberal post-metaphysical theology.

Habermas' debates with theologians are not generative for his own project: it has remained unchanged by these encounters. At the same time, theological resonances are more audible in his work than they are in the writings of other philosophers who happen to inherit the tradition of Christian thought. This is especially true of Habermas' early work, and it is no coincidence that this is the work most cited by theologians. In chapter 2, on the ideal speech situation, I examine some of these issues in detail, and try to show Habermas' proximity to and distance from Christian eschatology. In that chapter I also rehearse the principal Hegelian objections to his project. More important than these resonances, however, is the fundamental antagonism of Habermas' project to Christian theology, as I shall show in the middle chapters of this book. Chapter 3 considers the question of authority and tradition, and explains Habermas' understanding of 'distance' and 'reflection'. This is also an opportunity to compare him with Gadamer, through an engagement with his work in *On the Logic of the Social Sciences*. Chapter 4 reconstructs Habermas' understanding of the relationship between archaic religious practice and modern motivational deficits, and focuses in particular on his *Theory of Communicative Action*. Chapter 5 rehearses Habermas' defence of universalism, and looks in particular at the role of religious thought in it. This chapter also briefly poses a Schellingian challenge to Habermas' Hegelianism. Chapter 6 narrates Habermas' early Marxist ontology of peace and draws attention to his surprisingly substantial engagement with theology. Chapter 7 enquires into the relationship between 'religious' and 'mythic' thought. Habermas tends to identify them; I try to make things more complicated. Chapter 8 examines the relationship between religions and 'metaphysical' accounts. Again, Habermas tends to identify them, and I offer an alternative account. Chapter 9 is a brief rehearsal of Habermas' principal arguments against theologians, but as he does not engage with post-liberal theology, this generates rather limited insights.

The central chapters expose problems with Habermas' view of theology and of religion. It is, however, not enough merely to register these problems. His inadequate description of religion certainly invites a better account, and his approach to tradition calls for repair. Yet his concern with the encounter of different traditions in the public sphere persists. It is a 'meta-' kind of concern, in the sense that it draws attention to problems that are not internal to a particular tradition, and not merely shared by many traditions. The problem of coordinating different traditions is genuinely general. It is not just that many traditions have a difficulty in describing the public sphere; it is that there are many traditions which need a public sphere in which to debate. In some ways, Habermas' approach is formally similar to that of Nietzsche, who understood that problems arise when different traditions encounter each other in the public sphere. There is an important difference, however. Where Nietzsche saw only external conflict between value systems and internal conflict within individuals educated in the disciplines of religious life, Habermas sees possibilities for genuine argument and not merely conflict. Like Nietzsche, Habermas confuses 'meta-' issues concerning the public sphere with questions internal to traditions, such as the question of whether peace or violence is primary, or whether language itself is a bearer of hope or is just a bearer of whatever people have learned to make it bear. Habermas, like Nietzsche, thus makes strong claims from within his tradition while trying to appear objective. Just as Nietzsche tries to make his claims about violence appear as truths about reality, so Habermas sometimes attempts to present his claims about reason as realities which transcend the particularities of tradition. The 'meta-' questions about the encounter of traditions in the public sphere are thus mingled confusingly with metaphysical questions about reason, language and nature, even if Habermas tries to accomplish this post-metaphysically. For example, as Gordon Finlayson has argued, Habermas often makes strong claims about a break between morality and ethical life that allegedly opens up as a result of changing historical and social forces, whereas this break happens primarily within Habermas' own analyses and taxonomies (Finlayson 1999: 47–8). The outcomes Habermas attributes to historical cause and effect are sometimes more plausibly interpreted as the outcomes of Habermas' way of looking at the world, of his 'metaphysics'.

Nevertheless, with patience it is possible to learn from Habermas the importance of keeping questions about the public sphere in mind when dealing with metaphysical questions, while at the same time being careful not to confuse these issues. What distinguishes Habermas from Nietzsche is the primacy of cooperation over conflict in Habermas' account, and it is on this point that theologians and philosophers have most to gain from him. Habermas' claim is admittedly a metaphysical one which cannot be resolved contemplatively. In other words, his claim about peace cannot be defended against sceptical challenge. Nonetheless, it obviously makes a difference, when 'keeping questions about the public sphere in mind', whether this sphere is described as a place of hospitality or a war zone, and here it becomes evident that the most objective-looking 'meta-' questions are inevitably posed in languages shaped by a tradition's metaphysical commitments. Even this claim is hyperbolic, of course: what one believes to be 'inevitable under all circumstances' is itself just a thesis formed under historically contingent conditions within a particular perspective. Religion is significant for Habermas precisely because it is the realm where the hyperbolic is identical with the everyday; it is where traditional aspects of human life, including commitments to peace and practices of hope, are most intensely expressed. At some deep level Habermas grasps that everyday ethical language is marked by a hyperbolic surplus over what can reasonably be established by moral theory: people's claims routinely and significantly exceed the kinds of claim that could be redeemed by Habermas' rules for discourse. He also grasps that this excessive speech is often housed in religious contexts, and that the motivations of ordinary people are formed in such environments. His response is rather quirky: he elaborates an ultra-stringent moral theory for generating moral norms, and invites religious affiliations – which remain for him 'mythic', 'metaphysical' and 'non-rational' – to do all the work of getting people committed to them. This is recognised by many of Habermas' secular critics, although they are often puzzled that Habermas can hold such a view. In chapter 4 I reconstruct Habermas' narrative of how sacred and profane are related, and show how he arrives at his idiosyncratic account; and I expose the implausibly simplistic account of Protestant theology that Habermas has in mind when thinking about religious commitments.

Habermas, like Nietzsche, thinks that religion is one of the sources of modernity's inner problems. Whereas Nietzsche in the *Genealogy of Morality* associates Christian religion with self-destructiveness, however, Habermas associates religious thinking with 'metaphysical thinking'. Metaphysical thinking, for Habermas, is the kind of philosophy that strives to acquire the God's-eye view. Habermas also associates religious thinking with 'mythic thinking'. Mythic thinking is the kind that confuses natural and human, personal and impersonal, world and worldview. Finally, Habermas associates religious thinking with a language of hope and redemption, indispensable for modern life, which has not as yet been overcome by philosophical categories. It is only this last aspect of religion that Habermas thinks can contribute positively to modern social life. In my view, religion contributes *all too positively* in his theory. Far from celebrating its elevation to the status of privileged bearer of cultural norms, theologians should be profoundly suspicious of theology's lack of social critique, and its lack of metaphysical reserve, as it appears in Habermas' work. I shall present what Habermas says about religion in these areas, explain why he says it, situate his claims and arguments in the context of his overall theory, and place obstacles in the way of his more questionable judgements. I shall show that while his claims are not false, they fail to account for modern religious thinking that is not metaphysical and not mythic in his sense.

This brings us finally to the question of what resources theology can offer to those who wish to investigate Habermas' question about argumentation between traditions in the public sphere. Habermas' concern with argumentation is relevant to current theological developments. Since the 1980s there has been a renaissance of thought focused upon the significance of narrative (Hans Frei, Stanley Hauerwas, Nicholas Lash, George Lindbeck, John Milbank, Rowan Williams). Yet at times it is difficult to give a good account of the relationship of narrative to argumentation. Is narrative an alternative to argumentation? Are they complementary? Can argumentation be pursued narratively? These are difficult and obscure questions, and go to the heart of contemporary social and political anxieties. We in the economically rich countries are getting worse at arguing: listening to the news provides mounting evidence that politicians are impatient with processes of deliberation or with the due process of law. Newspaper reporters struggle to reconstruct arguments when official press releases are brief and punchy rather than deliberative. Reporters are themselves under pressure to be brief and punchy. The judiciary in Britain increasingly finds itself saddled with the responsibility of acting as a brake on hasty and destructive legislation by Government officials, while finding their authority questioned by those same officials because British judges are unelected. This is a very dangerous situation which reveals the fragile line between democracy and mob rule. If due process is part of that fragile line, and due process is coming under increased attack because it is 'cumbersome' or 'outdated', trouble is brewing. Matters are regrettably much the same in religious life. Church leaders in my own Anglican Church publish letters against each other, to the unedifying delight of the mass media, rather than debate patiently and charitably in synod: they impatiently try to bypass process. This is not a form of unstoppable cultural decline and it is certainly not an excuse for pessimism, but it is potentially damaging to institutions in ways that, if not irrevocable, are extremely costly. In a situation where argument is under threat, it is not enough to renew a concern with narrative. The quality of theological argument is by no means automatically put in danger by a renewed appreciation of the value of narrative: in many cases it substantially raises the level of debate. Yet it needs to be tempered with a constant eye on how good argument is to be promoted in a world of narratives that are not in harmony with each other. There need to be hospitable practices for coordinating rival narratives: the hospitality has to be bigger than the rivalry. Again, this is a metaphysical claim that cannot be resolved contemplatively.

To take a view on this question is to practise a form of politics, and there is no quiet spot where one can calmly watch from the sidelines. The world of 'competition' only promotes the flourishing of difference when it is situated within a framework of hospitality and trust, as one sees in the case of competitive sports, whose appropriately fierce rivalry is housed within a 'football association' or a 'baseball league' and so forth. Habermas cannot help much with the complex task of coordinating different narratives, as we shall see. He makes too strong a separation between narrative and argument, and instead of finding ways to handle the fact that the rules for argumentation are always particular to local communities, he wastes valuable energy searching for universal rules. Nonetheless, his attention to the details of argumentation is second to none, and his quite proper concern for procedure, while worryingly unfashionable, is something from which philosophers and theologians, in particular, can learn a great deal. Theology is an arena where disagreements can be more than usually painful, because they go to the heart of understandings of who God is, and where we, God's creatures, belong. Spending time with Habermas can prove instructive, even if he does not end up teaching theologians quite the lessons he had in mind, as I hope to show. Theology in turn has the potential to model certain virtues for others in society: first by showing how narratives can peaceably inform arguments, and second by embodying a commitment to giving debates the time and charity they need in order for good judgements to be possible.

Chapter 11 offers an alternative to Habermas' theory of communicative action. This alternative is not another theory. The preceding argument will have been that promoting genuine argumentation in the public sphere does not call for theory, but attention to actual practices where such argumentation successfully and peacefully takes place. This final chapter outlines, briefly and inadequately, a new and surprising practice that has been developed in the academy and beyond in recent years: scriptural reasoning. This refers to the practice, by members of different traditions (Judaism, Christianity, Islam), of reading scripture together. They read each other's texts as sacred, and – crucially for my thesis – find ways genuinely to argue with each other rather than merely juxtapose rival narratives. The practice of scriptural reasoners places hospitality above rivalry, but does not privilege consensus above disagreement. Scriptural reasoning presupposes radical disagreement as a condition of its practice, because to do otherwise would be to promote syncretism, which is damaging for all traditions. I conclude by wondering what philosophers like Habermas would make of this practice, and suggesting that practices like scriptural reasoning are vitally needed to heal religious divisions in the public sphere.

CHAPTER 2

The ideal speech situation

The ideal speech situation is one of Habermas' best-known concepts. It is arguably the topic most cited in theological works that
consider Habermas, and it is principally for this reason that it is
treated first. Theologians also tend to appeal to the ideal speech
situation as if it were one of Habermas' most enduring contributions
to an ethics of communication. This is remarkable, as Habermas
admitted problems with the concept before he wrote *The Theory of
Communicative Action*, and it had a life of barely more than five
years in his work from the early 1970s. This chapter will explain
some of the general themes in Habermas' work and suggest how his
ideal speech situation fits into it. There are three further reasons for
considering the ideal speech situation at the start of this study,
despite its brief life. First, it encapsulates some of the difficulties
of Habermas' attempt to steer 'between Kant and Hegel'. Second, it
contains some of his most theologically suggestive language, especially that of 'anticipation': I shall consider whether this is as
eschatological as it sounds. Thirdly, given that Habermas himself
abandoned the ideal speech situation over twenty years ago – in
name and in substance – its persistence in theologians' discussions
needs explaining and challenging.

Habermas' social theory has a therapeutic goal. He aims not
merely to understand social phenomena, but to alter them for
the better. His work stands firmly in the tradition of philosophy
influenced by Marx's challenge to intellectuals: philosophers have
understood the world, in various ways; the point is to change it. To
this end, Habermas has considered a large number of topics in social
theory from child development to systems theory. His most arresting claims are that money and power in modern societies have

'colonised' the lifeworld, and the idea that the ethical substance of religious traditions has to be distilled into procedural ethical rules appropriate to post-traditional societies.

Habermas has an ambiguous view of modernity: sometimes he seems to think of it as an edifice of post-traditional rationality that is always built on traditional land; at other times he describes it as the outcome of historical processes where traditional ideas have slowly (but not yet adequately) evolved into post-traditional forms of life. He has a correspondingly ambivalent view of tradition. On the edifice-building model, traditions provide the necessary foundations for rational life. Modernity is thus a question of generating norms that transcend traditional life so that members of different traditions can negotiate with each other without having to appeal to norms that only have authority for one group. Traditions provide the complex networks of meanings that make up social life, but modern conditions provide an *additional* requirement that different traditions must be able to coordinate action at a higher level than those particular complex networks. On the evolutionary model, traditions gradually give way to later post-traditional forms, and less rational forms of life transform themselves into more rational ones. Modernity is thus a question of switching from traditional norms to post-traditional norms. In sum: for the edifice model, traditions remain themselves, but are accompanied by post-traditional structures; for the evolutionary model, traditions transform from traditional to post-traditional forms. Habermas works with both models, and has never found a way of thinking that unifies them. He can thus be rather confusing to read. For our purposes it is enough to bear in mind that when one is reading what he has to say about 'rationalisation', he is generally using an evolutionary model; when one reads his 'discourse ethics' project, he is often using an edifice model.

The best way to understand Habermas is to consider his historical and intellectual context. Habermas grew up in National Socialist Germany, undertook detailed study of German Idealism, was heavily influenced by left-wing social theory (especially that of Horkheimer and Adorno), worked through the disappointments generated within Marxism after 1968, and devoted enormous energy to building bridges between 'analytic' and 'pragmatic' Anglo-American philosophy and German 'continental' thought. Habermas works squarely within the German traditions of thought, and this needs to be borne in mind when reading his meditations on modern culture. Many of the topics that fascinate Habermas are elaborated in the philosophies of Kant and Hegel, for example. The questions to which Habermas returns again and again, such as the relationship between morality, community and freedom, are familiar topics in German philosophy. More importantly, cultural critique is an integral part of German philosophy, and this distinguishes it from much British and American thought. Somewhat unusually, even for a German philosopher, Habermas also has a knowledge of Schelling, on whom he wrote his doctoral thesis. Schelling has been very much a minority figure in the usual surveys of German philosophy, which until recently tended to leap directly from Kant to Hegel and beyond. The Habermas known to theologians tends to be the author of the *Theory of Communicative Action* rather than the commentator on German philosophy and culture: it is important to recognise that the two sides of Habermas' thinking inform each other closely.

The main topic of this study is argumentation. For Habermas, this theme informs a host of discussions. Habermas is interested in the eighteenth-century question of how different cultural traditions relate to each other; he has analysed how different kinds of public sphere emerge and develop in Europe; he has investigated the relationship between law and democracy; he has produced a theory of rationalisation; he has developed a procedural ethics. Underlying these various studies is this question: when two parties communicate with each other, how can there be genuine argumentation instead of competing exercises of violence? It is easy to see why this is an important question. The philosophical tradition from Nietzsche onwards, particularly in its French forms (Deleuze, Derrida, Foucault), has claimed to expose alleged exercises of 'reason' as masks or ruses of power. This analysis of political interests is very persuasive. It is evident that when a powerful party enters into so-called 'debate' with a weaker party, the decisive factor on the outcome is often not the strength of the arguments, but the implicit threats of the stronger party. It is in the winning party's interest for it to *appear* that the negotiation was decided by arguments, because people tend to acknowledge the authority of the outcomes of debates more than the outcomes of brute force. Even very powerful totalitarian

governments have show trials which have the appearance of following rules relating to evidence and the formation of legally binding
judgements. The problem with this analysis of power is that it
makes 'reason' disappear completely. Is it true that *all* exercises of
reason are *only* masks for ruses of power? Are *all* arguments really
only a sham which disguises what would otherwise be naked expressions of violence? There is admittedly some slippage here between
'power' and 'violence', and this is characteristic of accounts which
aim to deconstruct reason.

For Habermas this is unsatisfactory. One should be able to specify
how violence is dressed up as reason. One should be able to indicate
when this happens, and when it does not. One should be able to
diagnose the *degree* to which such masks and disguises are used. To
do this, one presupposes that there is at least an ideal of genuine
argumentation, against which actual processes can be measured. If
there is *only* violence and its masks, then even the claim that 'there is
only violence and its masks' cannot be made argumentatively: the
claim itself is just another ruse. This may indeed be true, in which
case one would have to admit that university professors dress up
their discourse as argumentation for the same reason that dictators
hold show trials: to lend their pursuit of power an air of respectability and legitimacy. Habermas rejects this analysis. He claims that
even analyses of this kind presuppose an ideal of genuine argumentation. He claims further that such a presupposed ideal is evidence
of a commitment to *rational* debate, even if it rarely (never, even)
appears in its pure form. Habermas' overarching reason for making
these claims is readily intelligible: without it, one is unable to
critique corrupt practices *as corrupt*, or exercises of disguised violence *as disguised violence*. The notions of corruption and disguised
violence apply instead to everything: if everything is corrupt and
disguised violence, then nothing is. Social critique loses its bite.

The way Habermas advances this claim changes over his career.
To begin with he is interested in the power that such an 'ideal' has:
hence the ideal speech situation. Later on, under pressure from
critics who dismiss this as 'idealism', he switches to a concern with
the power that this kind of 'presupposition' can have. He also
emphasises more strongly that his approach is a 'detranscendenta-
lised' Kantianism, by which he means an attempt to recast certain

themes in German philosophy in ways much closer to American pragmatism. This change of tack is accompanied by other shifts of vocabulary. For example, the ideal speech situation is said in early descriptions to be 'anticipated' by those who enter into argumentation; later on Habermas says merely that undistorted argumentation is more or less 'approximated' by those who presuppose its possibility. It is worth paying attention to certain consequences of this change in terminology.

Two of the claims Habermas makes about the ideal speech situation are of special interest. (1) It is an ideal, but Habermas means 'ideal' neither in Kant's nor in Hegel's sense. We shall need to probe the meaning of ideal a little. (2) The ideal is 'anticipated', but Habermas does not mean 'anticipation' in the sense Kant uses of ideals. We shall try to discover the most appropriate way to interpret this word.

What is the ideal speech situation? It is an expression of the symmetry between partners in dialogue. For Habermas, symmetry is itself an expression of peaceability, and is emblematic of a commitment to rational debate. When two parties enter into dialogue, they have a commitment to treat each other not as 'things' in the world, which they can manipulate, but as 'subjects' whose freedom to determine their own courses of action is equal. Already we can see some major themes in German philosophy. One of the major debates of the late eighteenth century concerned how to interpret human action. Are we objects embedded in a web of causation, or are we free subjects who can determine our own goals and make judgements whose outcome is not predetermined? Kant famously described the realm of natural causation in his *Critique of Pure Reason* of 1781 and the realm of free moral action in the *Critique of Practical Reason* of 1788. Obviously any moral theory that draws on Kant's accounts has to show three things: first, how free moral action has an impact on the causally determined realm of objects; second, how any account of causal relations does not contradict the freedom of human action; third, how free acts are not merely arbitrary or meaningless. This requirement is commonly known as 'the unity of reason', and it is the guiding topic of German idealism.

Habermas offers commentary on this tradition by drawing on the social theory of Max Weber, who is himself commenting on the

Kantian tradition. To treat people as objects or 'things' is to engage in 'strategic' or 'goal-oriented' action. It is to treat social relations on a model of cause and effect: to seek control over others by using one's actions as a cause in order to bring about their actions as an effect. To treat people as 'subjects' is to engage in 'communicative' action. This model is often called 'inter-subjectivity'. It is to treat social relations on a model which describes the interaction of free and autonomous agents: to persuade others to act by using arguments which the other can freely and autonomously accept or refuse. The crucial difference between strategic and communicative action lies in the role of force and the symmetry or asymmetry that holds between the parties. For strategic action it is 'rational' to use violence to achieve one's ends: one seeks an outcome, not an agreement. 'When even the dictators of today appeal to reason, they mean that they possess the most tanks. They were rational enough to build them; others should be rational enough to yield to them' (Horkheimer 1982: 28). For communicative action the only force admissible is the force of the better argument: one seeks reasoned agreement, not merely an outcome. For strategic action each party may seek an asymmetry that will favour itself, because the balance of power may determine the outcome. For communicative action both parties seek symmetry, because otherwise certain kinds of reasons may not be contributed to the conversation because of fear of sanctions, or because one's right to speak has been revoked. If reasons are suppressed, then the agreement is not adequately rational. Having established a distinction between strategic and communicative action, Habermas' reader asks: what would an exercise of communicative action look like in practice? His answer is to elaborate the ideal speech situation.

The ideal speech situation is a description of what perfect communicative action would look like. Habermas describes it using highly suggestive language which contains a number of vaguenesses and ambiguities. We shall look first at *what* it is, as if it were realised as a concrete example of communicative action; after that we shall wonder *what kind of thing* it is.

As a German philosopher, it comes quite naturally to Habermas to specify the conditions that must obtain in order for something to exist. This is to elaborate the 'transcendental' conditions of an object. He thus lists the ideal speech situation's conditions. Habermas draws on a number of different sources in this discussion beyond the major figures in the German tradition, including Austin, Searle, Chomsky, Lorenzen and Kamlah. Habermas' handling of his sources is fascinating to track, as he is a prodigious reader and inventive interpreter of a diverse bibliography.[1] I shall keep things simple. There are four principal conditions:

1 All potential parties have equal opportunity to initiate or continue discussion.
2 All participants have equal opportunity to make claims, question them, clarify them, defend them and so forth.
3 All participants must make their attitudes, feelings and intentions transparent to each other.
4 All participants must have equal opportunities to perform what Austin calls 'illocutionary' and 'perlocutionary' acts: ordering and resisting, permitting or forbidding, making promises, giving or demanding accounts etc.

The 'equal opportunities' requirement is about symmetry. The other requirements discharge a variety of tasks. Participants should be able, over the course of discussion, to discover the difference between 'what is the case' and 'what appears to be the case'. Participants should act according to norms that are shared; when norms are not shared, the issues need to be made explicit. Participants should find, over time, that they 'express themselves' as persons and do not merely converse over some propositional topic: argument can be a way to get to know someone, and not merely a tool for achieving a goal. The standard trio of conditions that summarise this kind of interaction are truth ('that p' versus 'appearing that p'); sincerity (expressing oneself honestly); and normative rightness (observing moral norms). Any discussion that conforms to the four principal conditions listed above is an example of the ideal speech situation, which itself is the exemplar for communicative action (Habermas 1970: 371).

[1] The two best studies which investigate these matters in detail are McCarthy 1982 and Roberts 1992: 218–80. McCarthy deals extensively with the philosophers of language; Roberts has an excellent discussion of the Erlangen philosophers Lorenzen and Kamlah.

What makes the ideal speech situation 'ideal'? This question asks about *what kind of thing* the ideal speech situation is. Is it a lofty ideal to which we should aspire? Is it a real possibility which currently we fail to realise? Is it something Habermas dreamt up? To investigate this, some background in German idealism is indispensable. Habermas steers his project between Kant and Hegel, an aspiration he articulates on many different occasions. In this particular context he is handling two different meanings of the word 'ideal'. To sort this out takes a little time, not least because Habermas himself uses vague and suggestive language. The following long passage is full of interesting images and is worth considering carefully.

It is inherent in the structure of possible speech that when we perform speech-acts, we do so as if the ideal speech situation were not merely fictitious (*fiktiv*), but real (*wirklich*) – precisely what we call a presupposition. The normative foundation of agreement in language is thus both anticipated (*antizipiert*) and – as an anticipated foundation – also effective. The formal anticipation (*Vorwegnahme*) of idealised speech (as a form of life to be realised in the future?) guarantees the 'final' fundamental and counterfactual agreement; this is by no means only something that has yet to be completed: right from the start it must bind the potential speaker/hearer together. Additionally, agreement [with some held position] must not be mandatory if other arguments are to exercise an equivalent agreement-creating force. To this extent the concept of the ideal speech situation is not merely a regulative principle in Kant's sense: with the first act of agreement in language we must always already in fact make this presupposition. On the other hand, neither is the concept of an ideal speech situation an existing concept in Hegel's sense: no historical society is congruent with the form of life that we can characterise, in principle, by reference to the ideal speech situation. The ideal speech situation would best be compared with a transcendental illusion (*Schein*) except that this appearance is also a constitutive condition of rational speech, and not an illegitimate application [of reason] (as in the non-experiential use of the categories of the understanding). The anticipation (*Vorgriff*) of the ideal speech situation has the significance of a constitutive appearance which is at the same time the foreshadowing (*Vorschein*) of a form of life. Naturally, we cannot know *a priori* whether that foreshadowing is just a delusion (*Vorspiegelung*) or subreption – however unavoidable the suppositions from which it arises – or whether the empirical conditions for the realisation (if only approximate) of the supposed form of life can practically be

brought about. From this point of view, the fundamental norms of rational speech built into universal pragmatics contain a practical hypothesis.
(Habermas 1973: 258–9)

I offer this block of text in its entirety because it contains vocabulary that makes it interesting for theologians; moreover, its various claims are difficult to interpret if they are taken out of context; finally, it has not been translated into English before. We can distil seven of its claims:

a It is a fiction, but if it is treated as real, it becomes effective.
b Even though final agreement is never in practice attained, each participant must presuppose its possibility.
c Because it is always presupposed, it is not just a Kantian regulative ideal.
d Because it does not exist historically, it is not just an Hegelian existing concept.
e Because it is a requirement for rational speech, it is not strictly a transcendental *Schein*.
f A *Vorgriff* of it provides both a formally constitutive *Schein* with respect to the present and an intimation of the future: a *Vorschein*.
g It may be an unattainable delusion or it may be a realisable possibility as a form of life: we cannot tell in advance. This uncertainty is irrelevant: we cannot avoid presupposing its ideal existence.

How is the ideal speech situation ideal? By 'ideal' Kant means the concrete expression of an 'idea of reason'. The chief contrast here is between objects of consciousness (phenomena) and products of reason (noumena). Ideas are products of reason. That means they are not experienced as objects, but are things we imagine. We imagine them as a consequence of how our thinking works. Famously, God is an 'idea' for Kant. It is something we cannot escape imagining, but it is not something we can experience as part of the world of objects. The same is true of 'totality' or 'infinity': no-one has ever experienced these, and yet we cannot avoid entertaining them as ideas. The secondary contrast is Kant's commentary on the Platonic tradition of reasoning about forms: realities that constitute the world of appearances, but do not appear in it in their pure form,

are contrasted with concrete objects of experience. One can ask
Habermas: is the ideal speech situation a Kantian ideal? Is it a
product of reason which can never be an object of experience?
Habermas answers that it is not. If one treats a Kantian ideal as a
possible object of experience, then one has made an error. This is a
'subreption' or a 'transcendental illusion'. Thus if one speaks of an
'experience of God' one has, according to Kant, mistakenly applied
a judgement about objects of consciousness (e.g. sunsets and shivers
down one's spine) to a product of reason (God as an unavoidable
idea). Habermas insists that the ideal speech situation is not an
ideal in this sense. His warrant is that 'with the first act of agreement
in language we must always already in fact make this presupposition'. Somehow the ideal speech situation is 'constitutive' of argument, and Kantian ideals can only ever be 'regulative'. To be
constitutive is to be a condition for something: eggs are constitutive
of an omelette. To be regulative is to guide practice without existing: the 'perfect omelette' is regulative for the breakfast cook and
guides his practice with greater or lesser effectiveness. To deny
that the ideal speech situation is a Kantian ideal is to deny that it
merely guides practice: it already 'exists' in some way. Or rather,
participants *presuppose* that it exists in some way.

By 'existing concept', Hegel means (at least in Habermas' account
here) a concrete manifestation of reason's outworking in history.
The state is an example of an existing concept, in this sense. It is an
historical entity at the same time as being an expression of reason.
Understanding what Hegel means by 'reason' is a complex matter.
Until recently it was received wisdom among English-speaking
philosophers that Hegel imagines a vast overarching entity called
Geist which somehow instantiates itself as history and guides the
actions of great artists and heroes towards a final consummation of
reason. This is a very silly way of describing Hegel's philosophy
because it draws the reader's attention away from all the interesting
questions that Hegel asks. It is rather like describing Christianity as
belief in a vast overarching entity called *God* which somehow
instantiates itself in history and guides the actions of humanity
towards a final consummation in the end of time. Describing
Christianity in this way draws one's attention away from knotty
problems such as how one shows hospitality and friendship to

strangers, how one embodies God's reconciliation with the world in one's own relationships, how rich and poor, strong and weak, are to form integrated communities where wealth and power are exercised in ways that promote the flourishing of all, or how the world created by God is to be interpreted as our environment and not as raw materials for making money and weapons (or both at the same time). Hegel asks brilliant questions. How do we come to take to be true the things we take to be true? How adequately do our concepts capture reality? Is there any higher authority than the community? Is our grasp of an object always mediated by something that is neither 'us' nor 'the object'? What makes things and events intelligible or significant? Are concepts separable from the practices of using those concepts? Hegel uses 'reason' to investigate these questions. One can ask Habermas: is the ideal speech situation a concrete manifestation of reason's outworking in history? He answers: 'no'. His warrant is that 'no historical society is congruent with the form of life that we can characterise, in principle, by reference to the ideal speech situation'. In other words, there is no place on a map that you could visit to experience the ideal speech situation.

If the ideal speech situation is not an ideal in either Kant's or Hegel's senses, then how is it 'ideal'? This brings us to a vague formulation that has challenged many interpreters: 'The anticipation (*Vorgriff*) of the ideal speech situation has the significance of a constitutive appearance which is at the same time the foreshadowing (*Vorschein*) of a form of life.' The difficult words here are 'anticipation' and 'foreshadowing'. The secondary literature devoted to making sense of them is substantial.[2] All of them struggle with the word 'anticipation'. This is a word that Kant never uses in connection with ideas of reason, which supports Habermas' insistence that he does not mean 'ideal' in Kant's sense. What does it mean to 'anticipate' the ideal speech situation?

[2] Held 1980: 344; Kortian 1980: 127; Geuss 1981: 65, 85; Thompson 1981: 92–4; McCarthy 1982: 309; Bernstein 1978: 213; Benhabib 1986: 284; Roderick 1986: 78–9; Ingram 1987: 22; Ophir 1989: 221; Dryzek 1990: 30; Dallmayr 1991: 108; Marsh 1993: 522; Outhwaite 1994: 45.

Theologians are at an advantage here. The various resonances of 'anticipation' in twentieth-century philosophy have all contributed to the rethinking of eschatology in theology, especially as articulated in Jürgen Moltmann's classic *Theology of Hope* (Moltmann 1964). Ernst Bloch's notion of the 'anticipation' of future reality is fused, by Moltmann, with Gadamer's notion of the 'anticipation of meaning' to provoke an arresting redescription of Christian anticipation of God's future. Consider the following from Bloch's *Principle of Hope*:

Artistic *Schein* is everywhere not only mere *Schein* but a meaning of what has been driven further – wrapped in images, showable only in images – where their exaggeration and enfablement (*Ausfabelung*) represent a significant *Vor-Schein* of the real (*Wirklich*) circulating in turbulent existence itself, one that is specifically representable according to [a logic] immanent to aesthetics. (Bloch 1959–, 5:247)[3]

This finds its way into Moltmann's work in the following way:

hopes and anticipations of the future are not a transfiguring glow superimposed upon a greyed existence, but are realistic perceptions of the horizon of real possibility, which sets everything in motion and keeps it in a state of change. (Moltmann 1964: 20)[4]

Habermas is aware of Moltmann's work, but it probably does not represent a major influence on the ideal speech situation. Thinking along Moltmann's lines, however, can help the reader understand what Habermas means by 'anticipation'.

Habermas' use of *Vorschein* strongly suggests that he is drawing on a bibliography outside the mainstream of Kantian and Hegelian studies, and it is most likely Bloch who informs its use in the context of the ideal speech situation. Bloch's notion of a 'foreshadowing of the real' bears a close resemblance to Habermas' notion that to anticipate the ideal speech situation is also to entertain a 'foreshadowing of a form of life'. This bibliography, shared by Habermas and theologians alike, includes Walter Benjamin, Ernst Bloch, Max

---

[3] In the German, 'their exaggeration . . . turbulent existence itself' is in italics.
[4] The term 'real possibility' is a term of art taken from Bloch. Moltmann's relationship to Bloch is well known, and will not be emphasised here: see Moltmann 1975: 30–43; 1976; 1996: 30–3; Morse 1979: 12–15; Matic 1983: 276–83; Bauckham 1987, *passim*.

Horkheimer, Theodor Adorno and Herbert Marcuse. Theologians like Moltmann, Metz and Pannenberg, who are the same generation as Habermas, all draw significantly on this tradition of Jewish philosophy which is atheist in intention, but theologically rich in vocabulary.[5] The Jewish figures themselves are drawing on a tradition of Christian eschatological writing to assist in their interpretations of Kabbalah. These Christian thinkers include so-called 'mystical' figures like Eckhart, Böhme, Swedenborg and Oetinger. German intellectual history can be seen to repeat itself somewhat here. Just as the German mystics figured prominently in the German Idealist critique of Kant (especially Schelling and Hegel), so the Kabbalistic tradition (investigated vigorously by Gershom Scholem) figured prominently in the Jewish philosophical critique of neo-Kantianism, and in turn this Jewish philosophy figured prominently in the Christian eschatological critique of bourgeois political theology in the 1960s. The sterility of rationalism is in each case overcompensated for, as it were, by the wildness of the mystical texts. Schelling and Hegel are hard to understand because they use mystical traditions to evoke the non-rational 'ground' of reason; Bloch and Benjamin are hard to understand because they use Jewish mystical traditions to evoke the non-rational 'hope' that contradicts the horrific cause-and-effect actuality of 1930s Germany. Metz and Moltmann are actually fairly easy to understand, but quite often this is because they domesticate the wildness of the traditions on which they draw.

Against this interpretation of Habermas, one should bear in mind that in *Knowledge and Human Interests* (which predates the ideal speech situation) Habermas criticises the attempts by Bloch and others to use mysticism in this way (Habermas 1987c: 32–3), and Michael Theunissen judges that Habermas rejects the eschatological dimension of this thought as 'incompatible with a theoretically developed Marxism' (Theunissen 1981: 21). It is also worth noting that the mysticism of thinkers like Bloch and Marcuse is not oriented to God, but to nature. Yet although one should, therefore, not overestimate Habermas' proximity to Christian theology here,

---

[5] For discussion of some of the pitfalls in this kind of theology see Adams 2000.

Habermas' version of nature, namely *language*, does seem to have a revelatory character: we shall return to this at the end of chapter 4.

Habermas is heir both to the idealist critics of Kant (with their readings of the German mystics) and to the Jewish critics of neo-Kantianism (with their readings of the Kabbalah). Like his theological contemporaries he often tidies things up in the interests of clarity.[6] But even in Habermas, there persist forms of language that resist such tidying, and the notions of 'anticipation' and 'foreshadowing' are good examples of this. To put it more provocatively, Habermas' remarks on the ideal speech situation betray some experimentation with a kind of secularised eschatology. It is this, I think, which explains why the ideal speech situation has such a curious afterlife in theology long after it disappears from Habermas' own texts. Theologians recognise in it a faint echo of traditions with which they are familiar, most notably its aspirations to a healed world which they find articulated in theological speculations about the kingdom of God (e.g. Pannenberg 1969). This is not an original insight, admittedly. Quentin Skinner says much the same of Habermas' project as a whole (at least up to *The Theory of Communicative Action*): '[Luther's] has always been an inspiring vision, and the subconscious impact of such familiar images of sin and salvation [in Habermas' work] may even do something to account for Habermas's vast and somewhat bewildering popularity' (Skinner 1982: 38). However, I disagree with Skinner that Habermas' philosophy is 'a continuation of Protestantism by other means' (Skinner 1982: 38). The 'familiar images' are deceptive, and Habermas' outlook is incompatible with Protestantism, or any form of Christian imagination, as I shall show in later chapters.

In 1978, in a classic essay, 'A Reply to my Critics' (Thompson and Held 1982: 219–83), Habermas tidies things up significantly. This piece represents a shift away from the more ambitious claims made about the ideal speech situation, and establishes arguments that will later be worked out in the discourse ethics project. The essay is one of Habermas' longest, and is structured as specific responses to specific objections raised by his critics. His remarks about the ideal

---

[6] For a collection of essays in which this is not the case, see his extraordinary *Philosophical-Political Profiles*, Habermas 1983, especially the essays on Bloch and Benjamin.

speech situation are thus scattered somewhat. The two most important, for our purposes, are responses to Steven Lukes and to John Thompson.

Thompson raises questions about the strength of claims that can be made about the ideal speech situation. He focuses on Habermas' claim that the ideal speech situation is a necessary presupposition of communication. What does this mean? If the conditions of the ideal speech situation are not met, must we conclude that there can be no rational agreement? What about cases where we offer our agreement because we feel compassion (Thompson and Held 1982: 128–9)? Habermas readily concedes these points: 'I am not claiming that a valid consensus can *come about* only under conditions of the ideal speech situation' (Thompson and Held 1982: 272). There are all sorts of rational agreement that come about against the backdrop of shared cultural understandings and horizons of meaning. The more vital question is how one can secure rational agreement when these shared understandings break down or were never shared (as between members of quite different cultures):

Only when this disagreement is stubborn enough to provoke a discursive treatment of the matter at issue do we have a case concerning which I am claiming that a *grounded* agreement cannot be reached unless the participants in discourse *suppose* that they are convincing each other only by force of better arguments. (Thompson and Held 1982: 272)

In other words, one requires a commitment to the force of the better argument when other things that bring about agreement (shared values, existing commitments) are under threat. Typically, Habermas thinks less in terms of cultural variety and more in terms of modern scepticism about tradition, but the same reasoning applies to each. Habermas uses Thompson's critical questions to clarify his own concern with cases where traditional practices are inadequate (as he sees them) for securing agreement.

Lukes' criticism takes the form of two questions: (1) *who* are the 'participants' that Habermas names? (2) *What* are they supposed to agree about? (Thompson and Held 1982: 141). With respect to the first question, Lukes notes that 'ideally rational people in an ideal speech situation cannot but reach a rational consensus'; the problem is that ethical theories must deal with non-ideal people who are not ideally rational who engage in situations that are not the ideal speech situation. In regard to the second question, Lukes wants to know more about how 'generalisable interests' are related to interests that quite properly remain particular. Lukes tries to map Habermas' position against those of Rawls and Mackie. (It is worth remembering that this exchange took place before the publication of MacIntyre's *After Virtue* and the clarification of positions that Habermas calls 'neo-Aristotelian'. These take up and develop many of the same questions that Lukes poses.) Neither suits Habermas well, in Lukes' view. What, then, are participants arguing about: conflicts that arise within particular groups (which groups?) or general norms?

Habermas believes that Lukes' objections rest on misunderstandings. Habermas does not say so, but it seems that there are issues arising from the different idioms that English-speaking and German-speaking intellectuals use. Speakers of English tend to draw attention to problems in everyday life, and notice problems and ambiguities in the uses of ordinary language. Speakers of German are quite at home rendering problems in everyday life in abstract-sounding and rarefied concepts. German intellectuals readily see the ways in which particular phenomena reveal aspects of more general trends: concrete events are often described as emblematic of seismic cultural shifts. English speakers tend to use more modest language, even when pursuing similar questions. Academic life is much easier for the Germans here: they understand the English-language analyses without difficulty, but are also able deftly to retranslate the more bombastic German formulations into ordinary language when required. By contrast, English-speaking theorists have to undergo extensive education in the German tradition before they grasp that statuesque things like 'Reason' or 'World Spirit' actually perform the humdrum tasks of thinking about how people find their practices intelligible, or how minutiae relate to bigger pictures, and so on.

Habermas clarifies Lukes' alleged misunderstandings by translating his more Germanic expressions into more manageable English, but he also makes some concessions which represent a development of his thinking. First, he decides not to address at all the question whether the ideal speech situation adequately reconstructs the presuppositions of communication. Second, he confirms that 'practical discourse' of the kind exemplified by the ideal speech situation only has any content (at all) if participants in discourse 'bring with them' their traditions, histories, identities and so forth. Third, he retracts (his word) the following claim: 'no historical society coincides with the *form of life* that we anticipate in the *concept* of the ideal speech situation'.[7] These three concessions are worth exploring a little.

Habermas' decision not to defend the adequacy of the ideal speech situation is not merely a question of time, space and priorities. It is a recognition that the tasks elaborated in the ideal speech situation were already being discharged better elsewhere, most notably, in English, in Thomas McCarthy's big book on Habermas (McCarthy 1982) and, in German, in Robert Alexy's theory of argumentation (Alexy 1978). The first editions of both these works had just been published when Thompson and Held were soliciting essays for their collection. McCarthy and Alexy played a major role in helping Habermas down the road that would later be his 'discourse ethics'. Both advocate a shift away from the ideal speech situation towards alternative ways of reconstructing the presuppositions in communicative practice.

The concession that practical discourse requires traditions, histories and identities is a clarification of Habermas' existing views rather than a change of mind. Habermas had always insisted that attempts at universalisation were not a magical journey out of tradition or history, but an attempt to specify the invariant features that seem to underlie a variety of traditional practices. We shall return to this in the next chapter.

The retraction of the claim about historical and ideal forms of life is more significant. Habermas has learned from Albrecht Wellmer that problems emerge if one forgets how ordinary practices are related to an 'ethic of discourse'. Habermas acknowledges that it is a mistake to think that one can extract standards for an ideal form of life from an ethic of discourse. Although his remarks are extremely

---

[7] This form of words comes from an essay that is slightly earlier than the 'Wahrheitstheorien' essay cited above. The relevant wording in the latter is 'no historical society is congruent with the form of life that we can characterise, in principle, by reference to the ideal speech situation'. There is no significant difference between them.

abbreviated, it seems that Habermas is attempting to say something about the relationship between 'real life' and philosophical abstraction. The route is one-way: real life comes first, and philosophical abstractions (things like the ideal speech situation) are always subsequent. Thus the ideal speech situation is an idea which emerges 'under specific historical conditions, together with the idea of bourgeois democracy' (Thompson and Held 1982: 262). It is quite mistaken to think that one can travel in the opposite direction: achieving abstractions of this kind should not suggest that one has formulated an ideal form of life. Habermas agrees that there can be no such ideal. It is worth noticing that he is not merely admitting that the ideal speech situation is not an ideal form of life. He is denying that his way of doing philosophy yields *any* ideal forms of life. For this reason he takes back the claim that the ideal speech situation 'anticipates' or 'characterises' a form of life. It does not. Instead, it abstracts certain features of a particular historical form of life. This claim resembles some of the things theologians might say about eschatology, and I shall return to this later on.

Having noted Habermas' clarification and modification of his views, we should now turn briefly to the two most serious critiques of the ideal speech situation, which go substantially beyond the ones mounted by Thompson and Lukes. The first is 'Hegelian', and rehearses debates about *Sittlichkeit* (ethical life); the second is 'Schellingian', and rehearses debates about the scope of grounding. The two claims Habermas makes, and which these two styles of critique address, are (1) the rules of discourse presupposed by participants *transcend* the particular cultures in which they are found; (2) the ideal speech situation provides the means for agreement to be *grounded*.

The Hegelian critique is rehearsed by Gillian Rose, Herbert Schnädelbach, Fred Dallmayr, Robert Pippin, J. M. Bernstein and Gordon Finlayson.[8] The most salient of Hegel's critiques of Kant is the attention he draws to the relationship between rules and judgement (rule-following). Kant distinguished, in this context,

---

[8] Rose 1981: 35; Dallmayr 1991; Pippin 1997: 157–84; Schnädelbach 1991; Bernstein 1995; Finlayson 1999. For defences of Habermas on this question see Wellmer 1991: 164ff.; Matustík 1993: 34ff.

between determinate judgement and reflective judgement. Determinate judgements are acts in which general rules are applied in particular circumstances. Reflective judgements are acts by which general principles are discerned, after a number of particular cases have been examined. The important fact about rules or principles is that they require judgement in order to be applied. The important fact about judgement is that there is no rule that specifies how judgement is to be exercised: 'judgement is a peculiar talent which can be practised only, and cannot be taught. It is the specific quality of so-called mother-wit; and its lack no school can make good' (Kant A133/B172). The reason for this is evident: if there were a rule for judgement, then there would need to be a rule for this rule, and so on, in infinite regression.

Hegel's critique, in the *Science of Logic*, is aimed at the gap between rules, which Kant specifies, and judgement, which Kant refuses to specify and describes as an innate talent. The 'logic' in Hegel's title refers to rules for thinking. For Hegel rules and the judgement required for applying rules *belong together*. Kant's separation of pure and applied aspects of rules and the separation of external objects and internal appearances do not make sense for Hegel. For Kant, 'external' objects are knowable because they conform *a priori* to 'internal' rules for understanding. For Hegel this involves a contradiction: even for Kant the idea of the external and the nature of the internal are *both* described by (and therefore internal to) consciousness. Hegel rejects the notion of a 'ready-made world' (*eine fertige Welt*) distinct from thought. He also rejects the notion that truth means the agreement of thought and object. Objects cannot be 'radically beyond thought' (*schlechthin ein Jenseits des Denkens*) (Hegel 1999: 10–11). Rules and the application of rules are, for Hegel, best thought of like grammars and their use in living languages. If one leafs through a grammar, it seems to be a collection of 'dry abstractions' and 'arbitrary rules'. By contrast, if one has a sense of how grammars are part of living languages, and if one knows a number of languages and can compare their different uses of their peculiar grammars, then 'the spirit and culture of a people appear expressed in the grammar of its language. The same rules and forms now have a fulfilled, abundant, living value' (Hegel 1999: 25). Rules for thinking are not reserved to a discrete discipline alongside others which might be studied; they are a crucial part of all disciplines that can be studied. In Hegel's flamboyant language, logic is 'the universal holding in itself the riches of the particular' (Hegel 1999: 26). Even more strikingly, Hegel echoes Luther's translation of John 16:13: '*Geist* (spirit/mind) receives, through logic, the power which will guide it into all truth' (Hegel 1999:26).[9] In sum, Hegel insists that knowing *that* there is an object and knowing *what* it is happens all together in one 'self-conscious' act; similarly, knowing rules and applying them belong together (Hegel 1999: 10–27; 1969: 405ff.).[10]

Gillian Rose insists that recovering aspects of Hegel's thought enables social theory to renounce its preoccupation with methodology, which can only endlessly defer discussion of substantial moral questions. Social theory should abandon this concentration on pure procedure (what Hegel calls 'dry abstractions') and relearn from Hegel that its business is to make sense of actual forms of thought, 'living value', and digest the consequences of the fact that 'Hegel argued that the attempt to justify theoretical and moral judgements apart from their use is contradictory' (Rose 1981: 45). That is, justification and application are not separable. Rose's suggestion has been taken up seriously in different but related ways. The work of Pippin and J. M. Bernstein continues this Hegelian critique of Habermas; Dallmayr draws on Schnädelbach to mount similar arguments. I shall not rehearse these in detail.

The Hegelian critique poses some fundamental questions. (1) Can rules be abstracted from the contexts in which they are formulated? (2) Given that the judgement required to apply rules is not inherent in those same rules, to what extent can one specify in advance the contexts in which such judgement is learned? (3) Do not rules change when the contexts in which they are applied change?

Hegel, criticising Kant, insists that:

---

[9] All translations from the *Science of Logic* are my own. References to A. V. Miller's otherwise excellent translation are also given; Miller does not echo the biblical resonances as clearly as he might: I have used the King James translation of John 16 for effect. It is also worth noting a further resonance: Hegel's word for 'receive', *empfangen*, is the verb used for receiving the sacraments.

[10] For other relevant passages and their interpretation, see Rose 1981: 43–5 and Pippin 1989: 216–17.

1 Rules can be abstracted *but not separated* from the contexts in which they are formulated.
2 Judgement is learned in specific communal contexts ('ethical life').
3 Historical development changes both rules and patterns of judgement.

Habermas is aware of the potential for these arguments (whose thrust he accepts) to undermine his own theory. His attempts to defend himself, and his critics' doubts about his success, have been very well rehearsed elsewhere.[11] Habermas claims that he does not try to occupy a position external to tradition: instead he tries to show that the possibility of translation between traditions means that *there must be* something that unifies them all. Habermas admits that there are problems with procedural (i.e. Kantian) ethics that abstract rules from concrete forms of life: most importantly, such procedural approaches cannot articulate the good life in the way Plato and Aristotle could. However, Habermas insists that it is precisely because the abstract rules *must* always be applied in concrete forms of life that one can depend upon particular traditions to supply the substantial content that procedural approaches lack. Habermas' Hegelian critics object that rules that are abstracted from concrete forms of life *are still tied to those forms of life*. They cannot be abstracted into 'universals' that transcend forms of life. These Hegelian critics object further that Habermas' way of describing the relationship between general rules and specific traditional contexts tends to make it sound as if the general rules are what is really rational, while the specific commitments found in traditions are irrational and decisionistic (Dallmayr 1991: 120). Finally, Hegelian critics have pointed out that Habermas' most stringent formulations, in discourse ethics, do not merely explain our moral intuitions, but end up radically revising them, to the point where very few of 'our' (i.e. fellow theorists') moral intuitions are allowed to pass as genuinely 'moral' at all (Finlayson 1999: 46).

---

[11] Habermas' most explicit defence is Habermas 1990: 195–215. The most decisive criticism is probably Bernstein 1995: 176–91. For a Hegelian critique focusing on the excessive formalism of 'U' in Habermas' discourse ethics see Finlayson 1999.

In recent work, Habermas has tried to work through these problems, and he does acknowledge that there can be no moral theory, even a very procedural one, without agents who have conceptions of the good life that are specific to their traditions. This is because the things that matter, and which are the subject for moral debate, are precisely the things that are valued in traditions (families, children, care for the weak, hospitality to the stranger, entitlement to limited resources, justice and mercy and so on). Habermas fails to answer his Hegelian critics adequately, but his reason for persisting nonetheless is understandable: they fail to offer a better model for coordinating different traditions.

The Schellingian critique is aimed at Habermas' claim that his theory can uncover the universal rational grounding that unifies the practices of different traditions. Its basic observation is that Habermas conflates two discrete claims. (1) If there is translation between languages/traditions, *there must be something that unifies them.* (2) Theory *can uncover this universal thing.* It is quite common to find in so-called postmodern criticisms of Habermas the claim that there is no universal that unifies diversity. This is demonstrably false: if there is diversity, and if there is mutual intelligibility between diverse perspectives, then there is obviously something that renders this intelligibility possible. One might as well call this a 'universal'. The Schellingian critics (above all, Andrew Bowie) show this very well, as I shall demonstrate in chapter 5. The problem with Habermas is not that he believes in universals. *It is that he believes he can uncover these universals.* It is one thing to think that diversity is grounded in a unifying something. It is quite another to think that one can grasp this something in an explanatory way. Habermas should, according to Schellingian critics, acknowledge the necessity of universals, but should reject the idea that they can be 'got at' or grasped rationally.

The Schellingian critique thus complements the Hegelian one. The Hegelian critics insist that Habermas admit that 'procedural' abstraction is still tied to 'substantial' ethical life (i.e. actual historical communal practices) and cannot be generalised away from it. Habermas concedes this to a degree, but nevertheless wants to maintain that there must still be some universal something that underlies the diversity of such historical practices, and he claims that he can reconstruct it in his moral theory. The Schellingian critics insist that Habermas acknowledge that any universal grounding that underlies the diversity of traditions cannot be theorised.

If one combines the Hegelian and Schellingian criticisms, one gets a pretty good outline for an alternative to Habermas' moral theory. It holds that abstractions are necessary if one wants to reconstruct the rules that underlie practices of argumentation. These abstractions are still tied to the concrete communal practices in which they are situated. At the same time, there is a variety of communal practice in the modern public sphere, and members of these different traditions can and do find each other mutually intelligible. There is thus 'something' that unifies this diversity. However, this 'something' cannot be theorised, and it most certainly is not captured by the abstractions of theorists who are situated in a particular tradition. Rather, the possibility of translation and mutual intelligibility is a sign that moral argument is possible, and this possibility can only be described as a fact, and not demonstrated as a logical necessity. This is the position I advocate: it is outlined in a little more detail in chapters 10 and 11.

I suggested earlier that some of the claims Habermas makes for the ideal speech situation resemble claims theologians might make about the eschaton or the kingdom of God. Habermas' willing retraction of claims about forms of life poses some interesting challenges for theologians. When Christians pray 'Thy kingdom come', do they 'anticipate' or 'characterise' a form of life? Is the kingdom an ideal form of life? Having learned from the work of Bloch, Adorno, Rahner, Pannenberg and Moltmann, I would argue that it is not. The contribution that eschatology makes to theology is not the provision of blueprints for political action, but the constant reminder that the future which God makes possible cannot be deduced from the past we inherit. Eschatology is one of the many Christian modes of denying *both* purely mechanical causality *and* utter obscurity. The future can be thought of as a wholly predetermined product of cause and effect. At the opposite extreme it can also be thought of as a cluster of nasty surprises that no-one can see coming. The more one leans to the first position, the more one will invest in futurology. The more one leans to the second, the more one invests in nothing at all, because nothing will make any difference.

Christian eschatology makes (ungroundable) claims that the future will be the completion of all things in Jesus Christ; in other words, it will be the achievement of reconciliation and peace. These claims are part of a Christian outlook, and cannot be established independently; they cannot be defended against scepticism. At the same time, Christian eschatology refuses to say what the particular futures of particular societies will look like: it has no crystal ball. One should expect to find Christians investing in things which promote reconciliation and peace, because that is the (still immensely vague) future that they anticipate. To the extent that Christians fail to do so, we suggest to outsiders that we do not really believe the things we say in church in our liturgies.

Eschatology functions in quite a similar way to the ideal speech situation. Whereas the ideal speech situation is an abstraction from the concrete form of European life in which Habermas is situated, eschatological claims about the kingdom are abstractions from interpretations of scripture and liturgy, i.e. from the concrete forms of Christian life in which theologians are situated. The resemblance between the ideal speech situation and Christian eschatology is made possible by the overlap between 'European life' and 'Christian life' in this sketch.[12]

Of Habermas' quite proper retraction about ideal forms of life we need to note that this would not mean that the ideal speech situation does not affect 'real life'. It may not 'anticipate' or 'characterise' a form of life. In Christian terms, it anticipates the eschaton, which is certainly not a form of life in Wittgenstein's sense. Nonetheless, it functions as a means of diagnosing distorted communication and for guiding the imagination when it struggles to know what undistorted communication might be like. It is thus less like a cooking recipe and more like a photographic illustration of a dish; less like a blueprint for constructing a building and more like an artist's impression. Photographs of food or artists' impressions of buildings cannot tell you how to cook or construct. If you fry onions and then add salt you get a quite different result from adding salt before frying the onions: photographs know nothing of processes or time.

---

[12] For an emphatic version of this thesis, namely that Habermas' account of the redemptive power of reflection is a specifically Lutheran topic, see Skinner 1982.

Only a recipe or blueprint can show how to get from x to y. An artist's impression is not an 'ideal building'; it is an abstraction from, and an important component of, the concrete practice of building. Habermas makes a comparable claim about the ideal speech situation: it is an abstraction from, and an important component of, concrete practices of argumentation at a particular time in human history, in a particular geographical location. Habermas' problem is that his readers have been engaged in these practices for some time without knowing anything about an ideal speech situation, whereas most builders and architects *already* agree that artists' impressions are a useful component in construction. And it is precisely here that theologians make an interesting group of readers for Habermas: they *already* know that eschatology is a useful component in attempts to describe the world, and thus have fewer hurdles obstructing their appreciation of Habermas' work. Theologians are also less likely to mistake the ideal speech situation for a blueprint of the future, because they already know that 'Thy kingdom come' is not itself a programme of political action, but is rather a crucial component of, and enduring judgement upon, any concrete programme of Christian political action.

It is important to remember that these discussions refer principally to Habermas' earlier work. The ideal speech situation was presented in its most mature formulations in the early 1970s. It is more important, however, to note that Habermas abandoned the concept. This often seems not to be grasped in theological literature, so it is worth demonstrating it beyond doubt. We have already considered Habermas' replies to Steven Lukes and John Thompson, and his significant concessions and retractions in the light of them. These constitute the point after which Habermas uses other formulations to drive his theory. These concessions and retractions were made in 1978. By the time of *The Theory of Communicative Action* in 1981 the concept was not used at all. The nearest Habermas approaches it there is a brief remark about 'highly idealised speech acts' (Habermas 1984a: 328). By 1983, in his essay 'Discourse Ethics' (Habermas 1990: 43–115), he consigns it explicitly to the past: 'I tried at one time to describe the presuppositions of argumentation as the defining characteristics of an ideal speech situation' (Habermas 1990: 88). Finally, in a much more recent essay, 'Realism after the

Linguistic Turn' (Habermas 2003b: 1–49), Habermas rehearses his arguments about 'presumably universal but only *de facto* unavoidable conditions' and 'invariant features' (Habermas 2003b: 11–12) as well as the claim that 'communicative language still commits participants to strong idealisations' (Habermas 2003b: 17). But the ideal speech situation is not mentioned even for the sake of historical interest.

Any engagement with Habermas, especially by theologians who find it suggestive and attractive, needs to acknowledge that the ideal speech situation is not one of Habermas' enduring contributions to philosophy. It may be that Christian eschatological formulations might fare much better as models for mapping the anticipation of God's future onto current political practice, but perhaps this would only be persuasive for Christians, and not generalisable in the way the ideal speech situation was intended to be. We shall revisit the question of persuasion and plausibility in chapter 10.

Before moving on, it is worth suggesting one further reason why the ideal speech situation should be so prominent in discussions of Habermas despite its brief life. This is that it is relatively easy to understand. I have drawn attention to some of the problems surrounding words like 'anticipation' or 'foreshadowing', and these are interesting puzzles. The main contours, however, are rather easy to grasp. Habermas' presentation of the ideal speech situation is generally schematic with well-defined categories. This is also true of his discourse ethics project, which is a development and modification of the germs present in the ideal speech situation. It is perhaps understandable that Habermas' readers should focus on, and reproduce, those parts of his work that are simpler in conception and presentation. Unfortunately for philosophers and theologians, this is not where most of the interesting material on religion is to be found. Habermas' remarks about religion, and about the role of religious values in the public sphere, are generally embedded in much more difficult texts. This is not just because they are often concerned with knotty problems in classical metaphysics, or debates arising from problems in German Idealism (itself formidably difficult). It is often because Habermas himself, like all great thinkers, struggles to articulate insights that have not been thought before. The next six chapters are devoted to explaining Habermas' work on religion. We turn first of all to the question of tradition.

CHAPTER 3

Authority and distance in tradition

I shall argue that religion and theology are casual victims of Habermas' account of tradition in modern society. Habermas elaborates – at some length – the role of religion in society, but this religion functions primarily as a kind of ancestor to modern forms of thought. More importantly, this ancestor appears as a highly idealised concept in Habermas' theory, and it is not obvious how this concept relates to the messy particularities of Christian and Jewish histories in Europe, or to other religious traditions world-wide. Habermas shows limited interest in religious life and thought for their own sake: he does not conceive his task to be showing how Jewish and Christian practice feeds into contemporary social life. Rather, he understands his task to be that of identifying and repairing problems in 'post-traditional' societies. The most obvious problem is that moral discourse is always tied to particular traditions, and yet these traditions need to negotiate in the public sphere. What criteria are to be used to evaluate their claims? What authorities are judged appropriate as courts of appeal? These are the questions Habermas investigates in his consideration of tradition, and these are the contexts in which discussions of religion and theology arise. These discussions are incidental to his main theoretical interests. We shall consider his detailed remarks on religion in the next chapter. This chapter will elaborate Habermas' understanding of the problems with tradition in modern societies, especially his debate with Gadamer over the authority of tradition.

It is important to remember that Habermas grew up in a country whose politics embodied a violent regression to 'tradition', and

Habermas' thinking is heavily, if negatively, influenced by far-right theorists who all appealed to the authority of tradition: above all, Carl Schmitt and Martin Heidegger. To scholars educated in the ancient traditions, these figures do not appear 'conservative' at all, but as highly innovative radicals whose invocation of 'tradition' was a fantasy. In German art of the 1920s and 1930s one sees repeated attempts to make sense of urban industrialisation and the violent disenchantment of Germany's beautiful landscape. Descriptions of 'tradition' produced by intellectuals living in smaller towns like Heidelberg contrast strongly with attempts, by artists and film-makers overwhelmed by the industrial sounds and smells of Berlin and New York, to capture 'modern life'. The important point is that such contrasts are seen in the same period. The notion of 'tradition', not least that of 'Christian tradition', seems to Habermas, in some of his work, to be bound up with reactionary politics. Instead of exposing the hopeless and dangerous nostalgia embodied in right-wing misty-eyed descriptions of a 'tradition' that is a wish-fulfilling distortion of the real tradition to which its author genuinely belongs, Habermas has tended to peer at certain aspects of tradition with suspicion. Real European traditions are obviously messy and riven with contradiction as their members try to come to terms with changes in their material conditions. The fantasy traditions of right-wing rhetoric are simple, beautiful and morally stable. Rather than point this out, Habermas has perhaps sometimes colluded with the so-called 'conservatives' and allowed them to sustain their fantasies. When he speaks of tradition, in the sense of something that he believes should be superseded by modernity, it often appears to have many of the fantasy characteristics attributed to it by conservatives. I mention this early on, because any attempt to rescue traditions from their fate in Habermas' theory has also to rescue them from conservative fantasy and restore their messy, contradictory complexity.

The discussion of 'The Hermeneutic Approach' in *On the Logic of the Social Sciences* (Habermas 1988a: 143–75) is a relatively early text (1967) that sets out many of the issues that Habermas develops in later work. It is part of a long essay's wider argument about the role of 'universal' (Kant) or 'invariant' (Cicourel) dimensions of rules and norms that apply to social action.[1] Habermas' discussions before this point have focused on 'the transcendental structure of the lifeworld' (Habermas 1988a: 106), which identifies general features of any lifeworld, and on a 'general theory of ordinary language' (Habermas 1988a: 139), which recovers the pragmatic rules that operate in any given language. We have examined one idealised form of this in the previous chapter. It is the word 'any' in these enquiries that will interest us most: any lifeworld, any language. The section most pertinent to this study, on the hermeneutic approach, focuses on the relationship between universal reason and reflection.

'Reflection' is central to Habermas' account. It is a technical term in German philosophy: it means the process of becoming conscious of something that previously one did or thought unconsciously.[2] For example reading Isaiah 7:14 ('Behold, a virgin shall conceive, and bear a son, and shall call his name Immanuel') as an anticipation of the birth of Jesus is something that many Christians might do unconsciously. However, they can become aware that there are many different readings of this passage of scripture, in the rabbinic traditions, for example, and they can become conscious that their interpretation *is an interpretation*, rather than being something intrinsic to the text. This produces a different attitude to the interpretation, one that might even potentially call a particular interpretation into question. This is what is meant by reflection.

We are not concerned with reflection in all its forms, but solely with Habermas' account of what happens to traditions when their members become reflective. Habermas has a narrative of the transition from traditional to post-traditional societies, and this needs looking at. The texts in which he treats this question are many and varied, and the debates he enters – especially with Gadamer and MacIntyre – are sometimes complex. We cannot consider them all.

---

[1] For Habermas' discussion of Cicourel's *Method and Measurement in Sociology*, which he interprets in the light of Alfred Schütz, see Habermas 1988a: 98ff. For critique of Habermas' reading of Schütz see Harrington 2001: 94ff.

[2] For an excellent study of this concept see Roberts 1992. On Habermas see pp. 218–80, esp. pp. 237–48.

At the same time it is neither desirable nor necessary to try to make a mosaic out of his arguments in order to present an overview. Habermas tries to generalise about 'tradition' and 'religion' in ways that encompass the whole range of human cultures, at least in principle. This is surely unrealistic. I read Habermas as a commentator on European cultural and societal development, using conceptual tools that may be extended beyond Europe only if there is convincing historical evidence that other cultures have developed in similar ways. Because Habermas neither undertakes, nor draws on, such historical evidence, I shall assume that his insights apply only to Europe.[3] He also generalises about 'religion'; I shall assume that his remarks are intended to illuminate contemporary experiences in Europe, which may perhaps be assisted, or more likely modified, by drawing attention to ethnographies of non-European practices and beliefs. Furthermore, I shall assume that the categories he uses to describe European practices are derived from Christian and Jewish philosophy, and should only with caution be extended to other religious traditions. I read Habermas explicitly from a Christian theological perspective, and comment on that basis. If I make suggestions about how a 'Christian theologian' might respond to him, this is not in order to claim a privilege for Christian styles of reading, but in order to avoid making presumptuous claims on behalf of other religious traditions. For much of the discussion, I think that Jewish and Muslim commentators, for example, might come to some of the same conclusions as I do, but because I am unable to demonstrate it I hold back from claiming this directly.

Habermas' goal is to show that taking seriously the particularity of every concrete language, 'lifeworld' (Husserl) or 'form of life' (Wittgenstein) is not an obstacle to discovering general or universal or invariant features that govern them all. Before exploring some of the detail, it is important to note that Habermas does not claim that there is a universal language, or that there is a context-neutral perspective from which to judge languages (Habermas 1992a: 139).

---

[3] Some commentators have shown how the deficiencies of Habermas' analysis of the public sphere in Europe can be illuminated by looking at Islamic experiences of publicity (Eikelman and Salvatore 2002).

Rather, he wants to show that some notion of universality is implied in analysis of particular languages. This has much in common with what he elsewhere calls the 'unavoidable presupposition' of universality in all particular practices of ethical argument.

Habermas' chosen theme is that of translation. His wish is to reveal 'the unity of analytic reason in the pluralism of language games' (Habermas 1988a: 143). In later work this will be recapitulated as 'the unity of reason in the diversity of its voices' (Habermas 1992a: 115–48). The underlying claim concerns the fact that there are ways of getting from one language or lifeworld to another. Travel is possible, and although one is always located within a language (i.e. there is no context-free location), the very possibility of travel and translation is informative. Habermas wants to concede the individuality of every language right down to its basic structure. He also wants to concede that one often encounters untranslatable expressions when trying to get from one language to another. At the same time, there is obviously the possibility of translating things that are foreign, of making something intelligible even when it initially looks incomprehensible, and of putting 'in one's own words what at first eludes one'. Habermas infers from this that 'we are never enclosed within a single grammar. Rather, the first grammar that one masters also enables one to step outside it' (Habermas 1988a: 143). This 'stepping out' is not the occupation of a neutral space – later he will clear up any ambiguity by stating explicitly that 'we cannot step out of an objectively given horizon of interpretation at will' (Habermas 1987b: 77) – but the possibility of travel from one place to another. Habermas draws on Gadamer's evocative claim that 'thinking reason escapes the prison of language' (Gadamer 1989: 402). Habermas also echoes another of Gadamer's claims:

If all understanding stands in a necessary relation of equivalence to its possible interpretation, and if there are basically no bounds set to understanding, then the verbal form in which this understanding is interpreted must contain within it an infinite dimension that transcends all bounds. Language is the language of reason itself. (Gadamer 1989: 401)

Habermas puts it as follows:

Languages themselves contain the potential for a rationality that, expressing itself in the particularity of a specific grammar, reflects the limits of that grammar and at the same time negates them in their specificity. Reason, which is always bound up with language, is also always beyond its languages. Only by destroying the particularities of *languages*, which are the only way in which it is embodied, does reason live in *language*. It can purge itself of the residue of one particularity, of course, only through the transition to another. This mediating generality is attested to by the act of translation. (Habermas 1988a: 144)

The two claims are very similar. Gadamer speaks of 'the superior universality with which reason rises above the limitations of any given language' and 'the unity of language and thought' (Gadamer 1989: 402). He attributes a decisive break with previous theology and rationalism to Herder and Humboldt, who understood languages to be worldviews rather than merely tools for communication. What the 'theological' account of language prior to this was, Gadamer discusses later on. There, Gadamer suggests that for medieval theology 'the human relationship between thought and speech corresponds, despite its imperfections, to the divine relationship of the Trinity. The inner mental word is just as consubstantial with thought as is God the Son with God the Father' (Gadamer 1989: 421). Gadamer associates this 'inner mental word' with 'the language of reason'. The language of reason is the same as the 'hermeneutic experience', i.e. the awareness that the interpreter is able to travel between languages by a means of travel that is not restricted to any one particular language. Because of this association of inner word with reason, Gadamer loses interest in the connection between medieval accounts of language and accounts of the Trinity. Of more interest to his philosophical account is what this 'inner word' might be, and what its hermeneutical function is. Gadamer also finds medieval theology problematic in so far as its emphasis on an ideal inner word devalues, so he believes, the variety of actual spoken languages (Gadamer 1989: 422). Of more importance, however, and of greater relevance to our concerns, is the link Gadamer makes with reflection: this is important for Habermas' account of reason. Gadamer puts it as follows:

The inner unity of thinking and speaking to oneself, which corresponds to the Trinitarian mystery of the incarnation, implies that the inner mental word *is not formed by a reflective act*. A person who thinks something – i.e.,

says it to himself – means by it the thing that he thinks. His mind is not
directed back toward his own thinking when he forms the word.

(Gadamer 1989: 426)

To represent something to oneself by thinking it ('saying it to
himself') is not necessarily to be conscious *that* one is representing
something to oneself. It is not yet to understand a representation *as* a
representation. It is thought as a 'something'. To think 'tomato' is
not necessarily to understand that one is representing a tomato in
thought: one can perfectly well think 'tomato' without thinking
'representation of tomato'. It is on this point that Herder and
Humboldt, in the wake of 'the nominalist breakup of the classical
logic of essence' (Gadamer 1989: 435), and the later erosion of Latin
as the single dominant language of scholarship (Gadamer 1989: 436),
do something that breaks with theology, according to Gadamer.
Rather than connecting language with things, they are conscious of
language as a representation of things, and thus *as* worldview and
not merely as world. To understand that a worldview is a worldview,
and not the world, is to be 'reflective' in the technical sense we are
interested in. It is the same as understanding an interpretation *as*
interpretation rather than as the thing interpreted (Gadamer 1989:
439ff.). We shall return to this in the next chapter.

The act of reflection is significant. To be aware that languages are
languages, worldviews, particular ways of interpreting things, is to
discover 'a certain freedom with respect to language' (Gadamer
1989: 441). This is not to be able to escape from language: that is
unthinkable. Rather, it is to be aware that language is embedded
in tradition. To put it reflectively, it means to understand tradition
as tradition rather than as the only reality there is; to understand
worldview *as* worldview rather than as the only world there is.
Reflection makes one aware that there are other traditions and other
worldviews (Gadamer 1989: 442).

We can break off from Gadamer at this point and return to
Habermas, as we have enough to understand his use of the word
'reason'. His talk of 'destroying' and 'purging' (Habermas 1988a:
144) is drastic, but essentially repeats Gadamer's point that inter-
pretation/translation presupposes a 'freedom from language' that is
not inherent in only one language but rather transcends every

particular language. Like Gadamer, Habermas is interested in the results of reflection. He explores this by contrasting Gadamer's account of the hermeneutic experience with Wittgenstein's account of how the limits of language are the limits of the thinkable world. For Habermas, Gadamer's account does better justice to the reflective awareness *that* a language is a limit and *that* other languages spell the world differently. The reflective attitude means grasping that 'the language shows itself as something particular among particulars. Consequently the limits of the world that it defines are not irrevocable' (Habermas 1988a: 147). Habermas claims that this repairs a problem in Wittgenstein:

the language games of the young do not simply reproduce the practice of the old. With the first basic linguistic rules the child learns not only the conditions of possible consensus but also the conditions of possible interpretations of the rules, which enables him to overcome and *thereby also to express* a distance. (Habermas 1988a: 148, italics in the original)

At one level this is just a repetition of Gadamer's remarks about a 'certain freedom' from a particular language that reflection brings. But we already hear something else here: 'distance'. Habermas will make much of this in a way that will bring him into conflict with Gadamer. Habermas wishes to describe the possibility of the reflective agent placing himself or herself at a distance from any particular tradition, thus discovering resources for critique of that tradition. By contrast, Gadamer refuses to associate the 'certain freedom' from language with distance from the authority of tradition. The freedom from particularity is a purely formal consequence of reflection: one can only gain a perspective on a tradition by occupying some other tradition. To put it differently, Habermas and Gadamer disagree about the effect of discovering that reason is embedded in tradition while simultaneously suggesting the transcendence of tradition. Gadamer tries to balance the two: reason is absolute, but therefore cannot be thought; tradition is thinkable, but therefore cannot be absolute. The embeddedness of reason in tradition thus requires a good account of the relationship between thinkable and unthinkable, and between the particular and the transcendence of particularity.[4]

---

[4] Arguably Gadamer does not do such a good job as the early Schelling or the mature Schleiermacher. See Bowie 1990: 146ff.

Habermas is more boldly one-sided. He insists that reason's absoluteness produces a 'distance' from tradition. But he is more reluctant to acknowledge that reason's embeddedness in tradition produces something like a 'nearness' to reason in so far as it is thinkable. This would mean saying something like 'distance from one tradition is possible only because of nearness to another' or 'appeals to reason are always particular, and thus, *as appeals*, are not absolute'. Habermas knows that these statements are true, and even says something like them (see Habermas 1988a: 153). At the same time, however, he wants to do justice to the fact that members of traditions experience the hold of those traditions as greatly weakened. For Habermas it is not only the case that some traditions are distant because other traditions are close. He thinks it is also true that even the closest of traditions are somehow increasingly distant because of the reflective attitude that their members are able to take. It is this question of emphasis that generated the exchange between Habermas and Gadamer regarding the balance between the critique and the authority of tradition. Habermas sees critical gains in the distance from tradition, whereas Gadamer diagnoses traditional losses (things lost because of philosophical mistakes) in the Enlightenment rejection of prejudgements (*Vorurteile*). Though much has been made of this dispute, it is not obvious that their arguments are mutually exclusive, although their emphases are different.

Habermas wants to take from Gadamer the idea of the 'immanent connection between understanding and application', which he illustrates by discussing the interpretation of scripture:

In a sermon, the interpretation of the Bible, like the interpretation of positive law in adjudication, serves at the same time as an interpretation of the application of the facts in a given situation. Their practical life-relationship to the self-understanding of those addressed, the congregation or the legal community, is not added to the interpretation afterward. Rather, the interpretation is realised in its application. (Habermas 1988a: 162)

Using terms from C. S. Peirce, with whose work Habermas is familiar, one might say that the interpretation of scripture in a sermon is not merely a plain-sense reading but a pragmatic reading.[5]

---

[5] For an explanation of these terms, and this way of using them, see Ochs 1998.

A plain-sense reading would interpret the text in a straightforward way and would make sense of the actions described more or less on their own terms. For Habermas, a sermon does not do this. Rather it interprets the text so as to orient the congregation in some way to a contemporary situation. The text is interpreted in the light of, and for the purpose of addressing, a question posed by the community of readers. Habermas suggests that this is not a two-stage process, with interpretation followed by application, but a complex single action in which the text is interpreted for application to the readers' situation. Obviously Habermas (following Gadamer) is not suggesting that this describes all interpretations of scripture: his remarks here are restricted to his understanding of what sermons are. He thinks that sermons function in much the same way as legal rulings: a text/law is interpreted in order to address some task or other. Gadamer's account, which Habermas follows closely, makes it clear that not just any old text will do. The situation that calls for judgement, for 'practical knowledge' (Aristotle), cannot be addressed by selecting some text at random and hoping that an interpretation will yield assistance. The text needs already to be acknowledged as authoritative for this purpose. To be a member of a tradition, for Gadamer, is to recognise the authority of certain texts, the validity of certain rules for interpreting them and the competence of certain persons to use these rules in a way that is potentially binding on the community.

Habermas wants to ask some additional questions about rationality and about the difference between practical knowledge and technical knowledge (Habermas 1988a: 163–70), and it is these that concern us most because they contain Habermas' baldest remarks about the loss of traditional authority. It is worth noting that Habermas has changed his mind on some of the details since the mid 1960s when this essay was first published, but the broad thrust of his remarks about tradition has persisted in all his work.

We need first to be clear about the difference between technical and practical knowledge. The distinction is from Aristotle. Technical knowledge means knowing how to build a computer or play the viola. Practical knowledge means things like knowing why it is good to buy fair-trade coffee or how to show strangers hospitality. Habermas suggests that one major difference between these is that technical knowledge leaks away if one gets out of practice, where-as practical knowledge becomes part of one's character. Obviously there is some fuzziness over this: one does not forget how to ride a bike once one has learned (which is technical), and it is possible to get out of the habit of treating people fairly (which is practical). Nonetheless, the basic distinction concerns the development of skills and the development of character.

Habermas is interested in the relationship between these two kinds of knowledge (technical and practical) and tradition. Both technical and practical knowledge require training in rules established by and embedded in a tradition. However, Habermas wants to draw out the implications of the 'abstract' nature of technical rules as opposed to the 'concretised' nature of practical rules. Habermas points to how groups make judgements about whether to accept or reject such rules or, in his terms, how the rules are established 'inter-subjectively'. In the case of technical rules, he claims, the rule is formulated generally and in an abstract way. Habermas thinks that the marks of inter-subjectivity for a technical rule are like those for a theoretical proposition: a provisional definition of basic descriptive terms is offered; rules for applying these terms are drawn up; the potential variety of cases to which these rules might apply does not affect the meaning of the rules; individual cases are subsumed under the rules (Habermas 1988a: 165). By using this analogy, Habermas seems to mean that understanding a technical rule just means understanding how to perform the technical tasks for which it is suited, and that finding new contexts for its use does not affect that understanding. Habermas is rather hard to understand here, as he offers no examples to illustrate his claims. My sense is that the important aspect of technical knowledge, for Habermas, is its ability to apply rules to a wide variety of contexts, together with the fact that it would take relatively drastic changes in context before they fed back into rule-formation.

Habermas insists that things are otherwise when it comes to practical knowledge. Inter-subjectivity works differently here. It is not merely a matter of provisional agreement on basic terms and rules for using them. The contents of tradition are not 'provisionally agreed'; they must be understood by consensus. They are also not understood 'abstractly', regardless of context; the context of use has to be investigated in order to get clear about the meaning of traditional rules. Accordingly, any judgements are bound to the particular situation in which they are made: if a new context arises, the whole process begins again (Habermas 1988a: 165). Again, Habermas offers no examples, and it needs illustrating. Suppose a stranger comes to town when all the guesthouses are fully booked. Mrs Jones, who does not own a guesthouse, takes him in, but instead of charging the market rate she treats him as an honoured guest. The question might be raised: has Mrs Jones placed the commercial business of guesthouses in jeopardy for the local community? The basic terms for this discussion are not 'provisionally defined' in the same sense that the rules for making a table are. For Mrs Jones' community, the terms are things like 'hospitality', 'commerce' and 'responsibility'. These are agreed, Habermas would say, by consensus. But they are not agreed in advance: there is no meeting where members of the community gather to decide what they mean by these words in the same way that woodworkers might have a meeting to evaluate new techniques for table-making. Instead, the meanings of hospitality and commerce have to be determined in the concrete situation in which Mrs Jones finds herself. Habermas puts it like this: 'The global universal, which we must have already understood diffusely, determines the subsumed particular only to the extent to which it itself is concretised through this particular' (Habermas 1988a: 165). The global universal would be something like 'hospitality in general', which is 'concretised' in the act of showing hospitality in the particular case of the treatment of the stranger. The important aspect of practical knowledge is the dependence of rules upon context: the context provides vital cues for how judgement is to be exercised, so that it is almost meaningless to articulate principles in abstraction from the contexts in which they are to be applied.

Habermas also draws attention to the arbitrary nature of the beginnings of technical knowledge, in contrast with the process of arriving at practical knowledge which is not arbitrary but arises from the 'mediation of the past'. It is difficult to be quite sure what is meant here, but presumably he means that technical processes can begin anywhere and can then be sharpened and improved through testing. And once a process is settled, it does not need (though it may receive) further interrogation. With practical knowledge, new situations require constant 'renewals of inter-subjectivity' because, as just discussed, general concepts (like hospitality) only have meaning when they are applied in concrete situations. These renewals come about through repeated acts of understanding which are the result of engagements with and interpretations of the past. Technical knowledge can begin with an arbitrary decision simply to begin somewhere; practical knowledge begins with an engagement with an already-begun history of practice.[6]

For Habermas this difference raises a question about the rationality of tradition. In the philosophy of Hegel, history itself is understood as the process of absolute reflection. However, for post-Hegelian philosophy, history is not the history of reason's self-awareness. It is no longer obvious that history, and therefore tradition, is inherently rational. Once the idea of absolute reflection is prised away from the idea of history, tradition needs some other means of shoring itself up.

Here Habermas begins to elaborate his now-famous critique of Gadamer's account of the relationship between hermeneutics and scientific method. This is well-worn territory in literature on Habermas.[7] I shall offer a reading of the text at hand which not only tries to be clear about what Habermas actually says, but also tries to identify his motivation. It is important to bear in mind that the exchange between Habermas and Gadamer went through various stages, but it is not obvious that Habermas' argument develops with respect to the issues with which we are concerned, namely the effect of reflection on the reproduction of tradition, and so we need not concern ourselves with the details of the different stages.

Habermas agrees wholeheartedly with Gadamer's critique of scientism. Scientism is the belief that scientific method gives the

---

[6] I have not discussed Habermas' handling of the relationship between trial-and-error 'learning' and discursive 'agreement', which can be found in slightly later essays. For a good account and critique of this see Mary Hesse, 'Science and Objectivity', in Thompson and Held 1982: 100–1.

[7] See Thomas McCarthy, 'Rationality and Relativism: Habermas' "Overcoming" of Hermeneutics', in Thompson and Held 1982: 57–78; How 1995; Silverman 1991: 151–77; Teigas 1995; Harrington 2001.

observer a wholly detached perspective on the matter under investigation together with a methodology that yields statements that are independent of any interest held by the investigator. Gadamer criticises the methodology of the 'modern historical sciences' (as practised in 1960) for proceeding as if aspects of tradition – historical 'objects' – could be investigated without acknowledging that aspects of tradition are transmitted historically and that the investigator is part of that ongoing history and shaped by it. Habermas applauds this critique. At the same time he claims that Gadamer separates 'hermeneutical experience' from 'methodical knowledge'. For Habermas, Gadamer is too dependent on a Heideggerian account of the engagement of the subject in practical knowledge. Gadamer correctly insists there are good arguments for saying that the subject is indeed 'engaged' in tradition in all understanding; but this places the subject *too close* to tradition for Habermas. There needs to be a corresponding description that does justice to the proper 'methodological distancing' that is the mark of reflective understanding (Habermas 1988a: 167). Habermas is not denying that the subject is always engaged in a tradition, in Heidegger's sense. The problem is that Gadamer's account pays insufficient attention to the difference between being engaged while reflecting on that engagement, and simply being unreflectively engaged. Reflection means seeing tradition *as* tradition, and therefore taking up a perspective on it, even if that perspective itself comes from within the tradition. Habermas makes his criticism thus:

Gadamer sees living traditions and hermeneutic research fused in a single point. Against this stands the insight that the reflective appropriation of tradition breaks the quasi-natural substance of tradition and alters the positions of subjects within it. (Habermas 1988a: 168)

This is not very precisely formulated, and the ambiguity it permits motivated the exchange between Habermas and Gadamer that followed. Habermas could mean many things by this: at one extreme it could suggest that being a researcher takes one out of a living tradition altogether; at the other extreme it could mean that researchers *as researchers* have a different attitude towards the tradition that they are still fully part of. The problem is the lack of precision about the meaning of 'altered position' and the extent of the 'break' of tradition's substance. We shall not spend time probing Habermas' later clarifications. For our purposes we need only pay attention to Habermas' insistence that reflective action is different from unreflective action. Habermas claims that 'Gadamer knows that the hermeneutic sciences were first developed in reaction to a decline in the binding character of traditions'. He is talking, one must presume, about the late eighteenth century and the rise of tradition as a theme in the philosophies of Hamann, the Romantics and the Idealists. The question, for Habermas, is thus how one orients oneself to a tradition once one becomes conscious of the vulnerability of its binding character. He has already acknowledged that 'sociology cannot remove itself from the dimension of history any more than can the society on which it is based' (Habermas 1988a: 23). The question is what kind of orientation is appropriate within a history when 'the medium of tradition' has been 'profoundly transformed as a result of scientific reflection'. Thus the problem is that 'Gadamer fails to recognise the power of reflection that unfolds in *Verstehen*' (Habermas 1988a: 168).

Habermas insists on the possibility of taking up a reflective orientation to the very tradition to which one belongs, and this changes everything. When one reflects on the history of one's tradition, on its origins and its development, the descriptions of the world and the practices that embody them are 'shaken'. There are doubtless many ways in which convictions and practices embedded in traditions are shaken; Habermas is most interested in the loss of authority they wield. Gadamer connects authority with knowledge: one knows who has authority to the same extent that one has learned one's tradition and made it one's own. Habermas is not impressed with this. He has learned (he does not say from whom) that children internalise authority through patterns of reward and punishment and through identification with role models. Gadamer gives a good account of the handing down of tradition, but for Habermas it needs supplementing with an account of the behavioural mechanisms by which children are socialised. Behavioural accounts explain how certain figures become acknowledged as authoritative, but they do not *give reasons* for this authority. They can actually undermine such authority: awareness of the mechanisms of socialisation permits authority to be questioned. Habermas raises an awkward question: does tradition legitimate someone's authority in some further way, besides its establishment through the system of reward, punishment and ideal roles characteristic of education?

Habermas is puzzled that Gadamer legitimates prejudgements and forms of authority through appeals to the power of tradition. It is obvious to Habermas that tradition does perform this legitimating function to an extent. But it is also obvious to him that the mechanisms of socialisation by which this happens are behavioural, and once one acknowledges this, the legitimation they serve seems much less binding. Furthermore, there is the power of reflection, 'which proves itself in its ability to reject the claim of traditions' (Habermas 1988a: 170). In the musical *Fiddler on the Roof*, Tevye sings a song of praise to 'Tradition!' and asks in the middle of it, 'You may ask: how did this tradition get started? I'll tell you [*pause*]. I don't know.' Tradition is precisely what comes under threat in the story that follows because this kind of question is posed more and more insistently. *Fiddler on the Roof* nicely illustrates what Habermas means by 'reflection', namely the ability for such questioning to be raised consistently: 'reflection does not wear itself out on the facticity of traditional norms without leaving a trace' (Habermas 1988a: 170). In other words, even if norms survive the process of questioning, that process itself now marks the tradition, shapes the characters and practices of its members, and leads to such norms being 'shaken'. Habermas agrees with Gadamer that action precedes reflection: only once one has been educated in a tradition can one question it from within. But once that questioning gets underway, it unleashes considerable power such that 'authority can be stripped of that in it that was mere domination and dissolved into the less coercive force of insight and rational decision' (Habermas 1988a: 170).

We now have a broad account of the consequences for society of reflection becoming a normal attitude. It is associated with self-criticism and, particularly for Habermas, with a certain distance at which members of a tradition find themselves with respect to that same tradition. Reflection calls norms into question, because they are now understood *as norms*, and not just as truths given in the world. Furthermore, the mechanisms by which children are socialised into acknowledging norms can themselves be described reflectively, and this robs such norms of their taken-for-grantedness. Habermas insists that if they are to becoming binding again – a kind of second authority – this needs to be established by some means other than coercion. It is to this question that he devotes much of his later theory about language. Already in *On the Logic of the Social Sciences* Habermas suggests that language, and not tradition, is the larger category. He even experiments with calling it a 'meta-institution' (Habermas 1988a: 172). Language is, of course, some-thing one is socialised into, so it is not merely a 'meta' sort of thing, but is also the medium of ideology, and so hermeneutic experience is, in its critical form, a critique of ideology. We shall not investigate this further, as this has been done very well elsewhere.[8]

The main theme to have emerged in this discussion is that of 'distance'. It throws up a number of problems, especially about motivation. These need investigating. We thus turn to Habermas' discussion of motivation in his treatment of the relationship between the sacred and the profane.

---

[8] For an analysis of Habermas' approach to questions of the critique of ideology, not least its cognitive aspect, see Geuss 1981, esp. pp. 26ff.

CHAPTER 4

Sacred and profane

We have considered Habermas' remarks about tradition in the previous chapter. This chapter investigates the ancestral quality that he ascribes to religion and theology. It is important to remember that the focus of Habermas' discussions is not contemporary religious life and thought, or the development of traditions of ritual and worship. His aim is to explain the forms that moral values take in modern consciousness, and to address problems associated with commitments to moral norms. For Habermas, members of modern societies are properly critical of – he would say 'distanced from' – their own traditions, but they suffer, as a kind of by-product, from a 'motivational deficit'. They know that their traditions see certain practices as moral or immoral, but they find it hard (compared with their 'traditional' forebears) to see why they should be committed to or bound to these ways of seeing. Moral values are criticisable for, but less binding on, modern members of traditions, in Habermas' account. He believes that the origin of morality in 'the sacred' holds the key to these questions, and he thus elaborates the ways in which sacred forces become profane through reflection.

Theologians need not, *as theologians*, be very interested in 'the sacred' any more than in 'tradition'. 'The sacred' is just as much an anthropological and philosophical term as 'tradition'. There is no reason for theologians to be anxious about entertaining or even embracing the idea that in modern society there is a loss of the sacred. There may well be other, anthropological or philosophical, anxieties, but not theological ones. Christians are only interested in things like holiness, sacredness, even goodness, because they are learned from worshipping God, and only have any value and command allegiance because of a desire to worship God. Something can be 'sacred' without having anything whatsoever to do with God: the point of using concepts like 'idolatry' is to diagnose when this is disastrously and even tragically the case. Habermas learns his account of 'the sacred' mainly from Emile Durkheim, and it is his account that Habermas hopes to repair. I shall assume that something similar applies to the notion of the 'holy', which for Habermas is freely interchangeable with 'sacred'. Christians have no idea what the word 'holy' means other than as an expression of their transformed relationship with God and creatures. More weakly, Christians learn to use the word 'holy' in two different ways: first, in the context of worship, when addressing God as holy, as taught in the psalms; second, in the context of study, when learning from sociologists like Durkheim. It is difficult to say how these two different ways of speaking of the holy are related to each other, because it is difficult to reconstruct the histories of these uses and, more particularly, the histories of their relationship to each other. I assume that 'holy' and 'sacred' are theologically less important the more they are used as general categories or concepts. In what follows, Habermas uses them almost exclusively as general concepts.

Habermas' two principal resources in 'The Authority of the Sacred' (Habermas 1987b: 43–76) are Mead and Durkheim. We can identify three themes concerning the sacred to which Habermas pays attention. (1) The sacred is the source of motivation and 'being bound' to a community's values; (2) the sacred is the source of an attitude towards an objective 'truth'; (3) the sacred is the 'original' form of what later comes to be the 'performative attitude' of partners in dialogue. These three themes are mixed together to some extent in Habermas' account. In what follows I distil them and deal solely with the first. Our interest is in the relationship between communicative action and the power of social interaction to bind members of a community together. Habermas is often criticised because he is profoundly procedural and seems to lack good arguments for why people should *feel* committed to certain forms of moral action. I reconstruct his best attempt at addressing this issue.

Habermas' preferred kind of account is developmental. A broadly empirical approach would notice different practices, institutions and ideas in different contexts and might attempt to compare them and even generalise from them. Habermas wants more. His aim is to show that certain kinds of difference are not just differences, but different stages on a continuum of development. This is important to him, as he wishes to show that modern thought is not just different from archaic thought, but a more advanced development of it. Habermas wishes to do this because it allows him to describe certain features of modern society *as* developments, and this means that he can evaluate gains and losses. It also means that he can diagnose certain practices as falling short of such development, and his theory can then promote a better form of development. This is an interesting strategy. Presumably it would be possible to weigh gains and losses and then – and only then – decide whether to promote certain kinds of development. It might even be feasible to promote certain kinds of regression, if the losses were considered too great. Habermas does not consider this. He has a barbed-hook theory of rationalisation. It can go one way relatively easily, although it might need a push. But once it has gone in that direction, it cannot be reversed.

Habermas has a developmental account of communication ready to hand in the work of George Herbert Mead's *Mind, Self and Society* (Mead 1934). The details of Mead's description of the socialised child do not directly concern us here: Habermas' main interest is in supplementing it with a description of the development of societies themselves, and not only those socialised within them (Habermas 1987b: 43). The two initial questions to be investigated by Habermas concern changes in how group commitments are fostered and maintained, and the processes by which cooperation between members of a group is secured. Both of these questions have a fundamental bearing on Habermas' own project, and guide his reading accordingly. In the case of the first question, he knows that commitments are fragile things even in traditional societies, and he believes them to be exceptionally fragile in post-traditional contexts. His own project has to answer the question posed to all broadly Kantian ethical projects: why should anyone care? He thus sets himself the task of looking at how the sacred fosters commitments in traditional societies, and what alternative means exist when such orientation to the sacred loses its hold on people's imagination. The second question, regarding cooperation, lies at the heart of Habermas' theory of communicative action. His differentiation between 'strategic' and 'communicative' action is designed to distinguish different ways by which people influence each other's actions, and to demonstrate the necessity of recovering the non-violent, consensus-forming practices embedded in reason over and against the coercive, instrumental practices so typical of rationalised processes in politics and the workplace. We have covered these in chapter 2.

Habermas chooses Mead as his point of departure because Mead tries to explain the shift from gestures to symbols in human communication, and the transition from symbolically mediated interactions to those guided by norms (Habermas 1987b: 44–5). Mead does so, according to Habermas, by speculating about attitudes adopted by individuals in a society: 'to render comprehensible the emergence of one complex structure from another, Mead resorts to a single "mechanism", namely ego's taking the attitude of alter' (Habermas 1987b: 45). Mead claims that members of social groups are committed to moral norms not because of the threat of violent sanctions if they disobey, but because they learn to take the other's perspective, and this leads them to imagine a 'generalised other' whose position they can adopt. Habermas takes up this theme of non-violent assent to norms. At the same time, he wants to supplement Mead's explanation of how this happens because it presupposes that social groups are *already* constituted in certain ways that make it possible for their members to adopt such positions. Habermas wants Mead's accounts of, first, a shift towards cooperation and, second, the commitment to norms that is secured non-violently, but he also wants an account of how social groups *become* the kind of groups that make this possible.

Habermas chooses Durkheim as his source for providing an account of how group identities are formed, as 'collective consciousness' and as 'religious consciousness' (Habermas 1987b: 45ff.). Unlike Mead, whose instinct is to explain social commitments by examining the perspective of the individual, 'Durkheim analyses religious beliefs and patriotism . . . as the expression of a collective consciousness rooted deep in tribal history and constitutive of the identity of groups' (Habermas 1987b: 46). It is Durkheim's account of religion that, Habermas hopes, will enable him 'to complete the programme of reconstruction pursued by Mead'.

Habermas draws attention to Durkheim's description of 'structural analogies' (Habermas) between the sacred and the moral. The most salient features of these analogies are feelings of obligation and attitudes towards the desirability of morality and the sacred. There is not only an analogy between them: they are linked. For Habermas, Durkheim argues that 'moral rules get their binding power from the sphere of the sacred' (Habermas 1987b: 49). Habermas refers more strongly still to 'the sacred foundations of morality' (Habermas 1987b: 50).

It is not religious attitudes that interest Habermas primarily, but commitments to moral norms. His interpretation of Durkheim is thus designed to emphasise social commitments.

Durkheim looks for the intentional object of the religious world of ideas; he inquires after the reality that is represented in concepts of the sacred. The answers that religion itself gives are clear: the divine being, the mythical order of the world, sacred powers, and the like. But for Durkheim what is concealed behind this is society – 'transfigured and symbolically represented'. (Habermas 1987b: 50)

The important feature of the collective consciousness is that it both transcends the individual's consciousness and yet at the same time resides within the individual and is owned by the individual. Habermas notices a certain circularity in Durkheim's thinking: 'The moral is traced back to the sacred, and the sacred to collective representation of an entity that is itself supposed to consist of a system of binding norms' (Habermas 1987b: 50), but he thinks that nonetheless the account manages to clarify aspects of the 'symbolic structure' of the sacred.

How does this immanent and yet transcending consciousness work? Through symbols. Habermas describes Durkheim's approach to religious symbols as a way of identifying patterns of communication that are more than 'sheer collective contagion by feelings' and which 'have the same meaning for the members of the same group' (Habermas 1987b: 52). These symbols are enacted, learned and interpreted in ritual. This allows Habermas to bend his account of Durkheim towards familiar aspects of his own project:

When ritual practice is seen as the more primordial phenomenon, religious symbolism can be understood as the medium of a special form of symbolically mediated interaction. Ritual practice serves to bring about communion in a communicative fashion . . . the sacred is the expression of a normative consensus regularly made actual. (Habermas 1987b: 52)

Habermas permits himself some licence here. Durkheim speaks of 'collective' or 'common' sentiments which are affirmed during certain rituals (Durkheim 1995: 420, 424, 429). Habermas glosses this as the 'repeated putting into effect of a consensus'. This gloss enables him to make the connection he wants between the sacred and communicative action:

It is a question of variations on one and the same theme, namely the presence of the sacred, and this in turn is only the form in which the collectivity experiences 'its unity and its personality'. Because the basic normative agreement expressed in communicative action establishes and sustains the identity of the group, the fact of successful consensus is at the same time its essential content. (Habermas 1987b: 53)

Sacred ritual, for Habermas, enacts commitment to a consensus. This is not a communicatively achieved consensus (i.e. one arrived at through argumentation), but a 'normative consensus'. In other words, this consensus is a matter of *already-established* group (and therefore individual) identity rather than agreement that is the product of disputation.

This abbreviated account of Durkheim appears to Habermas to serve his purposes well. It does the job of filling in what Mead had left out or just presupposed. Habermas summarises the story so far:

Collective identity has the form of a normative consensus built up in the medium of religious symbols and interpreted in the semantics of the sacred. The religious consciousness that secures identity is regenerated and maintained through ritual practice. (Habermas 1987b: 53)

With our eye on the role of tradition vis-à-vis religion, it is worth noticing that 'religious symbols' are almost accidental in this account. The primary category is clearly 'identity'; the form it takes is 'consensus'; religious symbols are merely the 'medium' for consensus. Similarly, 'ritual practice' is merely the mechanism for 'securing' identity. It is not obvious that this way of putting things is well suited to describing the observed effects of worship on a community's self-understandings. It interprets all outward orientation, for example towards God, as no more than what collective identity is 'concealed behind' (Habermas 1987b: 50). Habermas does not say so directly, but it seems reasonable to assume that, in his account, what members of a society are oriented to, even in prayer, is in fact *themselves as a collectivity*. The normal word for this in theology is 'idolatry'. This is admittedly rather gory, but it explains why Habermas expresses anxieties about the sacred. From a Christian theological perspective he is right to do so: the sacred is *the* problem when it is divorced from true worship of God. Habermas fully understands that an orientation to one's collective consciousness *as sacred* is a problem. His whole philosophical project is devoted to articulating a form of ethics in the wake of the German nationalism he grew up with and has consistently opposed. His project is not only a story about religion (which may or may not be persuasive), but also an urgent critique of idolatry. It is thus worth reading his account of the decline of tradition not just as an historical or developmental narrative, which is how he presents it, but as theoretical scene-setting for his critique of nationalism.

It is for these reasons that Habermas is not at all content with Durkheim's account. He wishes not only to use it to fill in gaps in Mead, but to use Mead to address questions left unaddressed by Durkheim. Habermas wants to investigate *developmental* issues. How did religious symbols emerge? How does the monolithic consciousness of the collectivity become differentiated in later societies? He also wants to hold on to Mead's concern with the individual as member of the group, and not just as the stuff of which the collective is made, but for reasons of space I shall lay this aside.

Habermas' approach is not surprising. Mead had given an account of a shift 'from symbolically mediated to normatively guided interaction' (Habermas 1987b: 54). Durkheim's description of the authority of the sacred has nothing to say about this shift. It is clearly central to Habermas' project. Mead thus provides the link Habermas needs:

The further cognitive development advances, giving rise to an objectivating attitude by actors toward the world of perceptible and manipulable objects, the less communicative acts carried out with symbolic means can by themselves link together the actions of participants. (Habermas 1987b: 54)

This is not a subtle move. Habermas needs a quick way to account for how the formation of consensus changes from being *already* secured by collective identity to being *a task* for the community. His characteristic approach is to offer a narrative of rationalisation. In this case, it is a matter of drawing attention to changes in cognition: members of a community increasingly distance themselves from (take an 'objectivating attitude' to) the world they see and touch, and this erodes the capacity of symbolic interaction to bind their common life together. Habermas does not have strong arguments for this causative effect. Instead he 'conjectures' that something like the separation of sacred and profane can be seen at work in the separation of different kinds of communication:

religious signification, which makes possible a normative consensus and thereby provides the foundation for a ritual coordination of action, is the archaic part left over from the stage of symbolically mediated interaction after experiences from domains in which perceptible and manipulable objects are dealt with in a more and more propositionally structured manner flow into communication. Religious symbols are disengaged from functions of adapting and mastering reality; they serve especially to link those behavioural dispositions and instinctual energies set loose from innate programmes with the medium of symbolic communication. (Habermas 1987b: 54)

This is a familiar story in anthropological literature which suggests that technical and practical (in Aristotle's sense) operations are mixed together in 'religion' in less advanced societies, and that they come to be differentiated as those societies develop (although, of course, they are *already* separated in Aristotle). At the stage Habermas is describing, the main job of religious symbols is not technical, but behavioural: they bind the individuals to the community.

This account has a lot in common with Hegel's well-known remarks about religion, which will be explored in chapter 8. It is religion that binds society together, and this is a problem for societies that become self-reflective, because they discover that their traditions are, precisely, traditions and not the only possible way of ordering the world. Hegel's question is: what binds society together when religions become reflective? Habermas takes up this question in relation to Durkheim. This is a tall order, and Habermas becomes very abbreviated.

Habermas' story so far is that normative validity can be traced back to morality, and that morality can be traced back to the sacred. The sacred, it appears, cannot be traced back to anything more basic: it has the honour of being 'archaic'. Habermas also claims that ritual is central to sacred practices, less so for morality, and far less so for differentiated institutions relating to the production of normative validity. This is just obvious to Habermas, and he offers no arguments to support the claim. He now sets himself a tough task: he wants to hold on to aspects of the *coordinating* function of religion, while abandoning the *ritual* medium of religion. He simply assumes that the ritual plays an insignificant role in modern practices relating to normative validity. He thus needs another medium that can perform the coordinating function. He chooses 'worldviews'.

Habermas' account here is hurried and vague: 'worldviews function as a kind of drive belt that transforms the basic religious consensus into the energy of social solidarity and passes it on to social institutions, thus giving them a moral authority' (Habermas 1987b: 56). The main advantage that he can squeeze from this switch of interest from ritual (Durkheim) to worldviews (Weber) is that the latter are established and transmitted through linguistic communication. 'Whereas ritual actions take place at a pregrammatical level, religious worldviews are connected with full-fledged communicative actions' (Habermas 1987b: 56). Durkheim needs repairing because he fails to differentiate the 'pregrammatical' medium of ritual and the 'communicative' medium of worldviews.

The next move is crucial. 'Communicative action is a switching station for the energies of social solidarity' (Habermas 1987b: 57). Habermas is claiming that it is not only ritual that secures common identity, but also the communicative action embedded in the 'drive belt' of worldviews. In other words, members of a community can be bound together through the 'linguistically differentiated processes of reaching understanding'. If this is true, then Habermas has solved his problem in one impressive, and astonishingly brief, argument. The problem was that social solidarity is secured in religious cultures by ritual. Ritual is powerful stuff, but it is not reflective, and thus cannot be criticised. The problem with modern forms of communication is that although they are reflective, and thus can be criticised, they do not command solidarity; they do not bind their members together; they suffer from motivational deficit. Habermas seems to have found an ideal solution: a modern form of communication which generates social solidarity.

Unfortunately, Habermas offers no arguments to support his claim. His rhetoric suggests that communicative action has some kind of relation to the 'archaic' sacred context, and that the energies of the latter are somehow preserved in the new differentiated communicative processes of reaching agreement. There is, however, no account of how this preservation works, or of how effective it is. Habermas' argument here has a lot in common with the thrust of early parts of Alasdair MacIntyre's *After Virtue*, with which it is exactly contemporary. MacIntyre and Habermas claim that moral theory is binding because it is embedded in worldviews; MacIntyre tends, in *After Virtue*, to tie morality to narrative; Habermas shares this, but also ties morality to ritual. MacIntyre and Habermas diagnose the problem in the same way: modern morality is not supported by ritual or shared worldviews, but is fragmented. Their responses are different. MacIntyre argues along Hegelian lines for an acknowledgement of the 'universal' importance of tradition, and like Hegel tries to repair the fragmentation of traditions that he inherits. Habermas argues along Kantian lines for an acknowledgement of the benefits of critical reason, and tries to repair the motivational deficit this produces by connecting it up with its archaic sacred origins. The problem this raises is significant, however: what grounds are there for thinking that communicative action does, in fact, preserve the motivational energies possessed by the sacred? Habermas associates communicative action with social solidarity, and even describes it as a 'switching station', but offers no arguments to support this. When Habermas recapitulates his argument slightly later on in a summary, the claim is significantly moderated, and he says merely 'Only in and through communicative action can the energies of social solidarity attached to religious symbolism branch out and be imparted, in the form of moral authority, both to institutions and to persons' (Habermas 1987b: 61). We must leave the stronger claim to one side.

After an interlude exploring the ways propositional and illocutionary speech-acts function, Habermas returns to Durkheim's question of the relationship between the sacred and social consciousness. Habermas connects his previous discussion to investigations of truth. This can be summarised briefly. Habermas suggests that Durkheim 'traces the counterfactual determination of a spatiotemporally neutralised idea of truth back to the idealising power residing in the notion of the sacred' (Habermas 1987b: 71). This sounds complex, but refers principally to Durkheim's interest in the human capacity not only to know the world in the way other animals know it, but also to represent it and, above all, to represent 'an *idealised image* of its society' (Habermas 1987b: 71). Habermas glosses Durkheim as follows:

The normative consensus that is expounded in the semantics of the sacred is present to members in the form of an idealised agreement transcending spatiotemporal changes. This furnishes the model for all concepts of validity, especially for the idea of truth. (Habermas 1987b: 71)

Certain kinds of thinking present themselves as if they apply always and everywhere, and are not tied to their contexts of origin. The idea of truth – especially the kind of truth that contradicts appearances – has its origins in the idealisations of collective identity. The individual encounters the thinking of the collective over and against his or her own thinking, and thus has an experience of an 'objective' realm, i.e. a realm that transcends his or her own thought. Durkheim claims that people believe there is a 'world of absolute ideas' because of their experience of the collective's thinking: 'a glimpse of a whole intellectual kingdom in which he participates, but which is greater than him' (Durkheim 1995: 438).

Habermas briskly intervenes to steer the discussion away from the alarmingly reverential attitude towards society described by Durkheim, and towards the role played by criticisable validity claims. Habermas adds to Durkheim's idea of 'collective thought' the Peircean idea of the 'ideal communication community'. At the same time, he needs to find a way to show how 'knowledge' is no longer underwritten by moral authority. Habermas wants to show that claims about how things are in the world do not command assent because there is a moral demand to do so, but because the person who raises the claim tries to show that there is a combination of 'the objectivity of experience' with 'the intersubjective validity of a corresponding descriptive statement' (Habermas 1987b: 72). Once one understands the significance of combining the relationship of facts and claims with the concept of an idealised consensus, one has the notion of a criticisable validity claim.

There is a certain vagueness to Habermas' account here which makes it difficult to interpret: Habermas is revisiting territory relating to questions of truth that he had battled out with positivists in the 1960s and 1970s, and in an abbreviated way. Nonetheless, the general thrust is clear. Habermas draws attention to the difference between two types of claim and tries to buy some binding power for communicative action. His argument runs something like this. Case (1) is a claim raised in a community which has strong social commitment to unquestioned norms. I raise the claim that I conform to these norms, and invite the hearer to agree that I do conform. The idea that I might not conform to them is intolerable, so my claim was not really in doubt, and the hearer's assent was pretty much presupposed. Case (2) is a criticisable validity claim raised in a community where members are prepared to evaluate claims. I raise a claim and invite the hearer to consider whether or not I conform to certain norms. It may well be the case that I might not conform to them, so the claim needs to be evaluated, and a 'yes or no' position adopted. My claim is in doubt, and the hearer's assent may or may not be given. Habermas argues that case (2) can secure a much stronger 'yes' than case (1). This 'stronger' means that participants in the process are more powerfully bound to any positive outcome, precisely because they could have walked away if it had been negative. In case (1) a negative outcome is a disaster, and no-one can realistically say 'no' without massive social costs; for that reason, although they are *already* bound to the moral values of the group, participants in the conversation are not strongly bound to the particular positive judgement they make. They were more or less forced to make that positive judgement. In case (2) things are quite otherwise. 'A hearer can be "bound" by speech-act offers because he is not permitted arbitrarily to refuse them but only to say "no" to them, that is, to reject them for reasons' (Habermas 1987b: 74). The question of binding force is thus connected with the distinction between strategic and communicative action. Case (1) does not invite debate, and so is more a matter of my having an influence *on* the hearer. Case (2) invites real evaluation, and so is more a matter of reaching agreement *with* the hearer (Habermas 1987b: 74).

Finally, Habermas makes the connection with reflection. Not only am I able to invite my hearer to take up a 'yes or no' position, but I am able to internalise the whole process and imagine what it is like for another person to evaluate my criticisable validity claims. 'If ego makes *this* attitude of alter his own, that is to say, if he views himself through the eyes of an arguing opponent and considers how he will answer to his critique, he gains a reflective relation to himself' (Habermas 1987b: 74). I become self-critical. It is here that we can see why Habermas wants to chart the move away from an orientation to the sacred. The sacred secures social solidarity, but in a non-reflective way, i.e. in a way that does not invite criticism or a 'yes or no' position. The sacred commands assent; it does not promote argumentation. It is thus important to Habermas that an account of socialisation describe a shift from solidarity rooted in orientation to the sacred to solidarity rooted in the ability to win assent through argumentation.

We have seen how Habermas connects communicative action to the power of social practices to bind members together and to certain norms. For Habermas it is a matter of losing the binding power of ritual and gaining the binding power of assent that is hard won in argumentation. This means claiming that the power of reflection is not only a destructive power vis-à-vis social bonds, but potentially a source of construction. I do not wish to challenge Habermas directly on his argument here. Instead we can pose a more oblique question. Can there be criticisable validity claims raised concerning the sacred? In Habermas' account there is a clear development *from* the sacred *to* criticisable validity claims. Argumentation begins where ritual ends. It is interesting to ask why Habermas does not consider the possibility that argumentation and ritual might be two parts of a unified form of life. After all, this might do justice to the practice, in the patristic period, of argumentation *about* ritual. At the other extreme, it might help explain why the form of argumentation in university seminars is often obviously ritualistic. Whatever answer one gives to this question, however, Habermas' set of questions throws into sharp relief the necessity of allowing argumentation to proceed on the basis of 'agreement with' rather than 'influence upon' the hearer. This is especially difficult in matters relating to the sacred, precisely because disagreement often appears as something intolerable. At this early stage in my own argument I wish merely for it to be imaginable that there are situations where it might not be intolerable. Habermas seems to offer some help in this by drawing attention to the ways in which members of a community who argue, rather than agree in advance, can nevertheless be bound together by the force of the hard-won-ness of their 'yes'. In chapter 11, I shall reject this offer and, instead, take the bleaker view that participants in argument are bound, or fail to be bound, together because of *already-secured* commitments to hospitality and friendship, or their absence: precisely the sphere of Durkheimian collective consciousness from which Habermas wants to depart. At the same time, however, I shall try to hold on to his commitment to the raising of criticisable validity claims as a way of demonstrating some interesting aspects of hospitality that arise when partners in discussion seriously entertain the possibility that their friends may be wrong. This is the model I shall explore in the context of scriptural reasoning in chapter 11.

The second essay, on 'The Linguistification of the Sacred', is of particular interest to theologians trying to understand Habermas' approach to religion, and in addition to offering a brief summary of its main points, I shall try to make sense of Habermas' claim that communicative action is powerful because of the association it has historically with the sacred.

Habermas' main developmental claim is that the social mechanisms for integrating members of groups and expressing this integration pass from ritual to communicative action: 'the authority of the holy is gradually replaced by the authority of an achieved consensus' (Habermas 1987b: 77). This is a strong claim, or rather two claims. The broader claim is that the authority of the holy is replaced (by something). The narrower claim is that what replaces the holy is achieved consensus. Habermas is aware that there are many somethings that can replace the holy. Legal contracts are a good example. How are parties bound to a legal contract? In societies oriented to the sacred, they are bound by the norms underwritten by the sacred character of obligations. 'How can such a contract bind the parties to it when the sacred foundation of law has disappeared? The standard answer to the question, from Hobbes to Weber, has been that modern law is precisely coercive law' (Habermas 1987b: 80). Habermas rejects what theologians know as an 'ontology of violence' (Milbank) and instead insists that the rational alternative to coercion is consensus. His narrative, therefore, will be of the linguistification (*Versprachlichung*) of the sacred not as coercion, but as communicative action.[1]

Once again, Habermas turns to Durkheim for help. Durkheim insists that coercion does not bind people's loyalty to legal norms; it merely forces external conformity. Political systems break down unless the obedience they command has a moral core. What binds people to norms originally, for Habermas, is an orientation to the sacred; in modern societies this is replaced by a 'moral agreement' that makes explicit what was only implicit in the signs surrounding the holy: 'the generality of the underlying interest' (Habermas 1987b: 81). In other words, there is a shift from sacred to common will. Habermas glosses the latter as 'communicatively shaped and discursively clarified in the political public sphere'. The social institution which bears the subjectivity of the general interest (Rousseau) is the state, which has to find ways to legitimate itself if it is to avoid brute coercion. As it loses the authority of the sacred, it finds an alternative form of support: consensus achieved in the public sphere.

Habermas wants to describe the transition from sacred to secular bases of legitimation. He promotes the notion of the 'linguistification' of the sacred, or of the 'basic religious consensus' that 'has been set communicatively aflow' (Habermas 1987b: 82). It is not clear whether this is a causal explanation which will show us the initial conditions and the forces which lead from one state to another, or if it is a description of observed changes in attitudes, or if it is a speculative history which aims only at plausibility. Most probably it is the last, as Habermas is content with a level of generality that is

---

[1] Some authors (e.g. Roberts 1992) translate *Versprachlichung* with the elegant 'linguification'. As 'linguistification' has since become the standard translation, I have used the more cumbersome term.

high even by his own standards, and little empirical evidence is brought forward as support. Two kinds of question can be posed regarding such an account: what happens in the linguistification of the sacred, and why does it happen?

It is significant that the part of Durkheim Habermas chooses to engage with is a discussion of law, rather than messier matters like ethics or moral formation. Law is codified in external forms, even documents, that can be examined and revised. Moral formation happens in a more sprawling way and is much more difficult to pin down. This is a point learned from J. M. Bernstein, who suggests that Habermas' programme in the later discourse ethics works very well in the case of law (which turned out to be the direction of Habermas' subsequent work), but is unduly and unpersuasively 'strained in the case of moral norms' (Bernstein 1995: 228). It is thus worth noticing that Habermas' account of the linguistification of the sacred deals overwhelmingly with shifts in legal legitimation rather than, say, the processes by which children internalise moral norms through their connection with worship. It would have been better, although much more difficult, for him to have done the latter, as he would then have had to deal with cases where *modern* Christian children are taught to 'be like Jesus' or that 'nothing is hidden from God'. These cases presumably come under 'the sacred' in Habermas' sense, and it would be most interesting to know what they look like when 'linguistified'. This is particularly significant because Habermas is going to have something to say about the formation of character in linguistified situations, and his account is greatly impoverished by his reluctance to deal with the difficult case of modern religious formation.

What is linguistification? Habermas offers not a pithy definition but a set of discussions. A sketch is in order. Linguistification involves 'achieving' mutual understanding rather than 'already' having it (Habermas 1987b: 82); it means distancing oneself from the basic religious consensus (Habermas 1987b: 83); it is the process that 'sublimates mythical powers into transcendent gods and finally into ideas and concepts and, at the cost of shrinking down the domain of the sacred, leaves behind a nature bereft of gods' (Habermas 1987b: 83); it is the growth of a range of applications for moral norms, an increasing latitude in interpreting them, and the correspondingly increased need to justify such interpretations (Habermas 1987b: 84); it is not the achievement of solidarity by 'prior value consensus', but is 'cooperatively achieved by virtue of individual efforts' (Habermas 1987b: 84); for members of communities, their 'Convictions owe their authority less and less to the spellbinding power and the aura of the holy, and more and more to a consensus that is not merely reproduced but *achieved*, that is, brought about communicatively' (Habermas 1987b: 89); instead of relying on already-given practices for moral deliberation, 'Participants in interaction must *themselves* relate the relevant norms to the given situation and tailor them to special tasks' (Habermas 1987b: 90).

   The basic features are clear enough. There are two broad strokes. The first is to note a shift from things that are taken for granted (powers, gods) to things that are up for discussion (ideas, concepts). The second is to describe a shift from things that are already binding (traditional norms, the sacred, the holy) to things that need to become binding (consensus, products of communicative action). This allows Habermas to set up the problem (how do things become binding?) and offer his solution: 'Once a community of believers has been secularised into a community of cooperation, only a universalistic morality can retain its obligatory character' (Habermas 1987b: 90). This will be Habermas' discourse ethics project.

   Habermas' way of telling the story of linguistification is intended to do more than simply set up his own project. He also wants to infuse morality with power over the imagination, lest communicatively achieved consensus seem weak. For this reason he insists that 'Something of the penetrating power of primordial sacred powers still attaches to morality; it permeates the since differentiated levels of culture, society, and personality in a way that is unique in modern societies' (Habermas 1987b: 92). There are problems with his account, however. Most importantly, he is unable to back up this claim with good arguments, but hopes that the reader will allow Durkheim's account of the power of the sacred to carry over into his discussion of communicative action. Second, it is obvious to the reader that the more morality resembles the sacred, the more it retains the problems that Habermas associates with the sacred, above all its unquestionability. Thus when he suggests that 'the authority of the sacred is converted over to the binding force of normative validity claims that can be redeemed only in discourse' (Habermas 1987b: 93–4), the difficulty is not just that the claim is unpersuasive, but that it would be a problem for him if it were true: he is rightly suspicious of attempts to imbue social settlements with the aura of unquestionable sacred truths. Habermas equivocates, as perhaps he should, over whether 'warm' commitments are desirable as well as 'cool' acknowledgement of validity. On the one hand, most rhetoric that stirs up hot passions does not seek 'communicatively achieved' consensus, but appeals to 'normatively ascribed' agreement. On the other hand, it is a pale life that knows only cool reasons, and such a pale life is vulnerable to hot rhetoric. Habermas is perhaps a little like Ernst Bloch, who desired a 'warm stream' of utopian mysticism to accompany the 'cold stream' of Marxist theory. Michael Theunissen observes that, for the early Marxist Habermas, this is ruled out: materialism is not compatible with mysticism (Theunissen 1981: 21; cf. Habermas 1987c: 33). In later work, which we are investigating, Habermas seems less sure. His other claim, that the 'ideal' of an undistorted communication community has an 'empirical' influence in the actual communities in which actors find themselves (Habermas 1987b: 96), is more straightforwardly Kantian: ideals affect practice and guide it regulatively. This does not suffer from the same problem. (It suffers from a different one, namely the excessive separation of intellectual ideals from commitment to one's community.)

The narrative of linguistification is a narrative about the power of reflection. Habermas has so far indicated, with broad lines, but repetitively, that reflection causes a transfer of power from the sacred to the power of communicative action. It is worth repeating that this narrative does not necessarily place Habermas at odds with theologians. Theologians are not automatically committed to 'the sacred' as a sociological category. Indeed, to the extent that Habermas wants to wean people away from treating *society* as sacred, theologians can and should offer their support: they share this critique of idolatry. Moreover, to the extent that people *already* know what 'sacred' means and subsequently apply it to God or to their religious traditions, the category of the sacred seems 'bigger' than God, and for that reason alone theologians should place it under suspicion. The problem for theologians is not that Habermas rehearses the decline of the sacred, but that he has secularised the notion of God's power and, like Kant, granted it to the autonomous self.

Before going on to discuss 'universalism', it is worth pausing to ask what kind of power this 'power of the sacred' or 'power of communicative action' is. Where does it come from? Habermas does not adopt either of two atheist positions in his own tradition. He does not take Feuerbach's route and suggest that the power attributed to the sacred is, in fact, the power of human subjectivity projected onto an external object. As a result, he does not have to get into difficult questions about whether this subjectivity is the aggregate of individual subjectivities or some property of groups, or even of something vague like 'society'. Nor does he take Ernst Bloch's route and appeal to an entelechy in nature, which manifests itself in dreams and works of art. Habermas nowhere speculates as to the origin or nature of the power of the sacred, or the power of the linguistified realm of communication. Some guesses are possible, however. Habermas makes striking remarks in earlier work, in the appendix to *Knowledge and Human Interests*, that language is a kind of equivalent of divine grace:

What raises us out of nature is the only thing whose nature we can know: *language*. Through its structure, autonomy and responsibility are posited for us. Our first sentence expresses unequivocally the intention of universal and unconstrained consensus. (Habermas 1987c: 314)

In this very well-known and much-discussed early claim, language is the source of peace between persons and the cause of a kind of supernature. The existence of distorted communication is not a prior reality, but precisely a *distortion* – of something prior to that distortion that is not itself distorted. That something, for the early Habermas, is language, whose structure posits autonomy and responsibility; in other words it has a kind of agency and power, and is itself something unspoiled. It almost sounds as if language is a bit like the absolute, or like God. It is unlike the absolute in so far as Habermas claims that we can know its nature: it makes no sense to say one knows the nature of the absolute or of God.

This impressive yet vague claim is one that Habermas could not maintain convincingly: he became aware very quickly that claims like this are difficult to defend against scepticism, and in subsequent work his claims moved away from 'language' more consistently towards 'the pragmatics of communication'. Yet it seems that communication still holds some of this divine agency for Habermas even in *The Theory of Communicative Action*. This brings him very close to theology, or rather shows that he was already very close to it. Claims about communication that are of this order have much in common with the question of revelation, namely how we learn what we know of God. Habermas' 'knowledge' about the power of communication has a family resemblance to theological 'knowledge' of God. It is thus worth looking briefly at how some of these issues play out in some Anglican theology, and comparing them with Habermas. This is the debate with Anglican theology that Habermas never had.

Rowan Williams has usefully explored the philosophical and theological significance of tackling revelation as itself a topic of enquiry: not only can we ask how we learn; we must also ask how we learn about our learning (Williams 2000: 131–47). This essay on 'Trinity and Revelation' has, immediately, two things in common with Habermas' approach to communication. First, it is rooted in questions of reflection, in Habermas' sense. Second, it doggedly teases out the implication of acknowledging the *prior agency* of something that is not the first-person agent. Obviously there is a difference, because this something is language for Habermas, whereas for Williams it is intentionally left vague and circumlocuted: 'The point of introducing the notion [of revelation] at all seems to be to give some ground for the sense in our religious and theological language that the initiative does not ultimately lie with us; before we speak, we are addressed or called' (Williams 2000: 133). Williams is just as interested in the philosophical as the theological implications of this 'sense' (what kind of sense?) of prior agency, so he does not hastily seek to fill this something with apparently – but ultimately not very – informative words such as 'God' or 'the absolute' or even 'language'. There are good reasons to hold back here: 'God' can only possibly be informative if the speaker has *already* learned who God is; and the only possible grounds for confidence of such knowledge is on the basis of revelation – and what is precisely under consideration is the question of how we learn this learning. For Habermas it is language or communicative action that has prior agency, and which draws us 'out of nature' or 'serves . . . to *bring about* rationally motivated agreements' (Habermas 1987b: 107). For Williams it is, after Ricoeur, poetry which 'restores to us that participation-in or belonging-to an order of things which precedes our capacity to oppose ourselves to things taken as objects opposed to a subject' (Williams 2000: 133, quoting Ricoeur 1982: 101).

Williams is a most appropriate theologian to juxtapose with Habermas. His interest in Ricoeur is an obvious point of contact, as Ricoeur himself wrote a commentary on the debate between Habermas and Gadamer (Ricoeur 1973). Ricoeur and Habermas have also been used to illuminate each other by John Thompson (Thompson 1981). Both Habermas and Williams associate language/revelation not only with a certain priority of agency but with healing. Not only does poetry manifest 'an initiative that is not ours in inviting us to a world we did not make' (Williams 2000: 134), or, more prosaically, hermeneutic understanding 'leads to new processes of development within the horizon of developmental processes that have already taken place' (Habermas 1988a: 153); there is more than this. For Williams, revelation concerns 'what is *generative* in our experience – events or transactions in our language that break existing frames of reference and initiate new possibilities of life' (Williams 2000: 134). For Habermas, this is most obvious in the process of disagreeing and working through the difficulties that arise, through use of language: 'Protest in speech is thus the reverse side of hermeneutic understanding, which bridges the distance maintained and prevents communication from being broken off. In translation lies the power of reconciliation. In it the unifying power of speech proves successful against disintegration into many unrelated languages that would be condemned in their isolation to unmediated oneness' (Habermas 1988a: 151). The difference between Habermas and Williams does not lie at the level of something as straightforward, or at least seemingly straightforward, as a belief in God (Williams) and belief in language (Habermas). This is evident from the following:

revelation decisively advances or extends debate, extends rather than limits the range of ambiguity and conflict in language. It poses fresh questions rather than answering old ones. And to recognize a text, a tradition or an event as revelatory is to witness to its generative power. It is to speak from the standpoint of a new form of life and understanding. . .

Is this Williams or Habermas? The sentiment is common to each, although the vocabulary of revelation (rather than 'communication') recognisably belongs to Williams (Williams 2000: 134). The difference lies in the warrants for making these claims. Williams closely ties the generative power of language, theologically, to 'the experience of grace' and historically, to the narrative of God's initiation of a new community through Israel's Exodus. Habermas, by contrast, characteristically generalises and connects the power of language not to a specific historical event, and certainly not to divine action, but to the moment of any genuine discursive negotiation, i.e. the practice of placing things in question and arguing about how to handle them against more or less stable background norms. Williams thus appeals to a particular story, a specific narrative, and an identifiable memory of the generation of a new community. The Exodus is not merely an example of the generative power of language. It is the event which itself motivates the questioning which, in turn, produces the concept of 'revelation' which Williams is trying to explicate. It is not too strong an interpretation to say that, for Williams, if there had been no Exodus, there would be no concept of revelation. It might even mean that there would be no philosophical reflection on the significance of the generative power of language. This is an arresting train of thought. It suggests that it is inappropriate to *start* with a class of events named 'generative' and then to find examples which conform to it, such as the Exodus. Instead, it makes more sense to start with a puzzle of everyday life, in this case the question of revelation, and then to interrogate one's memory to find out which events threw up the puzzle, in this case the Exodus. It is because the particular event has echoes in history (Jesus is *like* Moses, or – as it has been traditionally put in Christian theology – Moses is a *type* of Christ) that the general question arises, for Christians, and it is only at this late stage that the conceptual puzzle – what is revelation? – is formed and initiates the enquiry.

Habermas goes about things not in the opposite way, but in a less consistent fashion. He interrogates his memory, after a fashion, in that he finds out that the modern experience of worldwide travel in the eighteenth century threw up cultural puzzles about translation and worldviews. He most certainly interrogates his memory when it comes to the event of German nationalism and the seeming inability of many German academics in the 1930s to know how to, or even want to, situate the specificity of German language and culture in the context of a world of varied languages and cultures in a peaceful fashion (e.g. his article on Heidegger: Habermas 1992b). Yet Habermas conceals the events that are historically significant for him in a way Williams does not. The extent of this can be gauged by how easy it is to find out which events are generative of the puzzles for Williams. Barely four pages into his discussion, one encounters the Exodus, and then the question of how to interpret the generative life of Jesus. It is infinitely more difficult in the case of Habermas. The reader has to know quite a lot about Habermas' background, especially his anxieties about German academia, in order to interpret his work as a response to a problematic history. Habermas has long stretches of theoretical material – even as long as *The Theory of Communicative Action* – without giving the reader even a hint that this work needs to be written because of failures by German professors of philosophy. It is worth noticing that Thomas McCarthy's otherwise excellent introduction to *The Theory of Communicative Action* names Habermas' motive as a desire to respond to 'fragmentation, discontinuity and loss of meaning' and the rationalisation of administration that threatens 'freedom and self-determination' together with a corresponding 'sense of having exhausted our cultural, social, and political resources' (McCarthy in Habermas 1984a: vii). This is not untrue, but it is no coincidence how closely they map onto distinctively *North American* anxieties. McCarthy does not mention the problem of German philosophy in the twentieth century at all, even though he would surely acknowledge, if asked, that this is indeed a significant background to Habermas' writing. Part of the reason is probably that Habermas himself does not mention it in his preface. 'The contemporary-historical motive behind the present work is obvious', Habermas says. The historical situation named turns out to be the problems in

the West arising from what he calls 'the social-welfare-state compromise' and the loss of confidence in Occidental rationalism which
seems to exact acute sociopsychological and cultural costs. Habermas
tells the reader that he wants to offer an alternative to neoconservatives who, when confronted with the colonisation of the lifeworld
by money and power, 'want to head off and muffle [such experi-
ences] in a traditionalistic manner' (Habermas 1984a: xliii). Again,
this is not untrue: clearly that is a major motivation for writing
the work. What remains obscure here is why there is any problem
with the neoconservatives' approach, from Habermas' point of view.
The problem is, obviously, that *German* philosophers who muffle
their cries of pain with cloth woven from tradition will be using
precisely the materials which caused such disaster in the 1920s and
1930s. Is the same true for French philosophers? Habermas freely
discusses some of this (although not the latter question) in inter-
views and in lectures, but it is striking that he does not think it
appropriate to begin a theoretical work with a frank statement of
the historical problems that render neoconservatism problematic
and even immoral.

Perhaps it is partly a question of readership. Habermas is not
writing only for Germans, or even those interested in German
political history. Williams, by contrast, is aiming a book called *On
Christian Theology* and an article titled 'Trinity and Revelation'
(which originally appeared in a journal called *Modern Theology*)
almost exclusively at Christians or those interested in Christianity.
I do not think that this entirely explains it, however. Although
Habermas repeatedly declares that one can never achieve a con-
textless position from which to critique any particular situation, he
nevertheless tries to generalise as much as possible, as early as
possible, in many of his discussions. As we shall see in the next
chapter, the religious specificities of Christian Europe will admittedly constitute, for Habermas, the initial conditions for certain
theoretical developments: but they will very swiftly be left behind.
My conjecture is that Williams can be confident of which scriptures
his readers have before them, probably only a shelf or two away
from his own article. Yet there is much more to this than a confidence that his readers share his sources. Williams' approach contains
a warning: not only are these scriptures authoritative for his readers,

but there is a constant danger that they will be read badly: as 'a centre of achieved, privileged, non-ambiguous language and practice in the midst of a fragmented reality' to be transmitted by those who 'have' it to 'those who do not possess it' (Williams 2000: 132). Williams is thus not simply appealing to a cultural resource, but drawing his readers' attention to scripture *as* scripture which renews the imagination and gives it surprising new life, rather than as a source of deadly certainty and positive knowledge that destructively enshrines existing ways of thinking and closes down discussion. By contrast, Habermas cannot be at all confident that his readers share any such thing. He has, as he says of modernity, to do all the work. Because he must establish not only the reliability of his arguments, but also the very bases from which they proceed (he even has to teach his readers what 'lifeworld' means before his argument can get underway), the specificity of his situation seems a distraction. The self-critical question theologians might ask, and this will be the subject of chapter 11, is what kind of appeals to scripture best foster friendly disagreement not only within Christianity but across different traditions, and make genuine argument possible. If this can be addressed persuasively, it might go some way to persuading philosophers like Habermas that specificity is not a distraction or, worse, a source of division, but a condition of good conversation.

This detour into Williams' account of revelation was sparked off by the question of what kind of power Habermas believes the sacred, and subsequently communicative action, actually has: why it precedes individual human subjectivity and what makes it powerful. In summary, I wonder if its power does not so much derive from the kind of power Durkheim describes in *The Elementary Forms* but is more like the power of revelation as described by Ricoeur. The supporting argument for this would be that Habermas actually comes from a tradition that appealed (at least until quite recently) to revelation rather than from the kind of aboriginal totemic society described by Durkheim. One corollary is that the so-called linguistification of the sacred might be not so much the rationalisation of the lifeworld as the displacement of scripture in the face of the historical discovery that there are different traditions with different scriptures, and that some way of organising moral debate needs to be found other than that which appeals to only one scripture. It is not that a basic religious consensus has been set communicatively aflow: it is that members of different religious traditions (not least within Christianity, in Europe) have to communicate with each other by means other than war (Toulmin 1990). Clearly this kind of claim needs filling out in more detail than I am able to do here. Instead of diagnosing the problem in more detail, I shall try later on to describe some candidates for 'other means' in a way that addresses Habermas' quite proper concern with the need for genuine argument in the public sphere.

CHAPTER 5

Universalism

Habermas' defence of universalism is not self-explanatory. It is much easier to critique universalist positions than to advance them, and given the significant number of lethal criticisms of Habermas' version of universalism, it might seem a puzzle that he sustains his attempt nonetheless. The broad outlines of the arguments will be summarised before looking at two essays in which Habermas presents arguments about universalism and – more importantly for this study – the role that theological roots play in it.

By 'universalism' I mean the attempt to identify dimensions of human action that are the same for all actors, regardless of local context or history. Habermas describes his universalist ethics as a continuation and transformation of religious worldviews. The problem of religious worldviews, for Habermas, is that they are irreducibly particular, and that their own universal claims are far from universalist in his sense. The universal claims made in Christian worship (e.g. 'Christ died for all') are raised, evaluated and redeemed *within* that tradition, and are not universalisable beyond Christianity. We are interested in the gains Habermas attributes to universalism, over against the particularity of traditions, so it is important to be clear how he transcends these particularities. Beyond this, it is possible that some forms of theological reasoning tend towards neither universalism nor its opposite but, under modern conditions, seek *an alternative to narrating from within only one tradition* the universal or the impossibility of the universal. Such an alternative might be the practice (and only subsequently the theory) of *coordinating different traditions* with respect to 'common objects of love' (O'Donovan), namely scripture and ultimately God. The 'universal' here would not necessarily be God, incidentally, but whatever it is that makes such coordination possible. Habermas argues for a universalism that *transcends* particular traditions. We might ask whether there might be practices which *coordinate* particular traditions (and thus are not restricted to only one tradition), but which are nevertheless always housed *within* any tradition that is amenable to such coordination. Such practices would not conform to what Habermas means by universalism, but would simply be shared *across* traditions. Habermas wants more than this; whether his concerns with public argumentation actually need more than this is a good question.

Habermas' argument for universalism is presented as a cognitive thesis (i.e. it makes claims to truth on the basis of how things are in the world). He fills out the meaning of 'cognitive' as 'the view that normative rightness must be regarded as a claim to validity that is analogous to a truth claim' (Habermas 1990: 197). 'They represent more than expressions of the contingent emotions, preferences, and decisions of a speaker or actor' (Habermas 1990: 120). However, the basis for this argument is moral. The notion that life-worlds (Husserl) or forms of life (Wittgenstein) are incommensurable is all too easily conscripted by the fascist corruption of Christian theology, namely

the ingredient of Lutheran radicalism in the project of 'authentic' Dasein, which secures its wholeness 'heading provisionally towards death'. This Protestantism at its nadir of secularisation gave way at the start of the 1930s to a decisionism purified of Kierkegaard and theological remains and marching in the trappings of antiquity. (Habermas 1983: 57)

This critique of Heidegger, elaborated further in later work (Habermas 1992b), helps explain his arguments with Gadamer, which we examined in chapter 3.[1] Habermas associates the idea of the 'authority of tradition' (Gadamer) with an unwillingness to critique any specific tradition in the name of values which transcend it. His argument in his earlier work is something like this: some cultures need reminding that they do not merely happen to be committed to certain communicative practices, as if by happy accident,

---

[1] See also the chapter on Heidegger in *The Philosophical Discourse of Modernity* which elaborates this in more detail: Habermas 1987a: 131–61.

but are inescapably bound to them by the very structure of human communication *as such*. Any culture which deviates from these practices can be called to account against a measure which stands over and against every particular culture. The counter-arguments are (a) members of communities are educated *in a community* and not in a transcendent zone of some kind; (b) their commitment to moral norms is inseparable from their identity and character formed in particular communities; (c) there is no access to 'human communication as such', only to particular instances of human communication. Habermas has further refinements in the light of these arguments: (ad a) members of communities are also educated in universities in which multiple communities are represented; (ad b) modern people can develop identities and characters as participants in a plural public sphere; (ad c) hypothetical reconstructions of 'communicative action as such' are legitimate generalisations if supported by evidence and argument. Clearly this kind of exchange could go on for some time. It has arguably been terminated, however, by J. M. Bernstein's sympathetic but profound critique: Habermas starts out in his early work with a hard line about formal universalism versus substantive particularism, but then, in his subsequent writings, gradually makes so many concessions to his communitarian opponents about the importance of substantive commitments as support for formal procedures that the original project is *de facto* abandoned and lives on only in rhetoric and not in argumentative substance (Bernstein 1995: 197–234).

We are not interested primarily in whether Habermas' thesis about universalism is persuasive. There is good reason to examine it even if it is not: Habermas describes the role of theology in his account of universalism, and we need to know what that role is. This is useful knowledge, whether theologians wish to pursue Habermas' line of argumentation or wish to oppose it in the name of the very theology he conscripts for his purposes. It is also useful because Habermas ties 'cognitive claims' very closely indeed to the idea of 'argumentation in general'. He claims that 'narrative' and 'argumentation' are opposed to each other. This is most obvious in his famous essay 'On Levelling the Genre Distinction between Philosophy and Literature' (Habermas 1987a: 185–210), in which he separates 'problem-solving' from 'world-disclosure' and warns against allowing the latter to obliterate the former. Again, there are two quite distinct critiques of Habermas possible at this point. Either one can accept that problem-solving and world-disclosure are indeed wholly separate, and argue that world-disclosure is the only viable use of language today. Or one can insist that some better account of the relation between science and poetry be developed, because Habermas' is too coarse.[2] We shall investigate these questions further in chapter 10. This chapter concentrates on the role of theology in Habermas' account of universality.

'The Unity of Reason in the Diversity of its Voices' (Habermas 1992a: 115–48) is about the relationship between the one and the many. It is for that reason that theological metaphysics plays a leading role in the first parts of the essay. Over the course of this study I am trying to place some obstacles in the way of Habermas' easy identification of 'theological' with 'metaphysical'. For the moment we shall try to follow the argument as he presents it, and try to discern to what extent Christian themes persist in his own secular argumentation.

The contemporary problem of unity, for Habermas, is the danger that it might be imposed by force, and buy its simplicity by suppressing other voices. The critics of metaphysics (Kierkegaard, Heidegger, Adorno) had tried to undo the unified 'dogmatic' view of the world found in German philosophy before Kant and the unified account of 'reason' developed by Hegel: the critics tried to get at those aspects of encounter in the world that cannot be reduced to concepts. For Habermas the new 'radical contextualism' of Lyotard or Rorty takes up this critique and rescues the diversity that has been suppressed: 'the non-identical and the non-integrated, the deviant and the heterogeneous, the contradictory and the conflictual, the transitory and the accidental' (Habermas 1992a: 115–16). The new postmodern positions which attempt this rescue are nonetheless not quite as anti-metaphysical as they seem. Habermas makes

---

[2] For all their differences, this is a major point of contact between Andrew Bowie (Bowie 1990), John Milbank (Milbank 1990) and J. M. Bernstein (Bernstein 1995). All three insist that world-disclosure is at the heart of the scientific use of language, although they have different sources: Schelling and Schleiermacher as interpreted by Manfred Frank (Bowie), Augustine as interpreted by de Lubac and Rowan Williams (Milbank), Adorno as interpreted by Gillian Rose (Bernstein).

the astute point that certain features of German philosophy from the early 1800s are being recapitulated, above all the 'negative metaphysics' that accompanied idealism in the notion of the absolute. The meaning of 'the absolute' in German Idealist philosophy takes a little getting used to. Roughly, it means the unthinkable that precedes the thinkable and makes it possible, or the identity of being that precedes its differentiation into things. The concept, which is not even a concept because that is too 'thinkable', was hotly debated in the early 1800s, most influentially by Schelling and Hegel.[3] Habermas has in mind Schelling's account of the absolute. The key feature of the absolute here is its unthinkability: it cannot be conceptualised and it is the condition of human determinate thinking, and thus cannot be its product. When Habermas says that the role played by the deviant and the heterogeneous in Lyotard repeats the 'negative metaphysics' of the absolute, he is referring to this resistance to conceptualisation or placement within a determinate narrative. It is for this reason that he makes the fascinating claim that the 'metaphysical priority of unity above plurality [Hegel] and the contextualistic priority of plurality above unity [Lyotard, Rorty] are secret accomplices' (Habermas 1992a: 116–17). Habermas means that both routes give too determinate an account of the absolute: either as 'unitary' reason or as 'plural' deviance. What is needed, instead, is an account which does justice to the relationship between the absolute and the determinate, unity and diversity.

Where does Habermas locate the absolute? In communication/language,

> the unity of reason only remains perceptible in the plurality of its voices –
> as the possibility in principle of passing from one language to another – a
> passage that, no matter how occasional, is still comprehensible. This
> possibility of mutual understanding, which is now guaranteed only proce-
> durally and is realised only transitorily, forms the background of the
> existing diversity of those who encounter one another – even when they
> fail to understand each other. (Habermas 1992a: 117)

It seems clear enough that Habermas' version of the absolute is this 'possibility of passing from one language to another'; it is

---

[3] For a good explanation of its role in Schelling's philosophy see Bowie 1993.

guaranteed 'procedurally' rather than substantively, and is a kind of 'background'. We looked in chapter 2 at Hegelian critiques of Habermas' Kantianism. Here we can look briefly at a Schellingian critique of Habermas' revised concept of the absolute. Andrew Bowie suggests that Schelling's arguments against Hegel might be applicable to Habermas' version of reason, because of a residual Hegelian moment that Habermas reproduces in his own account (Bowie 1993: 184–9). This moment is the way Habermas relates his theory to the practices of communicative action. The problem for Bowie, following Manfred Frank and Hilary Putnam, is that Habermas knows *too much* about the difference between problem-solving and world-disclosing uses of language. Problem-solving involves an element of 'intuitive' (i.e. untheorisable) practice, and world-disclosure can perform problem-solving tasks (e.g. the use of metaphor to address psychological problems in psychoanalysis). 'The crucial factor is the refusal to accept that the *theory* which attempts to resolve difference into identity, in consensus, can rely on a basis which the theory itself can circumscribe' (Bowie 1993: 188). This refusal is a good refusal: one should constantly refuse to think that theory can rely on a basis that the theory can secure. In other words, Habermas is right to ground his theory of communicative action in a reconstruction of *already-existing* practices, but he is wrong to think that his theory can *establish* that there are, or should be, such practices. The key word in Bowie's critique is 'circumscribe'. Theories like Habermas' cannot circumscribe (i.e. fully conceptualise and account for) the basis of communication; they can only *respond* to their prior existence. This will involve 'intuitive' and 'interpretative' aspects that are spontaneous and thus non-theorisable – a point Bowie has learned from long and detailed engagement with Schleiermacher.[4] This criticism applies directly to Habermas' version of the absolute as the 'possibility of mutual understanding': Habermas cannot *circumscribe* this, and his attempt to do so renders his project vulnerable to the same kinds of critique as Schelling mounted against Hegel.

---

[4] See Bowie's introduction to Schleiermacher 1998.

In other words, Habermas brilliantly diagnoses the problem with postmodern privileging of the marginal: even this is an overly determinate version of the absolute in disguise. He also helps his reader understand the need to revisit the philosophy of the absolute in a non-disguised way, and relate unity to diversity in a way that avoids the 'secret complicity' of the priority of unity and the priority of diversity. The problem with his solution in a theory of communicative action is that he is not content with the 'fact' of communication and desires to ground it in some further way. If one comes to terms with this discontent – and so gives up on a theory that can embrace or circumscribe communication – what is the positive result? For Bowie it is 'the realisation that one of the crucial factors about the practice of reason is its ability to look beyond anything that can be theorised' (Bowie 1993: 189). This is not a lapse into irrationalism but a proper attention to the *reserve* that philosophy must exercise in its attempts to enquire into the bases of human action. Those bases are the condition for such enquiry. They cannot be used as explanatory principles, because they are what would need explaining, and that is what philosophy cannot do. Habermas is thus making a mistake in trying to use the fact of communicative action as an explanatory principle. Communicative action is, indeed, a fact. We do, or can, understand each other. But this is not something that one can have a theory of, any more than one can have a theory of the absolute. How, then, does Bowie think one can account for different kinds of communicative practice, if not by an overarching conceptual and explanatory theory? The differences between practices 'can only be continually tested in the contingencies of real communication' (Bowie 1993: 189). The appropriate alternative to Habermas' theory of communicative action is thus some form of 'continual testing', *and not theory*. This is radical. I take up Bowie's suggestion, although in a direction he might find questionable, in the final chapter on scriptural reasoning.

We can now return to Habermas' arguments about the unity of reason in the diversity of its voices. If we accept that Schelling defeats in advance Habermas' attempt to ground reason in communicative action, we are freed from having to evaluate the detailed arguments that presuppose the success of this attempt and can, instead, concentrate on the role played by theology in his account.

How are the one and the many related to each other, for Habermas? Although he is heir to the Christian philosophical-theological tradition, his answer is not approached via the doctrine of the Trinity. Instead he comes at it through a clarification of the problems of metaphysical thinking, i.e. the attempt to *think* the one, or, as he puts it, 'to subsume the one itself under objectifying categories' (Habermas 1992a: 121). What is the appropriate response to these problems? To refuse metaphysical thinking. However, there are different modes of this refusal. One can, with Nietzsche, Heidegger and Derrida, adopt a 'negative ontological concept' of the one. This places a clear break between the 'effusive' one and 'discursive reasoning': they are pitted against each other in an attempt to think the one as 'absolute negativity, as withdrawal and absence, as resistance against propositional speech in general'. Habermas traces this line of argument back to Plotinus (Habermas 1992a: 121). One can also, with Adorno, adopt a privileging of the particular over against the universal. This is a reaction against the metaphysical attempt to describe particulars in terms of general features which objects possess or express: 'Metaphysics uses the concepts of genus and specific difference in order to break the universal down into the particular'; but the consequence of this is that 'the individual remains accessible only in the accidental husk that clings to the core of the generically and specifically determined being'. For this reason 'Metaphysical concepts break down in the face of the individual' (Habermas 1992a: 122). The reaction against this is to privilege the particular over and against the universal, a line of argument that Habermas traces back to Scotus and his account of *haecceitas*. Lastly, for Habermas, one can, with Horkheimer and Bloch, adopt a renewed materialism. This asserts that matter is 'an active power of negation that first generates the world'. Habermas describes this as an anti-Platonic line of thought, traced back through Schelling, presumably to Aristotle.

Habermas wishes to attempt an alternative to Plotinian negative ontology, the Scotist account of individual particularity and Schellingian materialism. I shall leave to one side Habermas' arguments against Schelling, as these have been expertly addressed by Bowie in the section previously rehearsed (Bowie 1993: 178–91). Habermas is interested in the transformations undergone by 'the one' in the nineteenth century. There are many candidates for what 'the one' might be: history, culture, language. Habermas associates the explication of these different candidates with the work of Herder, Humboldt and Schleiermacher. They attempted to describe how individuals (the particular) relate to their contexts (the universal):

It is, in an emphatic sense, individuals who are enmeshed in their histories, their forms of life, and their conversations, and who for their part convey something of their individuality to these engulfing, intersubjectively shared, yet concrete contexts. The particular of a specific history, culture or language stands, as an individual type, between the universal and the singular. (Habermas 1992a: 128)[5]

Hegel's philosophy is a response to this situation and also the last attempt to renew 'the unitary thinking of metaphysics'. Hegel 'adds the last imposing link to the chain of tradition that extended through Plotinus and Augustine, Thomas [Aquinas], Nicolas of Cusa and Pico, Spinoza and Leibniz' (Habermas 1992a: 128). Given this list of figures, it is surprising that Habermas does not acknowledge that Hegel's form of unitary thinking is an experimentally reworked account of the Trinity. Instead, Habermas describes it as an account of the 'absolute subject' in which reflection itself is made absolute: 'reflection as the self-reference of a spirit that works its way up out of its substantiality to self-consciousness and which bears within itself the unity as well as the difference of the finite and the infinite' (Habermas 1992a: 129). The important feature of this, for Habermas, is Hegel's move beyond a metaphysics of nature to a metaphysics in which history itself is part of the ontological totality. This involved a big hostage to fortune. Hegel's account of history was supposed to take contingencies and uncertainties into consideration, but these are not so easily absorbed, and they revenge themselves on any attempt to reconcile them with each other in advance (Habermas 1992a: 130).

Where do things go from here? Habermas offers two directions: instead of a model which integrates history (with all its contingencies)

---

[5] Bowie is again a good source for these debates, especially in his explanation of how 'spontaneity' relates to 'rule-following'. This is a version of particularity and universality that Habermas does not investigate properly. See Bowie's introduction to Schleiermacher 1998 and Bowie 1997: 104–37.

in advance, models emerge which privilege social labour and revolutionary practice (Marx) or Christian consciousness of sin and radical choice (Kierkegaard). (For reasons of space, the problems with Habermas' account of Kierkegaard will be left to one side.) Even these philosophies have a 'foundationalist residue', however, in the implied teleologies which cannot be grounded in the philosophies themselves. At the same time, a new historical consciousness found it harder to ignore the 'unforeseeably new and other' which constantly emerges in history, and this led to a yet more radical metaphysical reserve exemplified by 'the withdrawal into the theory of science' (Habermas 1992a: 131). Alongside the neo-Kantianism of natural science, with its refusal of metaphysical structures of meaning, went another withdrawal, this time on the side of the *Geisteswissenschaften*: 'Historicism . . . declared the context-dependent knowledge of the interpreter and of the narrator to be the domain of a plurality that escapes the claims of objectivity and unity for knowledge' (Habermas 1992a: 131). The products are scientism in the natural sciences and historicism in the human sciences. These spell relativism:

histories triumph over the philosophy of history, cultures and forms of life triumph over culture as such, and the histories of national languages triumph over the rational grammar of language in general. Interpretation and narration supersede argumentation, multivalent meaning emancipates itself from simple validity, local significance is freed from the universalist claim to truth. (Habermas 1992a: 132)

This seems flatly contradicted by Stephen Toulmin's *Cosmopolis* (Toulmin 1990). Toulmin describes the rise in the 1600s of universalism, and the shift from local to general, particular to universal, whereas Habermas describes in the 1900s the switch from general to local, universal to particular. Toulmin thinks that the early modern trend towards universalism is repeated in the twentieth century each time after the world wars, whereas Habermas thinks that it is reversed. The apparent contradiction here is explained by looking at the figures they have in mind: Toulmin is thinking of the Vienna Circle and analytic philosophy, whereas Habermas has in mind developments in Germany (he does not specify which).

Habermas again raises the question: what is the relationship between narrative and argumentation? Habermas is unimpressed with the fashion for celebrating difference while devaluing the importance of argumentation that proceeds according to named criteria. We shall see why in the next chapter: once argumentation is devalued, the public sphere potentially becomes a Hobbesian war zone. Habermas' solution, which we shall look at further in chapter 10, is to prise apart narrative and argumentation as his opponents do, but to insist on the primacy of argumentation. The path he does not consider is the idea that narrative and argumentation are only ever relatively separable. It does not seem plausible to him that one might narrate, argumentatively, a relationship between science and aesthetics that does not reduce the one to the other. Habermas' defence of argumentation is sophisticated, however: he tries to get beyond an opposition of universality and particularity, by appealing not to universals known in advance (i.e. metaphysically) but to those that can be distilled out of *any* practice one looks at. 'For, although they may be interpreted in various ways and applied according to different criteria, concepts like truth, rationality, or justification play the *same* grammatical role in *every* linguistic community' (Habermas 1992a: 138). This is the kind of claim that is vulnerable to Schelling's critique: Habermas 'circumscribes' (in Bowie's sense) the bases for his theory, instead of allowing them simply to be the contexts within which piecemeal, 'spontaneous' (in Schleiermacher's sense) practices of testing can be continued. Interestingly, Habermas does make two close passes at this kind of admission, before slipping back into the priority of problem-solving theory. The first concerns contingency; the second – of central relevance to this study – concerns the role of religious language.

First, the 'placing' of contingency:

Communicative reason, too, treats almost everything as contingent, even the conditions for the emergence of its own linguistic medium. But for everything that claims validity *within* linguistically structured forms of life, the structures of possible mutual understanding in language constitute something that cannot be gotten around. (Habermas 1992a: 139–40)

Habermas gives 'everything' to contingency with one hand, in a most promising fashion, only to take it away again with a strong claim about 'the structures of possible mutual understanding'. If his arguments for doing so are not persuasive, his reasons for attempting it must be taken very seriously indeed. 'More discourse means more contradiction and difference. The more abstract the agreements become, the more diverse the disagreements with which we can *nonviolently* live' (Habermas 1992a: 140). Habermas is alarmed that universalism is exclusively associated, by his critics, with the repression of dissenting voices by a totalitarian central power. He argues that it must instead be associated with providing a means of coordinating all the different narratives that occupy the public sphere, no single one of which can perform the task *for everyone* of interpreting the world and helping people understand their place in it.

Another attempt to get at the contingency of communicative action is made: communicatively acting subjects

already find themselves within the context of a lifeworld that makes their communicative actions possible, just as it is in turn maintained through the medium of these processes of reaching understanding. This background, which is presupposed in communicative action, constitutes a totality that is implicit and that comes along prereflexively – one that crumbles the moment it is thematised; it remains a totality only in the form of implicit, intuitively presupposed background knowledge.

(Habermas 1992a: 142)

Habermas seems to imply that 'the totality' can only be grasped intuitively, and so not circumscribed by a theory; at the same time he steers his reader towards 'unavoidable and idealising presuppositions of action oriented toward reaching understanding' (Habermas 1992a: 143), thus negating the contingency that makes his suggestion potentially non-Hegelian. There is a constant slide back into claims for a knowledge that Habermas cannot possibly have, in this case the knowledge that presuppositions are unavoidable. It is not true that it is 'only when the totality of the lifeworld . . . is hypostatised as the speculative idea of the One and All' that the problems begin; they are there as soon as anything in the lifeworld is called 'unavoidable' rather than 'the practices there in fact are'. Habermas defends himself vigorously on the question of unavoidability, and in recent work concedes that certain conditions are only '*de facto*' unavoidable (Habermas 2003b: 11). I shall argue that it is enough to acknowledge the 'fact' that certain contingent practices happen to arise, and that the role of theory is best restricted to interpreting them.

Second, the role of religious speech. Habermas sees in the 'negative metaphysics' of Lyotard an 'equivalent for the extramundane perspective of a God's-eye view': a perspective radically different from the lines of sight belonging to innerworldly participants and observers (Habermas 1992: 144–5). In other words, the old religious metaphysics contrasted the human view with the divine view, and gave to philosophy the task of grasping and articulating the divine view. The new negative metaphysics contrasts the insider's view with the outsider's view, and charges philosophy with the task of gaining 'the perspective of the radical outsider'. Habermas argues persuasively that the new view is just as problematic as the old: they are equally metaphysical and claim too much knowledge. The old metaphysics affirmed the universal one and enforced conformity to it; the new metaphysics emptily negates the universal one by privileging the outsider. Habermas offers an alternative to both:

> Communicative reason does not make its appearance in an aestheticised theory as the colourless negative of a religion that provides consolation. It neither announces the absence of consolation in a world forsaken by God, nor does it take it upon itself to provide any consolation. It does without exclusivity as well. As long as no better words for what religion can say are found in the medium of rational discourse, it will even coexist abstemiously with the former, neither supporting it nor combating it.
> (Habermas 1992a: 145)

Habermas warns against *both* idolatries: the identification of God's perspective with the ruling power (metaphysics) and the identification of God's perspective with the marginalised (antimetaphysics). Instead he insists on refusing to take the God's-eye view at all. He calls for 'a type of emergence that cannot be intended', a responsibility that is nonetheless 'dependent upon the "luck of the moment"'. Habermas seems, in this context, to understand the full force of contingency: 'Philosophy, working together with the reconstructive sciences, can only throw light on the situations in which we find ourselves' (Habermas 1992a: 146). This seems an approach to communicative action which more correctly identifies our normal states of affairs.

We are thus left with two puzzles. Why does Habermas none-theless insist on a *theory* of communicative action which insists on the unavoidability of certain presuppositions instead of being con-tent to work with the contingent practices there actually are, regard-less of whether they are unavoidable or not? And why does he think that 'the consolations of religion' are invariably bound up with the adoption of the God's-eye view? It seems unthinkable to Habermas that religious traditions might have resources for healing the world that, like Habermas, renounce the God's-eye view in favour of a certain reserve and willingness to work with the contingencies of history, the 'luck of the moment' and 'the situations in which we find ourselves'. My argument later will not merely be that, of course, these resources do exist in contemporary post-liberal accounts of religious language. It will further suggest that interesting things happen when different traditions come together jointly to acknowl-edge their renunciation of the God's-eye view and to embrace the luck of the moment that enables them to read scripture together. Before that, however, we need to confront Habermas' repeated insistence that religious worldviews are no longer viable. We need to find out if his arguments are strong. If they are, then equally good arguments need to be mounted that can rescue practices like the reading of scripture as genuinely modern practices for healing divi-sions in the world. That is the subject matter of the next three chapters.

CHAPTER 6

Theology and political theory

Habermas believes that the modern era is characterised by the breakdown of 'religion' as a unifying force in political life in Europe. His reason for rehearsing this is now familiar to us: there are gains and losses in such a breakdown. The gains are increases in 'testing' and the shift from validity claims to *criticisable* validity claims. The losses are the fragmenting of shared worldviews, and the corresponding unavailability of universally acknowledged authoritative criteria for testing ethical claims. Habermas' purpose in continuing the 'unfinished project' of modernity is to maximise the gains and minimise the losses. In his earlier work, theology plays a major part in his discussions. His account of modern political theory in *Theorie und Praxis* (1963) is of special interest to theologians, because it traces the fate of the role of public argumentation from Aristotle to Hegel via Aquinas, Machiavelli, More, Hobbes, Vico, Locke and Kant. Most theologians who engage with Habermas tend to focus on his later theory of communicative action, and are surprised to learn that he has so much to say about Thomas Aquinas, for example. This material is especially relevant for understanding why Habermas thinks that religious traditions are a problem in the modern public sphere. The purpose of this chapter is to reconstruct Habermas' arguments, and show why he advances them.

Habermas' history of ideas has been expertly challenged on many fronts, but most of them concentrate on his alleged misrepresentations of Hegel and Marx or his misunderstanding of Nietzsche.[1]

---

[1] The literature is substantial. On Hegel see Rose 1981: 35, 41–5; Pippin 1989: 216–17; Pippin 1997: 157–84; Schnädelbach 1991: 281ff.; Dallmayr 1991: 37ff.; Bernstein 1995: 180. On Marx see Agnes Heller, 'Habermas and Marxism', in Thompson and Held 1982: 21–41. Heller

I wish to look at the part of his account which rehearses the history of ideas before Hegel, namely the overcoming of 'religion' before Kant. Habermas' account is impressionistic. Criticism of it is difficult: it is often not clear where he learned the story he tells, or which sources he might use to defend it. Another way of putting this is to say that Habermas' own narrative is mythic. 'Everybody knows' that religion was superseded by philosophy and art. Habermas seems to reproduce the kind of account he might, perhaps, have learned as an undergraduate. Consider the following:

> Unlike the range of early mythic narratives, the idea of God – that is, the idea of the unified, invisible God the Creator and Redeemer – signified a breakthrough to an entirely new perspective. With this idea, finite spirit acquired a standpoint that utterly transcends the this-worldly. But only with the transition to modernity does the knowing and morally judging subject appropriate the divine standpoint. (Habermas 2002: 148)

This chapter will explore the iceberg of which this short quotation is the tip. All the main problems are laid out here: the identification of theology with an appropriation of the God's-eye view; the non-trinitarian explanation of the idea of God; the broadly Hegelian language ('finite spirit'); the description of modernity as essentially post-Christian; and the implication that overcoming the God's-eye view in post-metaphysical thinking will be inherently non-theological. Instead of offering a comprehensive alternative mythic account, I propose to place some obstacles in Habermas' way. This should be satisfactory as preparation for later arguments about the encounter between traditions in the public sphere.

In 'The Classical Doctrine of Politics in Relation to Social Philosophy', Habermas aims to compare 'the old politics', associated with

---

echoes, and gives a better account of, the kinds of objection raised by the theologian Helmut Peukert regarding the loss of lives in a history of so-called progress (p. 40). Cf. Peukert 1984 and chapter 9 of this study; see also William McBride, 'Habermas and the Marxian Tradition', in Hahn 2000: 425–38; James Bohman, 'Habermas, Marxism and Social Theory', in Dews 1999: 53–86; Nancy Love, 'What's Left of Marx', in White 1995: 46–66. On Nietzsche see principally Owen 1994: 17–83. Owen's account is an 'extended reply' to Habermas' version of Hegelian critique; see also Tracey Strong, 'Nietzsche's Political Misappropriation', in Magnus and Higgins 1996, esp. pp. 132–3; Alexander Nehamas 'Nietzsche, Modernity, Aestheticism', in Magnus and Higgins 1996, esp. pp. 228–30.

the Aristotelian tradition, with 'the revolution in approach' initiated by Machiavelli and More and completed by Thomas Hobbes. It thus fills in some of the prehistory of his earlier *Structural Transformation of the Public Sphere* (Habermas 1989a). There are three aspects which undergo change, according to Habermas: the association of politics with the good life; the association of politics with the formation of character; and the association of politics with *phronesis* rather than with *episteme*. The ending of these associations in Hobbes goes hand in hand with changes in the religious life of modern Europe. Habermas' motivation for writing the essay is reasonably clear: he wants to retain the 'scientific' advances in social philosophy because these might aid the reconstruction of public politics in Europe after the Second World War. However, he does not want to pay the price demanded by Hobbes, namely the abandonment of 'the practical orientation of classical politics' (Habermas 1988b: 44). Habermas' essay is an attempt to renarrate the story so as to show how it might be possible to do good social science and thereby aid practical philosophy.

Hobbes' revolution in thought was decisive. The following brief rehearsal is of Habermas' interpretation of Hobbes; indeed, his whole essay is a commentary on chapter 29 of *Leviathan*, which opens thus:

> Though nothing can be immortall, which mortals make: yet, if men had the use of reason they pretend to, their Common-wealths might be secured, at least, from perishing by internall diseases. For by the nature of their Institution, they are designed to live, as long as Mankind, or as the Lawes of Nature, or as Justice it selfe, which gives them life. Therefore when they come to be dissolved, not by externall violence, but intestine disorder, the fault is not in men, as they are the *Matter*, but as they are the *Makers*, and orderers of them. (Hobbes 1996: 221)

Hobbes, according to Habermas, aims to use 'scientifically grounded social philosophy' to establish the correct order of the state; in so doing he separates politics from morality, and instead of emphasising moral instruction, he privileges scientific construction of order: 'The order of virtuous conduct is changed into the regulation of social intercourse' (Habermas 1988b: 43). Habermas learns from Vico's *On the Study Methods of our Time* and *The New Science* that this creates an increasing gulf between scientific knowledge and procedures for establishing moral norms. This rupture leads to decisionism in ethics (i.e. the privileging of individual choice instead of argument) because moral claims are disbarred from 'scientific' investigation. There is the further assumption here that such scientific investigation is increasingly the sole domain where evidence and argumentation are the normal means of adjudicating questions of truth. Vico, however, rejects the incursions of science into politics, and this is a problem for Habermas. Vico promotes 'prudence' (i.e. *phronesis*) in public life instead of the Hobbesian coldly scientific politics; but he fails to notice that the new scientific study of society ('social theory' in the twentieth century) yields potential benefits if they can be harnessed appropriately. Thus, Habermas wants Hobbes' scientific impulse *and* Vico's 'prudence': that will be the project elaborated twenty years later by Habermas in his discourse ethics and the explanation for his insistence that moral claims have a 'cognitive' content.

The heart of the matter for us is Habermas' account of how classical politics (Aristotle) became transformed into social philosophy (Hobbes). There is obviously a lot of history in between, and how Habermas traverses it is of interest to philosophers and theologians alike. To view it thematically, Aristotle distinguishes sharply between *polis* (which promotes public virtue) and *oikos* (which promotes private interest). So the question is: what is the hinge between Aristotle's distinction between, and Hobbes' identification of, the state and the 'commerce of bourgeois private individuals' (Habermas 1988b: 47)? Habermas' answer is: Thomas Aquinas.

Habermas' Aquinas is Aristotelian in so far as he identifies the state with the community that promotes the virtues in pursuit of the good life. He is not Aristotelian in so far as he fails to distinguish between *Polis* and *Oikos*. Habermas' Aquinas talks instead of *societas*, and his account of it is decidedly domestic. Furthermore, instead of Aristotle's 'political' safeguarding of public discussion and argument, Aquinas' chief good is *pax*: the peaceful life together of family members. Habermas ominously observes

The criterion of the well-founded *ordo* is no longer the freedom of the citizens, but tranquillity and peace – *pax*; an interpretation of that New Testament concept from a 'police' viewpoint rather than a political one.

The central question of the old Politics, concerning the *quality* of govern-
ance, has been dropped. (Habermas 1988b: 48)

The privileging of peace-keeping over free public discussion is
not a problem in Aquinas' politics because he still intimately associates ethics and politics, and he still sees the goal of communal life as
the learning of virtues in pursuit of the good life. He does this,
Habermas says, 'ontotheologically': through an account of natural
law. The *lex naturae* is the basis of the city's order: cosmic and social
lawfulness are intertwined, and they are known through the ten
commandments in scripture.

The problem arises, for Habermas, with the nominalist critique
of Aquinas (i.e. by the traditions stemming from Scotus and
Ockham). The nominalists fatally undermine Aquinas' account
(Habermas does not say how); furthermore, the thirteenth-century
social relations that made Aquinas' account plausible were themselves shattered, and this undermined the account's persuasiveness
(again, Habermas does not say how – perhaps he has in mind a
vague Marxian notion of the economic base that determines the
theological superstructure). Habermas calls this 'the broken bond'
(*das zerborstene Band*): the order of virtue is no longer guaranteed by
the order of nature. At the same time, European history in the
sixteenth century saw a split between *dominium* (exercised by
princes) and *societas* (privatised under the state). It is in this new
context that the work of Niccolò Machiavelli and Thomas More
lays the foundations for later political theory. The new question is
not 'what is the goal of the good life?' but 'how can the *civitas* be
ruled in an ordered way?' (Habermas 1988b: 49).

To simplify greatly, Machiavelli treats politics as the art of war,
and his theory is directed to explaining and teaching the strategic
management of power. More, by contrast, theorises the domestic
order that has now been expanded into the state. The old Aristotelian teleology which sought the meaning of politics in the pursuit
of the good life is abandoned: Machiavelli fills the gaps with the
Prince's interests, while More fills them with the interests of the
labouring citizens. God, so central to Aquinas' account (freely acknowledged by Habermas), has been replaced by the Prince and by
the citizenry. And the goal of these new gods is not a good life but,

explicitly, mere *survival* in the face of slaughter (Machiavelli) and starvation (More). (I wonder if it is here that one finds the origins of bureaucratic speech about 'social security' instead of the good life.) In both cases politics is divorced from ethics: 'Just like the techniques for securing power in Machiavelli, so in More the organisation of the social order is morally neutral' (Habermas 1988b: 54). In the language of German philosophy, this marks a shift from 'practical' to 'technical' questions.

Aquinas' social philosophy combined *dominium* and *societas*, i.e. the question of rulership and the question of social organisation. Machiavelli treated *dominium*, but ignored *societas*; More did the reverse. What they have in common is their contributions to splitting off what Aquinas had held together. Hobbes inherits this situation and, in a seventeenth-century English context, finds a new way of combining them that is quite unlike that of Aquinas: the task of *dominium* is now to safeguard the system of contracts between those who have commerce in *societas*. Hobbes also has technological superiority over Machiavelli and More: he inherits a rigorous methodological outlook from Descartes and Bacon which can be put to work in investigating society.

Habermas reminds his readers that in classical philosophy *praxis* (the area of practical judgement in the difficult arena of ethical and political life) and *poiesis* (the area of human manufacture of tools and objects) had been separate. Because Machiavelli and More treat political questions as questions of technique, this separation is overcome. What Habermas' Hobbes adds to this is a 'scientific' method for investigating and testing such questions of technique (Habermas 1988b: 60–2). And what follows in its wake is a radical reinterpretation of 'natural law'.

According to Habermas, Hobbes is not solely responsible for the 'diabolical inversion' of natural law seen in his work. He is able to imagine things the way he does because of key developments in theology.[2] Habermas attributes to the Reformation the chief of these

---

[2] Richard Tuck's editorial introduction to *Leviathan* attributes Hobbes' more immediate influences to Grotius and Seldon: Hobbes 1996: xxvii–xxix. Habermas, as usual, has his eye on the big picture.

ills, namely the 'positivisation and formalisation of the prevailing Thomistic Natural Law' (Habermas 1988b: 62). Habermas means that divine law and human positive law become identified and subsequently codified. In the secular realm this results in an unprecedented privileging of law as the regulation of private contracts between individuals. (How this relates to theological understandings of the covenant between God and humanity Habermas does not say.) To the two fears of enemies and starvation, Hobbes' period adds a third: of servitude. The new social philosophy is designed to theorise the 'protection' that can now be offered against these dangers. Hobbes' predecessor Althusius had offered an account of society that Hobbes subsequently developed: social relations originate in contracts. Habermas diagnoses the weakness of Althusius' version: although he speaks of contracts, he merely presupposes all the structures that underlie them, namely the obligation to honour them and the legitimacy of the authorities that police them. Hobbes is able to deal with these big questions head on: he makes natural law into a science for investigating and testing networks of obligation and, most importantly, the forms of political control that will secure their successful operation. In this scheme of things, the term 'natural law' has little in common with what Aquinas meant by *lex naturae*. Natural law comes to be associated with what Hobbes calls the 'state of nature': this is not the divine law-governed cosmos of Aquinas, but the evil state of man which receives gruesome elaboration in the account of the war of all against all in Machiavelli and in the Reformation's theological account of sinful human nature in a fallen world (Habermas 1988b: 63). (Habermas states this, but offers no examples: we shall return to his misleading account of the Reformation in chapter 8.)

The new natural law is the natural compulsion to avoid death at all costs: 'a modern physics of human nature replaces the classical ethics of Natural Law' (Habermas 1988b: 64). Then comes the climax of Habermas' theological narrative:

Under naturalistic presuppositions, the traditional determinants which have been retained are transformed and with a profound irony. For after all, the absolute Natural Law of St Thomas assumed that in the state of nature the ethics of the Sermon on the Mount had been directly realised:

that there was no domination: all are free; there were no social distinctions: all are equal; there was no personal and exclusive property: everything is common to all, all have a right to everything. Verbally, Hobbes accepts these determinates; but tacitly he replaces the subject of Law. In place of the *animal sociale* in the Christian Aristotelian sense of a *zoon politikon* he sets an *animal politicum* in the sense of Machiavelli, in order then to show quite readily that precisely the assumption of these rights, especially the right of all to everything, as soon as it is applied to a pack of 'free' and 'equal' wolves, will have as its consequence a state in which they mutually tear and devour each other. This subtle playing with venerable attributes reveals the radical rethinking of classical Natural Law, so that it becomes the actual absence of all right and justice for the natural environment, which lacks positive regulation and rational compacts. The conditions under which a community of saints was supposed to live, appear, in a diabolical inversion, as the conditions under which human beasts live in a continual life-and-death struggle. (Habermas 1988b: 64–5)

In other words, the natural law of Aquinas is based on scripture and an intensely complex theology of reconciliation, whereas Hobbes' is based on a 'scientific' account of human nature. Instead of the scriptural narrative of social peace and justice, Hobbes asserts the *realpolitik* of the war of all against all. This account is not ethical at all: it relies purely on biology, and its currency is 'sensation', 'instinct' and 'reaction'.

Fascinatingly, from the point of view of this study, Habermas recognises that the philosophies constructed by Aquinas and Hobbes are structurally very similar: what differs is the 'revelation' (not Habermas' term) they seek to interpret, and the rules for testing such interpretations. Habermas has an account of nature much closer to Aquinas than Hobbes: indeed, it is basically Augustinian. The theological problem (which he does not acknowledge) is that he, like Hobbes, abandons scripture and theology in favour of the 'scientific'. This leaves him in some difficulty in accounting for how he has learned what the world is like and how he proposes to teach others in turn. His account of the rules for testing his interpretation (but of what?) is also non-theological, in that instead of subjecting the interpretation of scripture to the tests of prayer, he subjects validity claims to the tests of communal argumentation. Nonetheless, theologians may appreciate Habermas' insight that Aquinas'

account of natural law only has the normative sense he intends
because it is rooted in scripture.[3]

Habermas goes on to complicate his account of Hobbes a little.
Hobbes does not restrict the scope of 'natural law' to biology.
'Natural law' refers not only to the biological nature of humanity
prior to the contractual constitution of society but also to 'the
normative regulation of their social cohabitation *after* this constitution' (Habermas 1988b: 66). With this equivocation, a cat is let out
of the bag: what Hobbes calls 'natural' turns out to look suspiciously
fabricated. As Habermas knows, and as his reader knows, once this
comes to be acknowledged much of the modern project comes
under heavy threat. What will be required is an account of political
theory that acknowledges the impossibility of claims about nature
underwritten by the God's-eye view and instead sets about giving a
good account of the relationship between justice and human political fabrication. That, of course, is what Habermas' later project
will be.

Theologians familiar with John Milbank's essay 'Political
Theology and the New Science of Politics' in *Theology and Social
Theory* (Milbank 1990: 9–26) may recognise parts of Habermas'
account, which Milbank reproduces quite closely. Milbank objects
that Habermas ignores the possibility that the realm of human
making might not be instrumental but poetic (Milbank 1990: 11).
Milbank suggests that this kind of thinking might yield a 'science'
that does not insist on an unbridgeable gulf between divine and
human making; the problem with Habermas, for Milbank, is that
although Habermas has learned from Nicholas of Cusa, he fails to
appreciate the trinitarian thinking that relates divine and human
knowing and doing. This may be true, but it does not do justice to
the heart of Habermas' problem: Aquinas' theology allegedly drew
its plausibility from the social relations that it mirrored, and once
those social conditions changed, the theology crumbled. For

---

[3] It is not obvious where Habermas had learned about Aquinas. It is possible that he reflects a
received view commonly taught in basic politics courses at the time (the late 1950s).
Probably he learned a lot from Ernst Bloch and from Wilhelm Hennis, whose habilitation
thesis (on precisely these themes) Habermas cites and which was being written in Frankfurt
while Habermas was a research student there.

Habermas it would be quite irrelevant that there might be persistent trinitarian accounts of divine and human action: he would claim that they cannot be sustained *persuasively* under the new social conditions. I think the main issue is that Milbank is influenced by Romanticism and tends towards the belief that politics follows from the imagination, whereas Habermas (at this early stage in his career) considers himself more Marxist and tends to assume that the imagination follows from politics. Thus Milbank's critique of Habermas will always be that his imagination is impoverished, while Habermas' critique of Milbank (were he to mount one) would be that his politics is imaginary. My argument is that Habermas hits the problem's nail on the head: social relations have changed, and no theology from a single tradition can by itself provide the resources for coordinating argument and disagreement in the public sphere. His solution certainly suffers from an impoverished imagination, however, because he does not consider the possibility that members of different traditions might bring their theologies together in a coordinated but non-unified way. As we saw in chapter 5, Habermas tries to unite the diversity of voices through reason. I shall try to show the consequences of coordinating the diversity of voices through the practice of scriptural reasoning, and not merely an 'account' of some imagined possibility.

The remainder of Habermas' essay must be set aside. In it, Habermas analyses Hobbes' shortcomings in a little more detail and rehearses the main theme: that scientific techniques in social philosophy were bought at too high a price, namely lack of access to practical reasoning. It is worth noting, in addition, that Habermas' interest in Hobbes is not the product of a chance encounter with a major figure from the past. There is good reason to suppose that it arises from Habermas' passionate opposition to the work and influence of Carl Schmitt. Schmitt's *Political Theology* of 1934 (Schmitt 1985) and *Leviathan in Hobbes' Doctrine of the State* of 1938 advocate the abolition of precisely the kind of public sphere that Habermas believes is so vital to the healthy government of the contemporary nation state. Instead of an arena of argumentation for resolving disagreements, Schmitt conceived of politics as the authoritative representation of the people by the total state and, perhaps, by an elite (Kodalle 1973: 39–43, 77–86).[4] It is an obvious point, but Habermas accepts Schmitt's belief that the opposite to dictatorship is discussion, but naturally argues *contra* Schmitt *for* discussion. Perhaps Habermas' desire to overcome religion stems partly from Schmitt's identification of medieval Catholicism with a kind of dictatorial model of 'representation'. But instead of repairing Schmitt's account of medieval Catholicism, Habermas blots it out. Central to Schmitt's argument was an investigation into Hobbes' understanding of sovereignty, his intention being to show that because politics is a war of all against all, a discursive public sphere – which he mocks as 'everlasting conversation' – can only lead to chaotic disaster (Schmitt 1985: 53ff.). Only a government exercising sole authority, and defended by force against both external and internal threats, can make a strong Germany. Schmitt's influence did not die with the destruction of National Socialism: it recurs in more contemporary attempts to describe appropriate forms of government in post-war Germany (Habermas 1989b: 134). I read Habermas' detailed analysis of Hobbes as an attempt to make it more difficult for the earlier English intellectual to be plundered by Schmitt for these purposes, to defeat Hobbes on those points where he seems to advocate arbitrary authority, and so defend the idea of a public sphere as a desirable model for German politics not just in the 1920s and 1930s (which went Schmitt's way) but in the 1960s too.

The points of interest for the purposes of this study are the account of Aquinas' role in the transformation of politics and the brief remarks about the role of Reformation theology in paving the way for a legalistic understanding of contracts between individuals. We shall return to these.

In 'Between Philosophy and Science: Marxism as Critique', on the meanings of 'critique' in the Marxist tradition, Habermas allows himself some leisure for theological speculation, whose mythic character he freely admits. This is a relatively long essay, not all of which is relevant for our purposes. I shall restrict my remarks to two sections, one on Hegel's account of the incarnation, and one on

---

[4] On Schmitt's 'medieval' elitism see McCormick 1997: 157–205, esp. 165. See also Schwab 1989: 62–7, Bendersky 1983: 37–9.

Vico's *New Science*. Habermas rehearses Hegel's theological account because he is concerned to rebut the characterisation of Marxism as a 'secularisation of a religious or philosophic faith' (Habermas 1988b: 199). With this warning – that Habermas is interested in Marxism rather than theology – the outlines of his account can be presented.

Hegel's account of divine estrangement and reconciliation has its origins in Jewish and Protestant mysticism: of Isaak Luria and Jakob Böhme (Habermas 1988b: 215). They present a 'remarkable conception of theogony and cosmology' in which God goes into exile within himself, 'emigrates into the darkness of his own groundless grounds' and 'becomes his other – nature, that is: nature in God'.

Through this folding within himself – an original self-dethronement – God lets himself out of his own hands, disappears, so thoroughly that Adam can oust him from his throne a second time, at the end of a process of restitution marked by God's creaturely agony. Under the compulsion to repeat this mythically, humanity becomes a Christ in Lucifer's promethean role. Humanity is left all by itself in history to accomplish the work of redemption: redemption of itself, of Nature and even of the overthrown God: and all through its own power. In humanity God has stopped being divine in the strict sense, while still being God. He has delivered himself over entirely to the risk of an irretrievable catastrophe. Only at this cost has he started the world process as history.

(Habermas 1993b: 246–7; 1988b: 215)[5]

This is a summary by Habermas of an article on 'Marxism and Gnosis', published in the preceding year (1962), by Ernst Topitsch.[6] The myth is of interest to Habermas because of the influence it had on Hegel's speculative metaphysics. It is part of the 'negative' moment in God which is central to Hegel's account of spirit in the *Phenomenology*. Theologians familiar with Barth's account of the way of the Son of God into the far country (Barth 1956: 157–210) will recognise what the Swiss theologian was trying to correct:

God's unconditional handing over of himself to history makes history into a totality of interconnections of crises, and does so perfectly. Nonetheless, a

---

[5] Where the German edition is cited, translations are my own; references to the English translation by J. Viertel are also given.

[6] For commentary see Theunissen 1970: 50. On Habermas' use of Hegel's narrative see p. 57.

transcendence within immanence is maintained because the lost God was admittedly once God. So God is prevenient to the snuffed-out past's remains in the historical present. In the crisis he precedes the crisis. Returning to himself, at first as a stranger, he is the one who catches up with himself and recognises himself. Hegel rationalises the mythical version as the dialectical logic of world history as crisis. Indeed, world history's smooth course just is the course of the smooth dialectic. In the end, though, God – freed through humanity, in the absolute *Geist*, to himself – knows that he knew everything beforehand. Even *in* history he had remained Lord *over* it. (Habermas 1993b: 247; 1988b: 215–16)

Habermas is struck by the twist Hegel gives to this so-called mystical account. Surely, Habermas suggests, the point of the myth is to narrate the descent of God into history to make way for a human historical subjectivity which replaces a remote heavenly divinity. Habermas calls this an 'atheistic God' (Habermas 1993b: 247; 1988b: 216). For Habermas, Hegel's version messes it all up: the recovery of God's lordship ruins the whole point of the myth of the birth of human historical autonomy. Habermas also makes the astute point that Hegel's version of the myth has God triumph so spectacularly, and so obviously *in advance* of the incarnation, that it is profoundly to be questioned whether God can really be said to have surrendered to history at all. Instead of bothering with the details of divine impassibility or the quite different question of Jesus' suffering, Habermas merely finds Hegel's account altogether too docetic, and favourably contrasts Marx's mythic account, in which humanity comes to discover that its life is the result of its own labour from which it has become estranged.

With this, Habermas hopes to show why Feuerbach's critique of religion (which Habermas for some reason dismisses as 'not very profound') was so influential on Marx and Engels. For our purposes the interesting point is the bleak choice that Habermas gives to the theologian: *either* the cross is illusory suffering because God triumphs over death in advance, and not in the resurrection, *or* God really is subject to history and thus cannot have been God in the first place. Hegel takes the first path, Marx the second. The theological tangles implied by this approach are formidable. Giving good accounts of the relationship between divine impassibility and the crucifixion, or between God's eternity and the temporality of crucifixion and resurrection, is a major ongoing task in the Christian theological tradition. The one-sidedness of a solely *epic* account, in which events unfold according to a grand scheme, or a solely *lyrical* account, in which everything is seen from the perspective of the anguished and destroyed innocent, is an ever-present temptation. Offering a truly *dramatic* narrative in which time and eternity, the Father's almightiness and the Son's crucifixion under Pontius Pilate are woven together (as in the Creed) is no easy task (Quash 2005: 30–50). Habermas here, as elsewhere, shows little interest in these matters.

The question of divine sovereignty and human autonomy is a major topic for Habermas in a later part of this essay, entitled 'The presuppositions of a materialist philosophy of history'. Habermas considers the question of divine sovereignty in Vico's account of human *poiesis*, examines its transformations in Kant and Hegel, and finishes with remarks on how Marx brings the process to completion. Habermas is interested, to begin with, in how Vico relates the claim that 'in God to know and to do is the same thing' to the idea that history is the realm of *human* making. Unlike God, whose conception of the world is identical to his creation of it, humankind first creates its world and only subsequently manages, perhaps, to comprehend it. The key point here is that human creativity/knowledge is inescapably *retrospective*. To see how this works, Habermas compares Vico to the Church fathers.

The two key themes Habermas takes up from patristic theology (he names no names) are (a) the unity of world history suspended between creation and eschaton and (b) the difference between the subject of history (God) and subjects in history (humanity). 'Subject' is being used here in the normal sense it has in German philosophy, namely the agent of some named activity. The first theme is the *saeculum*, the time between first and last, whose meaning is interpreted in the light of the history of God's reconciliation with the world. 'From the eschatological perspective – redemption from original sin – history, to be sure, retains the [sense of a] double ground: of the world and of redemption' (Habermas 1988b: 244). The second theme concerns God's sovereignty. God is the lord of history, Habermas says, and is to be sharply contrasted with humanity, who were in patristic theology merely subject (*unterworfen*) to it.

This 'patristic' view (Habermas does not associate it with medieval or modern theology) throws some light on Vico's definition of the philosopher of history: 'the historical world [has] quite certainly been made by men . . . And therefore its essence is to be found in the modifications of our own spirit . . . for there can nowhere be greater certainty than where he who also creates the things also gives an account of them' (Vico 1948: book 1, §349, quoted in Habermas 1988b: 243). Habermas notes that for patristic theology there could only be one philosopher of history: God.

Vico's *New Science* does without the Christian difference between God and humanity: 'the philosophy of history from now on is to do without the hypothesis of God as the subject of history; but in his place Vico was now left with the human race' (Habermas 1988b: 244). This creates some problems. Although humanity comes to replace God as the subject of history, it does not suddenly acquire all of the classical attributes such as omnipotence and omniscience: 'People make their history, yet they do not make it with consciousness. History remains ambiguous: the free act and the event, action and occurrence' (Habermas 1988b: 244). For this reason Vico holds on to divine providence, in such a way that historical development is said to coincide with it: providence is understood by Vico to be part of the nature of things, recognisable to 'the naked eye of reason'. Habermas describes human action as a circus trapeze act, with divine providence as the safety net. So long as nations do not control history *consciously*, they will always be caught by it. This, Habermas explains, is the meaning of Vico's account of the periodicity of history, the *corso* and *ricorso* of human action in time. Only divine providence guarantees that, however much civilisation may disintegrate from time to time, it will not be subject to historical regression. It will always be healed from outside itself: even in devastation, redemption can be discerned.

Of this scheme Habermas asks the obvious questions: why should one give or accept such an account of providence, and what happens if one abandons it? His answer, suggesting Nietzsche and Weber, is: one would despair of progress because the collapse of civilisation *would* now be seen as regression. But things are even worse: Vico's philosophy of history is, as previously noted, *retrospective*. One can only make sense of the past. If one wants – as the eighteenth century did – an account of history in which one can make predictions, one needs a way of justifying them. A retrospective philosophy of history is no help here, and for that reason Turgot and Condorcet went back behind Vico to Descartes in order to use his rigorous method. They imagined a kind of 'Newton of history' who would chart regularities and elaborate the universal laws of history. These would make a complete set with the laws of nature.

It is against this background that Habermas shows the significance of Kant's call for maturity. If humanity is just a spectator of its own history, where is the true subject of history, now that God has been lodged safely in the realm of noumena? If humans are to be the subjects of history, and not just subject *to* it, they must become mature and make their own history *consciously*. Historical consciousness becomes a crucial project. More than this, for Kant, historical subjects must 'imagine' a purpose to nature, a kind of providence: only thus can they act with confidence. But precisely here one sees the well-known problem of dualism in Kant's philosophy: between the law-bound realm of nature and the free realm of practical reason. 'The historical subjects are, as it were, split up into their noumenal and phenomenal aspects; they are the authors of their history, but still they have not yet constituted themselves as its subject – they are at once a causally determined species of nature and morally free individuals' (Habermas 1988b: 246). The problem of dualism is, of course, what Hegel set out to overcome with the dialectical account of history. Habermas' account of Hegel is extremely telescoped at this point: he says that being human, for Hegel, means incorporating or appropriating aspects of the world that were previously external or alienated. Hegel discovered in the contradiction between human making and the necessity of divine providence the driving force of a humanity which continually creates itself; this is the dialectic of a self-moving history (Habermas 1988b: 247).

There were two problems to be solved: the dualism of human action and divine providence, and the retrospectiveness of historical knowledge. Hegel solves the first, but not the second. It would be left to Marx to address the second by speaking not of the 'exertion of the concept' (Hegel) but 'labour' as the motor of history. For Habermas, Marx reconciles Vico, Kant and Hegel in the idea that 'the meaning of history can be recognised theoretically to the degree that human beings undertake to make it true practically' (Habermas 1988b: 248). In this, action and consciousness, retrospection and prognosis, historical conditions and freedom are all reconciled.

What happened to the theology of redemption in all this? Habermas asks. It is made 'functional' for philosophy of history by switching the subject from God to humanity. Habermas makes the interesting point that intellectuals had started, in the eighteenth century, to see themselves as if from outside because of the discoveries made during colonisation. Thus Voltaire's philosophy of history begins in China (Habermas 1988b: 250). This colonisation seemed to be creating what Habermas calls 'a growing global unity', but this is not brought about by salvation from God but by human social intercourse. It does not occur to Habermas that these might not be mutually exclusive.

In summary, Marxism received from Christian theology a narrative of the world's unity in time between origin and goal. It also inherited a conception of the difference between God's sovereignty and human ignorance. The latter was intolerable for a philosophy of history on several fronts. The task was thus to preserve the idea of unity, but substitute human action for divine providence. Marxism is the final working-out of Vico's *verum et factum convertuntur*: knowing and doing are convertible.

Of particular theological significance in this essay are the theme of God's sovereignty and the account of human action that Habermas offers in the light of it. Of particular interest is his leap from 'patristic' thinking to Vico; thus he passes silently over the development of trinitarian theology in the intervening centuries, a theology whose purpose was precisely to describe the relationship between divine and human knowing, and divine and human action. Given that these are the very themes tackled by Habermas, this is, as Milbank suggests of Habermas' other essay, a serious lacuna.

Despite the poverty of his theological narrative, Habermas poses a question that contemporary theology needs to take seriously: how do narratives of peaceability avoid Hobbesian violent technologies for peace-keeping? Habermas thinks that it is wiser to have as one's highest goal the protection of the public sphere as a locus of high-quality and uncoerced argumentation. Which is the higher good for a Christian community: promoting an open public sphere or keeping the peace? The English anthropologist Timothy Jenkins suggests, in conversation, that this kind of question is best approached by asking how communities organise three values into a hierarchy: these three values are order, freedom and human flourishing. Prisons and the armed forces, for example, organise their values with order at the top, then human flourishing, and finally freedom. Schools in Britain equivocate between order and human flourishing at the top, with freedom at the bottom. Civil-rights groups advocate a hierarchy of freedom at the top, then human flourishing, with order at the bottom. It is not obvious in advance how particular Christian communities arrange this hierarchy: one would need to take them on a case-by-case basis. For Habermas, the promotion of the public sphere places freedom at the top, and is silent on whether human flourishing or order should come next. It would be an interesting question to find out whether Aquinas places human flourishing or order at the top. In any case, prioritising 'peace' does not yield an automatic hierarchy. One can promote peace in order to privilege order, or freedom or flourishing, depending on how one conceives peace. Habermas raises these as urgent questions, and theologians hoping to improve upon his account of political theory can learn a great deal from him about rival readings of the Christian tradition. Habermas' most significant claim is that Thomist accounts of politics collapse not because of internal inconsistency, but simply because the social conditions no longer render their claims about the world plausible. Few theologians have tried to answer Habermas on this point; it is obviously insufficient merely to defend the consistency of Christian claims. There is work worth doing here.

CHAPTER 7

Theology, social theory and rationalisation

Is religious thought inherently 'mythic'? There are two principal theological answers to this question. The first makes a separation between 'myth' and 'rational discourse', and suggests that the mythic inheritance needs to be rationalised in order to be intelligible and persuasive to modern religious people. The second suggests that even the most rarefied rationalised discourses are still importantly 'mythic', in that they narrate a description of the world whose bases cannot be secured by theory: religious thinking is mythic because *all* thinking is mythic. Habermas is interested in this question, and he tends to take the first route. For theologians who take the second, therefore, it is interesting to know how separations between myth and reason are made by Habermas, and to evaluate how persuasively he executes this.

The contrast in 'Some Characteristics of the Mythical and the Modern Ways of Understanding the World' (Habermas 1984a: 43–74) is between the rational and the non-rational. Our task is to find out whether theology is inherently sub-rational in Habermas' account.

Habermas' description of mythic societies draws on the work of Lévi-Strauss, Evans-Pritchard, Maurice Godelier, Peter Winch, Steven Lukes, Alasdair MacIntyre, Robin Horton and Jean Piaget. Habermas has been heavily criticised from a number of angles.[1]

---

[1] One of the earliest critiques is Thompson 1981: 136–9. Thompson points out that Habermas does not account properly for drawing the analogy between ontogenetic (Piaget) and phylogenetic (Habermas) development, and rests on unexamined assumptions about the relationship between 'early' infancy and 'early' societies. Thompson also makes the excellent point that Habermas gets into trouble by wanting to have both Freud's and Piaget's

I intend to focus on the question of *testing*. That means paying attention not so much to how validity claims are raised and defended as to how they are placed in question: the mechanics of this process. I do not intend to spend much time on whether Habermas gets the contrast between rationality and non-rationality right. Instead, I shall draw attention to the different kinds of testing of claims that Habermas thinks are operative in different situations. This is important to the current study because it is arguably where Habermas gives his secularised account of the role of prayer in the interpretation of revelation. Where theologians tend to talk of the interpretation of scripture and the testing of this in prayer, Habermas speaks of raising validity claims and testing them in argument. Argument and prayer function very similarly in some ways, although the differences between them matter. For example, argument is not learned liturgically in quite the same way as prayer, unless one wishes to suggest that universities function socially in contemporary society in the same way that churches used to in earlier Europe. I shall refrain from describing Habermas' interest in universities as an 'ecclesiology' not because the claim is false, but because defending it in any satisfactory way would require resources unavailable in this context. I shall stick to the relatively simple point that prayer is oriented to God, whereas argument's highest court is a socially constituted body, and the difference matters. This is a point learned from Kierkegaard's *Fear and Trembling*, and I shall attempt indirectly to replay the disagreements between Kierkegaard and Hegel in considering the disagreements that should arise between theological accounts of argument and Habermas' version of things.

The role of testing is central to Habermas' account of mythic and modern understandings of the world. Quite late on in this essay, one discovers that the historical progression Habermas wants to describe is not two-fold, from mythic to modern understandings, but

---

accounts of the unconscious: these are manifestly contradictory on a number of points. For another relatively early critique of Habermas' appropriation of these figures, and for a strongly worded criticism in particular of Habermas' treatment of myth, which is 'cursory in the extreme given the length of the book as a whole', see Giddens, 'Reason without Revolution?', in Bernstein 1985: 95–121, esp. p. 100.

three-fold: mythic – religious-metaphysical – modern (Habermas 1984a: 67ff.). Given Habermas' discussions elsewhere about 'post-metaphysical thinking', the hyphenated form 'religious-metaphysical' should interest the theologian, as it naturally raises the question of whether it is possible to have a 'religious-post-metaphysical' world-view. We shall visit this question again in chapter 9, and discover there that Habermas knows certain kinds of post-metaphysical theology, but judges them to be unpersuasive.

Habermas' project to broaden the scope of 'rationality', by com-plementing the theory of 'strategic' action in Weber with a theory of 'communicative' action, requires him to investigate what conditions have to be met in order to describe social arrangements as rational. Are societies *differently* rational, or are some *more* rational than others? Habermas assumes that talk of different rationalities robs debate of important criteria for judging better or worse arguments; it also makes it too difficult to speak of 'universal' claims. Accord-ingly he argues strongly and at length for a conception of rationality that will permit judgements about *how rational* social arrangements are. His chosen strategy for this is a comparison of 'mythic' and 'modern' societies.

The question of rationality is not of direct interest to this study, so Habermas' arguments will not be rehearsed in the order in which he presents them. Instead, I wish to draw attention to the character-istics he attributes to 'mythic' thought. This is because many of the practices of modern Christian life seem, sometimes, to conform pretty closely to it, and it is worth finding out why this might be, and whether it is a bad thing (at least judged by Habermas' cri-teria). Habermas relies on Maurice Godelier's 'Myth and History' (Godelier 1977), and the first thing he learns from Godelier is that mythic thinking is extraordinarily *explanatory*. Habermas focuses on Godelier's account of the role of analogy. By analogy, 'everything can be explained within a symbolic order, where all the positive known facts . . . may take their place with all their rich abundance of detail' (Godelier 1977: 213, quoted in Habermas 1984a: 46). This need for explanation is particularly acute in the face of tragedy and pain: 'the experience of being delivered up unprotected to the contingencies of an unmastered environment' gives rise to 'the need to check the flood of contingencies – if not in fact at least in imagination – that is, to interpret them away'. This is achieved, again, through analogy, where impersonal forces are anthropomorphised (Habermas 1984a: 46–7). There are many interesting aspects to this claim, but for our purposes the most important one is the surprising fact that the need for explanation, which one would normally attribute to modern societies, is projected by Habermas (Godelier) onto mythic societies as something that they seem to need very badly.

This is merely a building-block in Habermas' argument. His real interest is to associate rationality with the differentiation of 'value spheres'. This is a constant theme in Habermas' writings. It concerns the differentiation of human activities in modern society. Following Weber and Emil Lask, who follow the lead set by Kant's writing of three separate critiques relating respectively to scientific knowledge, moral reasoning and aesthetic judgement, Habermas insists that modern societies make a clear distinction between scientific questions of 'truth', moral questions of 'rightness' and expressive questions of sincerity or 'truthfulness' (Habermas 1984a: 71). Habermas also sometimes speaks of the different 'cultural subsystems' in a society: things like science, law/morality, music, art, literature (Habermas 1984a: 72). The more firmly Habermas insists on these divisions, the easier he is to criticise,[2] but the basic insight is sound: modern societies do encourage specialisation by professionals in these areas, and this has both costs and benefits. Habermas' big hostage to argument is his belief that such specialisation is a mark of increased rationality.

The main mark of mythic societies, for Habermas, is their failure to make such distinctions, above all between nature and culture (Habermas 1984a: 47–53). Natural phenomena are anthropomorphised and treated as agents with interests and wills; cultural phenomena like kinship and status are attributed to the natural order of things. The important point, however, is not what Habermas attributes to mythic societies. It is the strong contrasting claim he makes about modern societies, which, he insists, do not do these

---

[2] See Bernstein 1995: 231–4. For an account of the complex interrelations between aesthetics and subjectivity, which makes it difficult to defend the strong separation between value spheres Habermas insists on, see Bowie 1990.

things. Modern societies differentiate between language and world (Habermas 1984a: 49). By this he means that modern agents are conscious of the difference, following Frege, between the 'sense' (meanings) of expressions and their 'reference' (what they point to in the world). Habermas does not mean that modern societies construct the world in some way other than through language. Rather, he means that modern people do not confuse reordering sentences and reordering things in the world (which is the 'mistake', for Habermas, of those who practise magic). This leads to a profound point, which is of interest to this study:

> a linguistically constituted worldview can be identified with the world-order itself to such an extent that it cannot be perceived *as* an interpretation of the world that is subject to error and open to criticism.
>
> (Habermas 1984a: 50)

This is an important indication of Habermas' interest in testing. The problem with not differentiating between nature and culture, world and language, sense and reference, is that one fails to distinguish *world* from its *interpretation*. In other words, modern societies are better than mythic societies at *testing* their interpretations of the world. This is a hermeneutic point, and I do not want to suggest only that Habermas is adapting theological tools used to treat the question of *scripture* and *interpretation* for philosophical ends, which he trivially has in common with most philosophers interested in hermeneutics. More than this, I encourage theological readers to consider what kind of 'scripture' he works with, and the means he advocates for testing its interpretation.

Habermas' usual technical term for an interpretation of the world is 'validity claim' (*Geltungsanspruch*), and his usual term for testing is 'openness to criticism' (Habermas 1984a: 50). We are interested in the mechanics of the process by which interpretations are tested. In theology, scriptural interpretations are tested through argumentation and prayer. What equivalents does Habermas have for the criticism of validity claims? The question for him is whether criteria for testing are universal or specific to traditions:

> Validity claims are in principle open to criticism because they are based on formal world-concepts. They presuppose a world that is identical for *all possible* observers, or a world inter-subjectively shared *by members*, and they

do so in an abstract form freed of all specific content. Such claims call for the rational response of a partner in communication. (Habermas 1984a: 50)

The basic distinction is between 'world' and 'world-concepts', i.e. between 'world' and 'interpretation', between 'reference' and 'sense'. Interpretations (validity claims) can be tested (are open to criticism) because they are *recognised as interpretations*. The 'world' is *presupposed by everyone* as *the same for everyone*; 'interpretations', by contrast, are different for everyone, and are the things that need testing. Habermas suggests that because everyone presupposes that the world is the same for everyone else, they have a conception of something that exists independently of interpretation ('freed of all specific content'). If we think of 'the world' as 'like scripture' (in that it needs interpreting), we might say that everyone reads the same scripture, but they interpret it differently and thus need to test their interpretations.

Here lies the problem with 'mythic' societies, in Habermas' view. Because they fail to distinguish between world and interpretation, this process of testing is unavailable:

> it has been observed that the members of archaic societies tie their own identities in large measure to the details of the collective knowledge set down in myths and to the formal specifications of ritual prescriptions. They do not have at their disposal a formal concept of the world that could secure the identity of natural and social reality in the face of the changing interpretations of temporalised cultural traditions. (Habermas 1984: 51)

Habermas means that myths and rituals are interpretations of the world, and that premodern societies confuse them with the world itself. This is, incidentally, what he means in a later essay when he associates rationalisation with 'the reflective treatment of traditions that have lost their quasi-natural status' (Habermas 1987a: 2). He also makes the slightly stranger-sounding claim that they have a problem because they tie their identities to such interpretations rather than to 'a formal concept of the world'. This implies that such a formal concept is a condition for cultures being able to preserve their identity when their interpretations of the world change. There is some ambiguity about the meaning of 'preserve' here. Presumably Habermas means that cultures would experience changes in their interpretations as less of a crisis if they were able to recognise their interpretations as things they make rather than as properties of the natural world. To a theologian's eye, this sounds rather like the question of doctrinal change (which just means: changing interpretations of scripture and ritual). Communities which recognise that their doctrines are human artefacts, rather than being intrinsic to scripture and on the same level, are better able to adjust to cultural change and tend not to experience it as the breakdown of the community's identity. If Habermas does mean this, it could have been better expressed as follows: communities which tie their identity tightly to their *current* interpretations of scripture, which they identify with scripture itself, have a harder time adjusting to cultural change than communities which tie their identity to their particular history of *changing* interpretations of scripture, which they recognise *as* changing interpretations. Putting things in this light also helps explain why Habermas' theory of communicative action has proven so popular with many Roman Catholic theologians; perhaps they feel that their tradition some-times has an 'archaic' experience of cultural change. Of course, this would have the added implication that doctrines, because they are interpretations (validity claims), should be tested (open to criti-cism), rather than asserted. Some theologians might find this a useful way of thinking too. Most importantly, however, the insight that interpretations can be understood *as* interpretations makes a new qualification of validity claims thinkable. There is a difference between *criticisable* validity claims and mere validity claims. To make a criticisable validity claim is for the speaker already to acknowledge that the hearer can evaluate what is said, using argu-ments, and may well come to reject it if there are good reasons.

This translates quite easily into the language of doctrine. It makes a difference whether doctrine is seen as (a) a validity claim or (b) a criticisable validity claim. In the first case the speaker may or may not invite argument and potential dissent: perhaps a lot hangs on the attitude of the speaker, the existence of threats of sanctions and so forth. In the second case, the speaker's very utterance presupposes the possibility of debate, and invites argument. Habermas thinks that modern thought means a development away from (a) towards (b). More plausible is the idea that (a) and (b) coexist rather unhap-pily in contemporary society, and that problems arise especially when a speaker thinks that he or she is uttering (a) and a hearer thinks that he or she is hearing (b). This more or less characterises confusions about ecclesial authority in nearly every Christian tradition where pronouncements can be made *ex cathedra*. A legal judgement is not a validity claim: it is an adjudication. But in matters of ecclesial authority there is often some blurring of the boundaries between validity claim (whether criticisable or not) and adjudication. It seems obvious to me that the job of the General Assembly of the Church of Scotland or of the papacy is legal: to settle disputes *for the time being* and *for some particular context* in order to preserve catholicity (i.e. contain disagreement within a unified body). If this job is supplemented by other tasks that are intended to produce documents or institutions *in advance of any actual dispute*, for example drafting guidelines, experimenting with new doctrines, alterations not only to legislation but to the composition of the legislature, then problems loom. The authoritative body will have to raise *criticisable* validity claims. This will confuse both speaker and listener, because they are both used to the practice of *settling* disputes, which is not a criticisable matter. There is the danger of slippage between the speaker's existing *ex officio* authority as adjudicator and his or her – drastically reduced – status in the new role as a potentially persuasive partner in dialogue. It is confusing to raise a criticisable validity claim while wearing full ceremonial dress. Again, it is understandable that theologians might find Habermas helpful in addressing these confusions. Habermas helps theologians understand that there is a big difference between raising criticisable validity claims and making final (for the time being) judgements. This helps show why it is (or should be) fruitless for journalists to ask the Archbishop of Canterbury for his 'personal opinion'. Similar issues operate in questions of doctrinal development. Innovation in matters of doctrine involves raising criticisable validity claims rather than making final judgements. For that reason, it seems advisable that General Assemblies and Popes should not innovate.

Habermas reminds his reader that validity claims are humanly made, and that problems arise when they are attributed to the natural order. Modern societies are better than mythic societies at handling questions of this kind. Along with some strong claims about the rationality of modern society versus mythic society, which has received adequate critique elsewhere from anthropologists, social theorists and philosophers, Habermas has a useful discussion of Evans-Pritchard's 1937 account of witchcraft among the Azande. Evans-Pritchard's work evoked rival interpretations from Peter Winch, Robin Horton and Alasdair MacIntyre, and Habermas finds it instructive to explore some of their debate as a way of getting at what is rational about modern societies. Of particular interest to this study is his discussion of the Zande experience of being pressed, by the anthropologist, to account for apparent inconsistencies in their accounts of magic and oracles. Habermas is interested in the question of rationality; we are more interested in the character of the testing of interpretations of the world.

Evans-Pritchard argues that the Zande do not lack logic when they explain how magic and oracles work in their diagnosis of why a member of their tribe has become sick. The contrast between Zande and European reasoning does not lie at the level of logical operations: the Zande argue just as logically from premises to conclusions. Instead, it lies at the level of what they consider is in principle *testable*. The belief that sickness is caused by witches, and the system of discernment that arises from this belief, is not something the Zande consider testable. To use Habermas' terms, they attribute their humanly made interpretation to the order of nature. Nonetheless, the anthropologist raises for the Zande the possibility that this belief might be open to question:

Using the example of Zande ideas concerning the inheritance of magical powers, Evans-Pritchard discusses contradictions that inevitably arise from certain fundamental assumptions of their animistic worldview. And he leaves no doubt that the Azande themselves experience unavoidable absurdities as disagreeable as soon as they enter upon a stubborn consistency check such as the anthropologist undertakes. (Habermas 1984a: 60)

One might say here that every worldview, every ecology of interpretations, throws up aporias. In some societies these are noticed; indeed, their members may have habits and routines dedicated to noticing them. In other societies, such aporias are not noticed; they may even have techniques for avoiding the kinds of 'consistency check' that Habermas speaks of. For Habermas, this is the difference between modern and mythic societies: he describes this willingness or unwillingness as a difference in rationality. However, he is actually describing two things: *tools* for self-criticism and *willingness* for self-criticism. Doubtless the one accompanies the other, but they are nonetheless formally distinct. Habermas does point towards this:

a demand of this kind [of stubborn consistency check] is *brought* to bear upon them [the Zande]; it does not arise within the framework of their own culture; and when an anthropologist confronts them with it, they generally evade it. (Habermas 1984a: 60)

Habermas interprets this as evidence of irrationality. Of far greater interest, however, is the implication that tools for self-criticism are not enough. They need to be accompanied by a willingness to use them. In the case of 'doctrinal change' (the consciously undertaken changes in humanly made interpretations of scripture/ritual), this would mean that it is not enough to *recognise* that doctrines are humanly made. There is also a need for the *desire* to act on this recognition. I mention this because the difference between 'argumentation' and 'prayer' is precisely about this double requirement. It is not just a question of motivation to be bound to norms, but also willingness to undertake self-criticism. For the moment, it is sufficient to notice Habermas' account of the *origin* of critique. For the Zande, its source is external: the anthropologist. For modern societies, by contrast, critique is part of the worldview itself: the culture is self-critical. This is what Habermas seems to mean by 'rational' (Habermas 1984a: 62).

What, then, is the deciding factor? What is it that modern societies do, that mythic societies do not, that leads to self-critical attitudes to validity claims? Unless some account can be given of *how* self-critical attitudes arise and are propagated, it is difficult to know what to do with the information that there is a difference between mythic and modern societies. Habermas wishes not only to *describe* differences in rationality, but also to *promote* increases in it. The term he uses to describe the transmission of rationality is 'learning processes' (Habermas 1984a: 66ff.).

Habermas' discussion of learning processes suggests that the difference between mythic reliance on external testing and modern capacities for internal testing lies in contrasts in how people are taught to think, and is just one of those skills that is or is not taught in a culture. He is not content with such an account, however, because it lacks the *evolutionary* dimension that he believes adds weight to his argument about communicative action. He thus has a long section speculating that what Jean Piaget found to be the case in the cognitive development in individuals might have some analogy in the cognitive development of an entire culture (Habermas 1984a: 66–71). For our purposes this adds nothing to the main insight, and I shall ignore it.[3]

What is much more relevant is his introduction of the concept of the 'lifeworld' (*Lebenswelt*). This is a concept Habermas takes over from Husserl's phenomenology.[4] Its meaning for Habermas encompasses a society's horizon of imagination, together with its store of 'background convictions' (Habermas 1984a: 70). The important feature of the lifeworld is its relation to 'reflection', namely the activity of becoming conscious of things that were previously undertaken or thought about unconsciously. The lifeworld is *unreflective*; that means: it is the domain of things taken for granted, practices handed down without question, and hierarchies of goods that are not queried. It is, in other words, the world that we do not notice because it is what we expect to see and hear.

Habermas' discussion of the lifeworld is the place where he invests all of his most positive descriptions of the role of tradition in reasoning. These were considered in chapter 2 on the ideal speech situation and in chapter 3 in connection with his disagreements with Gadamer. For the moment, the relevant points concern the traditional setting against which validity claims are raised and redeemed. The lifeworld is, by definition, unproblematic. No-one would question aspects of the lifeworld because they would not notice them. It would be as absurd as a thirteenth-century Frenchman entering a church and being surprised to find crucifixes inside. (Quite a lot of humour works by treating aspects of the lifeworld as if they are terribly surprising.) Habermas believes that as societies progress, the

---

[3] For other discussions by Habermas of learning processes see two sections in *On the Logic of the Social Sciences*: Habermas 1988a: 68 (on Chomsky and child development) and 131–2 (on Wittgenstein and learning the grammar of language games); see also his fine tribute to Karl Jaspers on the role of universities in *The New Conservatism*: Habermas 1989b: 99–125.

[4] For an accessible analysis see Roberts 1992: 268–70.

lifeworld does less and less of the work of providing background agreements. More traditional societies contain arguments about interpretations of the world (validity claims) by situating them against a broad normative consensus. People already agree about the basic issues and do not even notice that they agree because things are just obvious. The extent of this prior agreement shrinks as societies become more advanced, more rational (as Habermas sees it). The lifeworld does less of this normative work as worldviews become 'decentred' (Habermas 1984a: 70). This is one of the concepts Habermas takes over from Piaget: its original context is the development of the child who learns to see things from other people's perspectives, and not only his or her own. Habermas speculates that something like this is true of societies as they begin to see themselves from other societies' point of view. This is the same strategy he uses with respect to Mead, which we looked at in chapter 4.

> The more the worldview that furnishes the cultural stock of knowledge is decentred, the less the need for understanding is covered *in advance* by an interpreted lifeworld immune from critique, and the more this need has to be met by the interpretive accomplishments of the participants themselves.
>
> (Habermas 1984a: 70)

Habermas means that once members of one society face up to the reality of perspectives from other cultures, the contents of their own lifeworld are open to question: the things taken to be true cease to be so easily taken to be true. He draws from this the conclusion that the burden of understanding one another, which in traditional societies is borne by the lifeworld, cannot be borne by it in more differentiated societies because the parties engaged in argument have less of this lifeworld in common: they come from different cultural backgrounds, with different cultural assumptions. Thus they must bear this burden *themselves* and allow the process of reaching understanding itself to do some of the work. Habermas draws a contrast between 'normatively ascribed agreement' (i.e. the agreement provided by a shared lifeworld) and 'communicatively achieved understanding' (i.e. the agreement reached in argument between partners who do not share such a lifeworld). He uses this contrast, once again, as a way of differentiating mythic from modern societies, and as a criterion for measuring rationality.

This implies some radical changes to the way members of a society view their own traditions. The lifeworld is unreflective. But encounters with other cultures ('decentring') force reflection upon occupants of a lifeworld. Habermas draws a strong conclusion:

> The cultural tradition must permit a reflective relation to itself; it must be so far stripped of its dogmatism as to permit in principle that interpretations stored in tradition be placed in question and subjected to critical revision. Then internal interconnections of meaning can be systematically elaborated and alternative interpretations can be methodically examined.
>
> (Habermas 1984a: 71)

This is an argument about tradition developed in *On the Logic of the Social Sciences* which we considered in chapter 3. Here we need only pay attention to the connection Habermas makes between rationality and a self-critical attitude to one's tradition. He seems to mean that modern people are self-critical about their interpretations of the world; it is important to remember that, in an earlier argument, he had pointed out that they also have a still more basic view of the world that is 'freed of all specific content': i.e. the presupposition that there is a world being interpreted that is the same *regardless of interpretation*. Thus even these members of different cultures still share a 'world', even if they do not share a 'lifeworld'.

The final part of Habermas' discussion ties these observations to issues in classical philosophy. In chapter 6 we looked at the change in social philosophy from the Aristotelian emphasis on the good life which unifies a society to the Hegelian insight that philosophy needs to work hard to do this work once this unifying 'religious' bond is broken. Habermas realises that one of the tasks performed by the good life is to provide a standard by which to measure a society's actual practices. One can ask: how well do they conform to the good life? He also realises that once (if) it ceases to perform this role, it becomes difficult to judge societies, because all criteria are culturally specific: there is no context-free criterion for such judgement. Nonetheless, Habermas does not wish to give up on such judgement altogether and so he adopts a line of argumentation that echoes Adorno's idea that although one cannot know the good life, one can know the damaged life and infer from it what an un-damaged life might be like. Habermas suggests that one can use a model of sickness and health. He does not press it strongly at this point. He merely raises the possibility that one might continue to make judgements on this basis (Habermas 1984a: 73).

In summary there are two main points. The first concerns the ability of a culture to understand that its interpretations of the world are humanly made interpretations and they can be distinguished from the world which is being interpreted. The second concerns the necessary relationship between being *able* to subject such interpretations to criticism and being *willing* to do so. A third, subsidiary, point is that the possibility for self-criticism, which arises from encounter with different cultures, causes a *reflective* attitude to things that previously had been taken for granted. This diminishes the role of the lifeworld in securing normative agreement; in its place the parties in discussion must reach such agreement *communicatively*, i.e. by *establishing* basic agreements rather than relying on their prior existence. I wish to connect this with the relationship between scriptural interpretation and prayer. Habermas' account of the 'world', in the sense of the 'abstract form freed of all specific content', functions like scripture; the lifeworld functions like scriptural interpretation that does not recognise that it is interpretation; communicative understanding functions like scriptural interpretation that realises that it is humanly made; and the relationship between capacity and willingness for self-criticism functions like prayer. The main difference, in Habermas' secularised version, is the elimination of God and the substitution of the community of interpreters as the ones addressed by such criticism. This seems to me a triumph for Hegel's *Sittlichkeit* over Kierkegaard's *Fear and Trembling*.

For the moment, we return to Habermas' own discussions. I noted above that Habermas does not merely operate with a dualism between 'mythic' and 'modern' societies. He has a tripartite model which moves from 'mythic' to 'religious-metaphysical' to 'modern' societies. The previous essay contrasted 'mythic' and 'modern' worldviews. The second relevant essay in *The Theory of Communicative Action*, 'The Disenchantment of Religious-Metaphysical Worldviews and the Emergence of Modern Structures of Consciousness', treats the difference between the second pair in the triad. Where the first essay engaged with anthropological debates, this one rehearses the account of religion given by Max Weber.

I do not propose to summarise Habermas' *systematic* account of Weber's theory.[5] Our interest is, at this point, solely on the narrative Habermas gives (drawing on Weber) of the shift from 'religious-metaphysical' to 'modern' consciousness. The background question behind this analysis is: could there be a 'religious-post-metaphysical' consciousness, or is the idea incoherent given the terms of reference within which Habermas describes social thinking? To put it differently, an examination of Habermas' essay may shed some light on the scope of the 'religious' in his thinking.

Habermas delights in Weber's aptitude for categorisation, and develops a number of the latter's contrasts. For a sociologist, however, there are some striking lapses of perception, and some of these are worth confronting in advance. A good example is Weber's distinction between 'material' and 'ideal' interests: between 'worldly goods' (Habermas) such as prosperity, security, health, longevity; and 'sacred goods' such as grace, redemption, eternal life. Early on in Habermas' essay about the contrast between religious-metaphysical and modern consciousness, the distinction between worldly and sacred goods is made quite strongly. We have already seen in chapter 4 how Habermas handles the concept of the sacred. Yet there is something strange about the emphatic way this distinction is made. To anyone brought up saying the psalms each day, the distinction between health and redemption makes a kind of sense: clearly my influenza of today is not of the same order as my need for reconciliation with God. Nonetheless, the idea that bodily health is 'worldly' and freedom from guilt 'sacred' is bizarre. They are both entirely worldly *and* sacred; for Christians this is obvious from the fact that the sacrament of the Eucharist – the paradigmatic reception of God's grace in the Catholic tradition – is performed in the

---

[5] Habermas' interpretation of Weber in this essay has been fundamentally challenged because it fails to acknowledge Weber's debts to Nietzsche: Owen 1994: 84–139. The presuppositions in Weber's account have themselves been radically questioned against the backdrop of Hegel's account of ethical life: Rose 1981: 18–21. For a representative critique of Habermas' systematising, see Dallmayr 1991.

sharing of bread. The Lord's Prayer is also profoundly obvious on this point: 'give us today our daily bread; forgive us our sins': they are prayed for *together*. Physical health and divine reconciliation are distinct, but they do not belong in vastly different categories. A Weberian analysis of the Lord's Prayer is perfectly possible, but it should result in describing it as a prayer about 'material' and 'ideal' interests *as a whole*. It would be a strange business to divide up its various petitions on a case-by-case basis, given that the prayer lies at the heart of 'the sacred' in worship. One of the differences between social theory and theology concerns the way these kinds of distinction are drawn. The difference is, however, not that one makes the distinction and the other does not; the difference is that both make the distinction, but make it differently. For Weber/Habermas, the distinction is of kinds of goods; for theologians, the distinction is of different kinds of description of goods. In this respect, the theological account appears more 'rational' in Habermas' sense: that is, it recognises the humanly made quality of such description and is able to switch between different kinds of description, rather than attributing such description intrinsically to objects (cf. Rose 1981: 19). This is true to the extent that Habermas is unable to describe 'grace' as a worldly good. Putting this initial query behind us, we can now ask what can be learned from his contrast between 'traditional' societies and 'modern' societies.

Habermas immediately raises the question of what theologians call doctrinal development, namely changes in interpretations of the world; what he calls 'new ideas, new grounds, new levels of justification' (Habermas 1984a: 192). For Habermas, 'traditional' societies do not prosecute doctrinal change through 'regulated argumentation' but through the influence of 'charismatic' figures. This line of argumentation presupposes some familiarity with Weber's contrast between charisma and routinisation. Habermas follows Weber surprisingly closely, and draws a contrast between 'prophetic word' and 'doctrine capable of being passed on as tradition'. (In the terms I have been using, *both* of these are 'doctrine', in that both are interpretations of nature/scripture; this should not be allowed to interfere with understanding Habermas' contrast.) It is surprising that Habermas should do this because on this account the period of patristic theology would not count as 'traditional' but as 'modern' by virtue of its conciliar procedures. If the last two thousand years of Christian history are to be counted modern, it is not obvious how much work the concept can do, as things like natural science and technological advance would not be marks of the emergence of the modern, but merely developments within its long history. Habermas does not consider this kind of issue in the current essay.

What Habermas is trying to get at is different kinds of process for 'legitimation', i.e. ways of defending interpretations and courses of action through argument rather than brute force. The sort of interpretations that call for such legitimation that are of particular interest to Habermas in this context concern *theodicy*, i.e. the attempt to defend descriptions of God and the world (previously just held-to-be-true) in the face of competing descriptions. Quoting Friedrich Tenbruck, and drawing on Robert Bellah and Rainer Döbert, Habermas speculates that

'The rational constraints that religion is supposed to follow arise from the need to have a rational answer to the problem of theodicy; and the stages of religious development are increasingly explicit conceptions of this problem and its solutions' . . . the contents of worldviews reflect various resolutions of the theodicy problem. (Habermas 1984a: 195–6)

What Habermas understands by 'the theodicy problem' remains tantalisingly unsaid at this point. Instead, Habermas' attention is fixed on elaborating something called 'the direction of religious development'. Habermas' Weber offers a linear account *from* the initial problem of theodicy (again, unspecified) *to* the disenchantment of interpretations of the world. The '*direction* of religious development can be explained through the inner logic of the core problem and of the structures of worldviews' (Habermas 1984a: 196). This implies that, in the conflict of competing descriptions of God and the world, certain types of account, 'solutions' in Habermas' words, will tend to dominate. What types of account? For Weber, they are those that lead to a capitalist economic ethic. Habermas finds this too restricted and wants to give a *general* account of such development, in line with his interest in *evolutionary* narratives of rationalisation.

Habermas wants more juice than can be squeezed out of the notion of 'inner logics'. The problem with 'inner logics of worldviews', for Habermas, is precisely that they are 'inner'. For a general account of worldview development, it is not sufficient merely to have a handful of societies which actually develop (but might not have) along a particular route, e.g. towards capitalism. It is much more satisfying to be able to specify a 'general logic' which particular societies can be said to follow in different ways. Habermas knows quite well that he cannot have a context-independent account of such a general logic, because he will always be occupying a particular context. Nonetheless, he thinks he can say more than just that worldviews have their own logic which produces developments in interpretations of the world. What might this 'more' comprise?

Habermas draws a distinction between two different approaches to the study of the world religions: the comparative and the systematic. Weber mostly conducted the first; Habermas wants to see how far he can get with the second. Precisely what this distinction means, Habermas does not tell us. Instead we are offered, at last, a sketch of what is meant by 'theodicy':

> Rationalisation is tied to a theme that is common to all world religions: the question of justifying the unequal distribution of life's goods. This *basic ethical problematic*, which bursts the bounds of myth, arises from a need for a religious explanation of suffering that is perceived as unjust.
>
> (Habermas 1984a: 201)

This account of theodicy surprisingly makes no reference to God, and actually serves no useful purpose for Habermas' argument. It is not at all clear on what grounds this ethical problem is 'basic', or whether this claim needs to be true for Habermas' own project to be persuasive. Besides this, Habermas shows that he (and Weber?) needs some rather basic theological education: he repeats the idea that the world religions try to 'explain' suffering, rather than address it in interpretation of scripture, in description of the world and in practical habits of healing and hoping.[6] Habermas also repeats a badly one-sided description of the practice of confessing sins, namely as a process for determining why and how suffering had

---

[6] For a sharp critique of this deficient way of thinking see Lash 1996: 219–20: 'Dear God! What kind of madness is it that supposes pain to call for "answers"? Agony seeks healing, not riposte.' Weber did not think like this; neither does Habermas.

been brought on (Habermas 1984a: 201). It is very difficult, using this language, to give a good account of why this practice is sometimes known as the 'sacrament of reconciliation', which explicitly connects the action with healing rather than explanation, and presupposes the reality of God's action. Habermas' description is badly distorted. It also shows no awareness that the kind of theology developed in the book of Job or in the psalms is markedly different from that of Leibniz, even though both address questions of human suffering and God's identity. Habermas unhelpfully lumps them all together as instances of 'explanation'.

Habermas is interested in why there is a shift from 'tribal' cults whose solutions are oriented to 'collective exigencies' to the 'new idea' where it is *individual* misfortune that calls for explanation. He suggests that the rise of the individual whose suffering is soteriologically significant (he confusingly has in mind Calvin's account of double predestination) arises from 'learning processes' that are responses to the conflict between tribal ideas of justice and the 'new reality of class societies'. That is: changes in theodicy are a secondary effect, traceable to the genesis of the urban state (Habermas 1984a: 201–2).

How far does this take us in addressing the 'more', or the 'systematic', that Habermas needs for his general account of the development of worldviews? He takes the next step by setting up a distinction between 'theocentric' and 'cosmocentric' worldviews.

The question of the justification of manifest injustices is not, however, treated as a purely ethical question; it is part of the theological, cosmological, metaphysical question concerning the constitution of the world as a whole. This *world order* is so conceived that ontic and normative questions are blended together. In this framework of religious-metaphysical thought about the world order, quite different solutions to the same problem have been found. Weber contrasts above all the two basic conceptual strategies: one, the Occidental, employs the conception of a transcendent, personal Lord of Creation; the other strategy, widespread in the Orient, starts from the idea of an impersonal, noncreated cosmos. Weber also refers to these as transcendent and immanent conceptions of God. The 'God of Action' is developed in an exemplary way in the form of Yahweh, the 'God of Order' in Brahman. The faithful must enter into a different relationship with the Lord of Creation than they do with the static ground of the cosmic order. They understand themselves as *instruments of God* and not as *vessels of the divine.* In the one case the believer seeks to win God's favour, in the other to participate in the divine. (Habermas 1984a: 202)

This is easily summarised. The problem faced by members of the new urban states is the unequal distribution of goods and the experience of as-yet meaningless pain. There are two theological 'solutions' to this problem. The first is Jewish and the second Hindu. The Jewish version sets God over and against creation and understands human action as a seeking of reconciliation with God, who has become estranged. The Hindu solution identifies God with the cosmic order and understands human action as an effect of divine action. (Weber never completed his studies of Christianity and Islam, and so Habermas holds back, for the time being, from speculating about how Christian and Muslim responses to the problem might be described.) The key feature of both approaches is the lack of differentiation between 'ontic, normative and expressive' aspects of their descriptions of the world order. That is, they fail to distinguish between how the world is, what people should do, and how it affects one individually.

The next pair of contrasts is between affirmation and rejection of the world. Judaism and Christianity (which has quietly appeared unannounced in Habermas' narrative) are paired as world-rejecting because of their alleged 'dualism', which is somehow associated with their being concerned with 'salvation'. Habermas is, once again, content to follow Weber here, and gives no account of how dualism and salvation relate to each other as themes.

We still lack the promised 'general' or 'systematic' account. Habermas continues to delay this, and instead rehearses Weber's criteria for judging the rationality of a religion. The following is from Weber's *Religion of China*:

To judge the level of rationalisation a religion represents there are two principal yardsticks, which are in many ways interrelated. One is the degree to which the religion has divested itself of magic; the other is the degree of systematic unity it gives to the relation between God and the world and correspondingly to its own ethical relation to the world.

(Weber 1964: 226, in Habermas 1984a: 205)

The rationality of a religion can be gauged by its lack of magic and its degree of consistency. This does not suit Habermas' purposes at all well: he wants to locate the difference in identifiable learning processes that overcome mythic thought. Habermas excuses Weber on the grounds that the latter is more interested in ethical than cognitive matters. Habermas is nonetheless content to follow Weber's lead, and summarises the effects of this increased rationality:

> in the main cultic domains it blocks the development of a personal communication between the faithful and God or the divine being. The manipulative techniques for compelling God, which live on in the sublime form of the sacrament, dominate in place of worship and prayer.
>
> (Habermas 1984a: 205)

It is important to note that Habermas has not yet told his readers how Christianity is best described in the polarity between Jewish and Hindu thought (i.e. between action and order, between instruments and vessels, between supplication and participation). It is also worth noting that Habermas does not actually mention Christianity by name, and the Weber text under consideration is primarily about Confucianism and Taoism. From his talk of 'sacraments' one must assume that Habermas is here talking about Christianity. What he says is striking. Christianity, in Habermas' account, not only tends towards the polar extreme of Judaism, but far excels it in its account of the difference between God and creation. Not only is there a gulf between them: there is no point even in shouting across it, because God cannot hear. With a confidence one almost admires, Habermas describes Christianity as a religion of 'the sacrament' rather than of prayer and praise. Now, every student of theology knows that it is difficult to explain what a 'sacrament' is, and it is no easy matter to describe 'prayer'. However, to reduce the one to 'manipulative technique' and the other to 'personal communication' might not be the most obvious starting point for an illuminating exploration. One would certainly find it difficult to account satisfactorily for what is sometimes called the 'prayer of humble access' ('We do not presume to come to this your table trusting in our own righteousness, but in your manifold and great mercies') which is uttered almost immediately before 'the sacrament' is received by the congregation. And quite what one would make of the singing of the Sanctus ('Holy, holy, holy, Lord God of hosts!') which precedes it must remain the most baffling of puzzles. The real problem here is not Habermas' lack of theological education but an unwillingness to pay attention to detail. This is a *sociological* matter. Christians disagree very colourfully and painfully over how to make sense of sacraments and prayer; different traditions (Coptic, Orthodox, Roman Catholic, Protestant) have distinctive theologies; there are noisy arguments within Protestant theology over these matters. Such variety is not new, and it was not new when Weber was writing in the 1920s.

Complaining about Habermas' sociological shortcomings is, however, no substitute for argument, and the task is to give a charitable account of his discussion. Perhaps it is better to ask *why* he rehearses this description of Christianity, and enquire into how it might help his search for a general account of religious development. We should assume that it serves some useful purpose.

Habermas is almost exclusively interested in the notion of disenchantment rather than the quality of worship. 'The magical world of ideas is an impediment to the adoption of an objectivistic attitude toward technical innovation, economic growth, and the like' (Habermas 1984a: 205). That is, disenchantment makes it possible to think coolly about technology and exchange because they are no longer part of the 'too-hot-to-handle' (Lash) domain of the sacred. And in regard to these issues, Habermas wishes to press beyond Weber's almost exclusive focus on religion as an ethical worldview towards some consideration of what Habermas calls 'cognitive' matters. It is precisely his interest in cognitive development that motivates his desire for a general account of religious development.

Habermas returns to the question of 'the degree of systematic unity' (Weber) that religious worldviews provide for their members. By this, Habermas means the way the manifold of experience is unified socially, especially in the face of contradiction and incoherence. Habermas calls it the 'point of unity', and this is the preparation for forging the first major link in his generalised account of the development of rationality:

This principle is represented as a God of Creation or a Ground of Being that unites in itself the universal aspects of 'is' and 'ought', essence and appearance. Indeed, worldviews count as the 'more rational', the more clearly they make it possible to grasp or to deal with the world – be it as the temporal world or as the world of appearances – under *one* of these aspects, which are still unseparated in the realm of the supramundane.

(Habermas 1984a: 206)

Habermas means that religions show signs of being more rational when they separate 'is' and 'ought', 'essence' and 'appearance'. Such separation, for Habermas, is one of the stages on the way to 'modern' thought, which is evolutionarily later than the 'traditional'. In language familiar to theologians, this means that it is necessary for traditions to separate 'dogmatics' from 'ethics' if they are to achieve increased rationality. On Habermas' scheme, Karl Barth's insistence that 'ethics is dogmatics' is a regression in social development. It is important to understand clearly why Habermas insists on this separation, not least because he would probably not describe Barth's theology, or for that matter MacIntyre's philosophy (both of which challenge such separation), as 'irrational'. Instead he would say that they fail to appreciate the benefits that such separation brings for cognitive and moral development.

Habermas is not as precise as he might be in his account of the separation of 'is' and 'ought'. What he seems to want to say is that rationalisation is about telling the difference between the world that is to be interpreted, the humanly made interpretations of that world, and the ethical motivations that follow from those inter-pretations. The ambiguity arises in how one is to fit 'is' and 'ought' into this. Habermas implies that conflating 'is' and 'ought' goes together with confusing 'world' and 'worldview'. This need not be so, however. If one understands that 'is' is a humanly made inter-pretation of the world just as much as 'ought', then 'is' and 'ought' could be held together perfectly rationally, in Habermas' sense. Similarly, if one recognises that 'dogmatics' is a humanly made interpretation of scripture, then there is no problem in saying 'ethics is dogmatics'. Here, the distinction between scripture and scriptural interpretation is more useful than 'world/worldview'. This is because Habermas' use of the word 'world' is counter-intuitive, and one has to work hard to remember to use it the way he does. There is great pressure on the imagination to think that 'world' means 'how we see the world', which is obviously a humanly made interpretation. Habermas emphatically does not mean this. For him, 'world' means the thing interpreted, not the interpretation. He would strenuously insist that no-one encounters the world except in some interpretation or another: he is an exemplary Hegelian in so far as he understands that there is no reality independent of its mediation through concepts. His point is different: it is that people with different worldviews can be taught to recognise that their worldviews *are worldviews* and are distinct from the world that they interpret. Talking of scripture and scriptural interpretation is easier to comprehend. Were Habermas to say that it is more rational to recognise the difference between scripture and scriptural interpretation than to think that they are the same thing, most readers would understand very quickly what Habermas is trying to say. Habermas' world/worldview distinction turns any 'worldview' into something asserted. A worldview is just an interpretation, whereas rationality, for Habermas, consists in differentiating worldview from world. It makes little sense, in this scheme, to talk of more or less 'rational' worldviews, except in so far as they are more or less consistent, or produce better or worse theodicies (according to some criteria – but which?). A consistency check is a pretty minimal thing, considering the vast influence that a worldview has on every conceivable area of human thought and action.

Habermas is certainly on to something in his distinction between world and worldview, or as he says elsewhere, 'the possibility of distinguishing between what is true and what we hold to be true' (Habermas 1992a: 138). There is surely a difference between arguing with someone who sees their worldview *as* a worldview, and someone who thinks that they are describing the only conceivable world there could be. I am perceived in the first case as someone with a different interpretation, whereas I am a pervert in the second. This is going to make a difference to the quality and tone of debate. To repeat: Habermas could achieve his ends better by speaking of the difference between scripture and scriptural interpretation, because he would not need the potentially misleading concept of 'world'. He would not have to give up discussion of 'reality' because there is the perfectly serviceable Renaissance notion of the two books of nature and scripture. 'Nature/scripture' can do the job much better than 'world', so long as readers of these books remember that all reading is interpretation. It also has a further benefit: there really are different scriptures, interpreted in different traditions, and not only different interpretations of scripture, and understanding this makes it easier to see why it is difficult to achieve good ethical debate between members of different traditions. Habermas is forced into suggesting that somehow partners in dialogue must transcend their traditions at the same time as admitting that this is impossible: he employs problematic concepts like 'unavoidable presuppositions' or 'quasi-transcendental ideas' or 'hypothetical commitments' of the kind we encountered in chapter 2. The concept 'nature/scripture' is much better because it renders the differences of perspective much more clearly visible. Of course, it raises its own aporias: one has to have a good account of how people with different scriptures can argue, and one still has to find (and here Habermas is excellent) criteria for evaluating the strength of arguments. But it is more obvious that such criteria have to come from *each* scripture-plus-tradition, rather than from some super-scripture, which all too obviously does not exist. Naturally, one has to give up on universal criteria on this model, but so does Habermas on his in so far as he acknowledges the *hypothetical* nature of such universals.[7]

Habermas' reliance on Weber is especially significant in Weber's notion that an 'objectivating' attitude to the world is one of the outcomes of 'religions of salvation', by which he means traditions that operate with a sharp distinction between God and the world. Alongside devaluing action in the world (which sounds a distinctly *Protestant* theological danger, although Habermas does not say so), the world is also viewed abstractly. Habermas notes that this is not enough to produce ethical rationalisation (i.e. the separation of 'is' and 'ought'). For this to happen, the theological presuppositions have to be attenuated and a *positive* rather than withdrawing attitude needs to be taken towards the world. The quality of this 'positive' attitude is striking in Weber's account, however. The world-rejecting religious traditions sometimes develop attitudes towards the world that promote 'mastery' of this devalued and objectivated realm.

---

[7] Pippin notes that this reconstructive interest in the hypothetical distinguishes Habermas from Karl-Otto Apel, but although Habermas moves away from some of the more problematic Kantian positions, he does not adequately address the problems Hegel poses for such an approach: Pippin 1997: 177.

Weber associates this attitude with religious traditions that construe human action as 'instrument of God' rather than 'vessel of the divine' (Habermas 1984a: 207).

At this point, Habermas once again risks a disagreement with Weber. Weber had wanted to explain how capitalism had arisen in Europe and not elsewhere, generating pressure to explain why other cultures did not 'rationalise' so far. Habermas notes that Weber implausibly speculated that the Chinese lacked the means for rationalisation because of the persistence of their 'magical' investment in the emperor. This is implausible because it is known (as Weber did not know) that Chinese theoretical accomplishments far outstripped those of Europe for many hundreds of years until around AD 1400. Habermas at this point once again suggests that analysis from the 'ethical' point of view (Weber) can be corrected by analysis from the 'cognitive' point of view (Habermas). Once again, Habermas emphasises Weber's insight that the condition needed for the next stage of rationalisation was an urban, non-feudal state.

The foregoing is enough for Habermas to attempt to forge the second major link in his generalised account of rationalisation:

Worldviews can count as the more rational, the further the world of appearances is distilled out from abstract points of view as a sphere of the existing or the useful, and is purified of other – normative and expressive – aspects. A cognitively rationalised worldview represents the world as the totality of all forms and processes that can be made contemplatively present to the mind. (Habermas 1984a: 210)

The first link was the separation of 'is' and 'ought', and the corresponding ability to conceive the world with reference to only *one* of these, rather than taking them together. This second link is the separation of the 'useful' from the morally right or the desirably good.

By this stage in the discussion, a number of contrasts are in operation, and Habermas has been diagramming them to show where the different world religions appear. Habermas has distilled things down to two axes: an *active* versus a *passive* attitude to action in the world, and a *negative* versus a *positive* evaluation of the world. Christianity, for example, is active and negative, whereas the ancient Greeks were passive and positive. Thus Christians aim for mastery whereas Greeks aim for contemplation (Habermas 1984a: 211). Again, Habermas wants to formulate a cognitive-evolutionary thesis that can *generalise* religious development rather than rely on contingencies that suggest that sometimes developments happen, and sometimes they do not. He continues to do this by combining his cognitive analysis with Weber's ethical analysis. He does it in the following way.

Rationalisation can take one of two forms: cognitive *or* ethical. Weber's account was one-sided in considering only ethical rationalisation, that is, the differentiation of 'is' from 'ought'. It needs complementing by a consideration of cognitive rationalisation, that is, a differentiation of different kinds of processes in nature (e.g. magical versus natural causation). Christianity and Judaism allegedly differentiated 'is' and 'ought', and 'decentred' their worlds that way; the ancient Greeks differentiated different kinds of empirical processes (that is, they developed sophisticated theories), and 'decentred' their world that way instead. This serves Habermas' *generalised* account very well: the most rationalised position is one which differentiates *both* axes: 'is' and 'ought' *and* a differentiation of different kinds of observed processes in nature (Habermas 1984a: 212–13). Of course, this kind of rationalisation does not belong to any *single* religious tradition. What Habermas wants to describe is the coming together of Greek 'theory' and Christian 'mastery' in the one European culture. Along the way, he has a nice aside: 'Naturally, the Christian religion can just as little be reduced to ethics as Greek philosophy can to cosmology' (Habermas 1984a: 213). This is wishful thinking. It is unfortunately all too easy to think of examples where Christianity is precisely reduced to ethics: there are philosophically respectable but theologically disastrous interpretations of Kant that point in this direction, for example.

It is right at the end of the argument that we find what we are looking for: signs of a distinction between 'theological' and 'metaphysical'. Our original query had been whether it is thinkable to have a 'religious-post-metaphysical' outlook. Habermas offers the following:

The unity of rationalised worldviews that refer, in a theological vein, to the creation, or in a metaphysical vein, to the whole of what exists, is anchored in concepts like 'God', 'being', or 'nature', in ultimate principles or 'beginnings'; while all arguments can be traced back to such beginnings, the latter are not themselves exposed to argumentative doubt. In these basic concepts, descriptive, normative, and expressive aspects are still fused; precisely in these 'beginnings' there lives on something of mythical thought. (Habermas 1984a: 214)

This is fascinating. Habermas is attributing to (now partially rationalised) religious traditions the capacity to distinguish between interpretations ('arguments') and that upon which interpretations are based ('beginnings'). Interpretations are open to criticism, whereas their source is not. This inability or unwillingness (Habermas does not differentiate) is attributed to the persistence of the 'mythic'. Habermas contrasts this with more fully rationalised thinking ('modern modes of thought') which

do not recognise any such preserves, any such exemptions from the critical power of hypothetical thought, either in ethics or in science. In order to remove this barrier, it was first necessary to generalise the level of learning that was attained with the conceptual apparatus of religious-metaphysical worldviews, that is, to apply the modes of thought achieved in ethical and cognitive rationalisation consistently to profane domains of life and experience. (Habermas 1984a: 214)

In other words, 'modern' thought subjects *everything*, even basic presuppositions, to criticism. But this assertion leads in a direction that is not at all congenial to Habermas: it replays one of the problematic situations inherited by the German Idealists, namely the question of how to have criticism without radical scepticism.[8] This is obviously not what Habermas wants: his goal is rather a generalised account of ethical and cognitive rationalisation.

Habermas gains his generalised account in an interesting way. He rehearses Weber's account of *ethical* rationalisation, and the deployment of Protestant theological commitments, as determining factors for the rise of the 'mastery' of capitalism. At the same time, almost as footnotes to Weber, he rehearses a complementary account of *cognitive* rationalisation, deploying Greek metaphysical commitments as determining factors for the rise of the 'theory' of modern

---

[8] For a short, accessible discussion of the situation inherited by Kant's successors, see Beiser, 'The Enlightenment and Idealism', in Ameriks 2000: 18–36.

science. It is a most interesting rhetorical strategy, not least because if one rigorously separates out the claims made about cognitive development, and dissociates them from the detailed commentary on Weber, one notices that he substantiates his claims about cognition almost never. They have the same speculative quality as Weber's remarks on religion, and are just as precarious. The difference is that Weber did not try to be 'systematic' in Habermas' sense. In addition he wrote in much greater detail, across a much broader range of data. Weber's account, more detailed and less systematic, is superior to Habermas' generalised theory of rationalisation, and it is perhaps not surprising that Habermas' cognitive theory has not been as influential as Weber's capitalism thesis. This, however, is not what primarily concerns us. Our question concerned Habermas' narrative of the decline of the 'religious-metaphysical' worldview in Europe. The long analysis of his argument demonstrates a negative conclusion: Habermas is really not interested in this decline!

Habermas is interested in a generalised account of rationalisation. The speculative narrative about religion, which is barely defended, is a wholly secondary matter. Habermas' basic thesis does not stand or fall with the truth or falsity of his *historical* narrative, but with the cogency and consistency of his schematic account of the differentiation of value spheres. Religion is just a casualty of his systematic intentions, and a relatively strong claim is in order: *it is a mistake to take Habermas' remarks on religion here too seriously.* He may well believe what he says about the decline of the 'religious-metaphysical' worldview, but he devotes very little theoretical energy to defending the aspect of *decline*. Habermas just is not concerned at any deep level with this. There is thus no need for theologians to argue against him that religious life is 'rational'.[9] Habermas' primary concern is a generalised account of rationality, and his arguments are at least worth considering (even if they are not finally persuasive). His account of the decline of religion is of a wholly different and lower order, and nothing he says here is of sufficiently careful formulation to warrant detailed rebuttal.

---

[9] See Rothberg 1986; Browning and Fiorenza 1992; Marsh 1993.

This helps explain Habermas' surprise and discomfort at being invited to hear theologians defend their traditions in the light of his theory of communicative action. This theory presupposes, but does not actually demonstrate, the overcoming of religion. It functions as a 'beginning' or 'ultimate principle', in his own sense above. He thus has no real arguments that one could dispute. If one analyses one of his few detailed engagements with theologians, an essay called 'Transcendence from Within' (Habermas 2002: 67–94), one notices immediately that he largely ignores all the contributions that try to defend religious rationality; instead he homes in on the contributions that tackle his rationality thesis more generally. We shall see this in chapter 9.

Reading Habermas' account of rationality may teach theologians a number of things, but they will learn very little about religion. Indeed, they might well come to suspect that their native distinctions between scripture and scriptural interpretation can be put to work in interesting ways as an *alternative* way of considering the question of what Habermas calls 'rationality'. Such a dialogue with Habermas has yet to take place.

CHAPTER 8

Modernity's triumph over theology

In his later work, Habermas is more explicit about why he thinks that even contemporary theology cannot perform a useful role in questions of modern ethical theory. In his refinements of the discourse ethics project, religion still plays a major part in his arguments, and it is important to clarify what this part is. Because of the connection he makes between theology and metaphysics, and because ethical theories in modernity must be post-metaphysical, Habermas claims that theology is no good for contemporary ethics. This is not to say that he knows no examples of post-metaphysical theology, and in chapter 9 we shall look at how he debates with some post-metaphysical theology. Rather, Habermas refuses to acknowledge that post-metaphysical theologies are genuinely theological, in the sense of being tradition-bound interpretations of scripture and ritual. Habermas also believes that philosophical interpretations of God's being and action are not just successful interpretations but are *too* successful: they make it unnecessary any longer to speak about God. If a post-metaphysical theology were to be viable, for Habermas, it would have to avoid interpreting God away using other concepts, and yet avoid being unintelligible to modern forms of self-consciousness. He thinks that it cannot be done, and the reasonings behind this are rehearsed in some of his later work. This work is the focus of the current chapter. In my view, Habermas indulges in some questionable readings of the philosophical tradition, and some sharp criticisms are called for.

This chapter will consider two later essays: 'Modernity's Consciousness of Time and its Need for Self-Reassurance' (from *The Philosophical Discourse of Modernity*) and 'A Genealogical Analysis of the Cognitive Content of Morality' (from *The Inclusion of the*

Other). The main theme to be investigated, as before, is the notion of the overcoming of religion in modernity: not only how Habermas describes the benefits and costs, but also trying to hear how he describes the process by which this overcoming happens.

The essay 'Modernity's Consciousness of Time' is the first of the twelve lectures in *The Philosophical Discourse of Modernity*. Its purpose is to lay out a two-fold thesis: (1) modern people see their present as a break with the past and the beginning of the future – the 'new age'; (2) their reflective attitude to the past means that the latter has no binding authority; the unity of the world and authority to describe how people ought to live, which previously resided in religion, thus has to be sought elsewhere: *out of modernity itself.*

Characteristically, Habermas' discussion of religion comes at the *start* of his main narrative. It is thus a kind of scene-setting rather than the nub of the matter, and is best read as such. The whole essay serves as scene-setting for the later lectures, so the discussion of religion is scene-setting for scene-setting: not an approach that promises much in the way of insight into religion *as* religion. It merely serves to set up a narrative about something Habermas considers non-religious, namely the self-reliance of modern thinking.

'Modernity's Consciousness of Time' starts from where our discussion of Weber in *Theory of Communicative Action* left off, although in the intervening time the reader has been offered the remaining volume and a half of *The Theory of Communicative Action*, parts of which we have discussed in the previous chapters. Habermas begins, again, with Weber's question concerning how one can explain that European developments in all of the 'spheres of value' did not occur elsewhere (Habermas 1987a: 1). Again, Habermas rehearses familiar arguments about 'disenchantment' and the 'disintegration of religious worldviews'. This is a pattern. Habermas *begins* with religion as a useful foil for his real interests, which are to draw as strong a distinction as possible between 'modern' and 'traditional' thinking. Our subsidiary question is: how important is this foil to his argument, and could he do without it?

Habermas wants to contrast his approach with that of the classical social theorists. Naming Durkheim and Mead once again, Habermas sketches their picture of the changes that bring about modernity. These are characterised by the reflective treatment of traditions that have lost their quasi-natural status; by the universalisation of norms of action and the generalisation of values, which set communicative action free from narrowly restricted contexts and enlarge the field of options; and finally, by patterns of socialisation that are oriented to the formation of abstract ego-identities and force the individuation of the growing child.

(Habermas 1987a: 2)

Some of this is already familiar to us. Habermas is speaking, in the first part, of the differentiation between world and worldview which enables members of traditions to recognise their traditions *as* traditions, i.e. as humanly made interpretations of the world. There is also some material we looked at in the previous chapter on tradition: it concerns the 'universalisation' and 'generalisation' of norms and values. This refers to Habermas' thesis about the shift from *substantive* to *procedural* issues in ethics.

Habermas also wants to distinguish his approach from certain others. One is research into modernisation (he names James Coleman as a typical representative) which, Habermas claims, tends to abstract modernity from its thick European history and cast it as a 'neutral model for processes of social development in general' (Habermas 1987a: 2). We saw in chapter 1 that Habermas insisted on this right at the start of his study of *The Structural Transformation of the Public Sphere*. Two other approaches named here are that of Arnold Gehlen, especially the latter's idea that Enlightenment processes continue to drive societal development even though its cultural motivations have long since died, and 'aesthetically inspired anarchism' (Habermas names no names), which tries to break down modernity's edifices because it sees all of them as tyrannical. Habermas rejects such approaches because they treat the origins of the present as a past era consigned to a no longer relevant history. Such approaches not only fail to notice continuities as well as breaks, but also – as a result – give a misleading account of the relation between modernity and rationality. Much better than these, Habermas thinks, is Hegel.

We are not primarily interested in Habermas' use of Hegel, but in the prehistory – the decline of metaphysical thinking before the Enlightenment – Habermas narrates. Nonetheless, the two are not so easily separated in the essay under consideration, because Habermas' account of that prehistory is Hegel's. This is odd, and therefore worth paying attention to. It is odd because there are surely more reliable guides to the history of religion in Europe than Hegel. Habermas' choice of Hegel is not one he directly justifies. The reader is told that Hegel was the first thinker to confront directly the problem of modern self-consciousness; the reader is also told that Habermas contrasts his own theory of communicative action with Hegel's account of reason and ethical life. These are both good reasons for exploring Hegel as a major source for a contemporary investigation into the philosophical discourse of modernity. Nonetheless, it is striking just how much of Hegel's philosophy of history Habermas rehearses as an authoritative description of European thought. It is true, as Habermas points out, that Hegel's categorisation of history into Antiquity, Middle Ages and Modern Period still shapes the way professorial chairs are described in the contemporary university. It may also be true that Hegel's description of the modern age as a 'new period' distinguished from previous periods still holds sway over contemporary imaginations. It may be true further still that 'Modernity can and will no longer borrow the criteria by which it takes its orientation from the models supplied by another epoch; *it has to create its normativity out of itself.* Modernity sees itself cast back upon itself without any possibility of escape' (Habermas 1987a: 7). It may even be true that 'Hegel was the first to raise to the level of a philosophical problem the process of detaching modernity from the suggestion of norms lying outside of itself in the past' (Habermas 1987a: 16). Nonetheless, it is not obvious that Hegel's account of the rise of subjectivity is useful for Habermas' purposes. Habermas summarises Hegel as follows:

The key historical events in establishing the principle of subjectivity are the Reformation, the Enlightenment, and the French Revolution. With Luther, religious faith became reflective; the world of the divine was changed in the solitude of subjectivity into something posited by ourselves. Against faith in the authority of preaching and tradition, Protestantism asserted the authority of the subject relying upon his own insight: the host was simply dough, the relics of the saints mere bones. Then, too, the Declaration of the Rights of Man and the Napoleonic Code validated the principle of freedom of will against historically preexisting law as the substantive basis of the state: 'Right and *Sittlichkeit* came to be looked upon as having their foundation in the actually present will of man, whereas formerly it was referred only to the command of God enjoined *ab extra*, written in the Old and New Testament, or appearing in the form of particular right . . . in old parchments, as *privilegia*, or in international compacts.'

(Habermas 1987a: 17, ending with a quotation from Hegel's *Philosophy of History*: Hegel 1991: 440)

Habermas does not cite Hegel as it were at a remove, to indicate merely how Hegel describes modernity. This is Habermas' account: a narrative he himself owns and reproduces as authoritative. But is it really Hegel's? The key works by Hegel upon which Habermas' summary in this passage is based are the *Lectures on the Philosophy of Religion* and the *Philosophy of History*. The reference to Luther and reflection might seem to offer some material to assist the generous reader in reconstructing Habermas' account of the religious/metaphysical worldview, but this passing comment is really all he offers. The footnote he attaches to the comment merely refers the reader to the whole of Hegel's lectures on the philosophy of religion! (These are vast and complex.) Hegel's only noteworthy remarks about Luther in that work are in the context of a discussion about the relationship between 'absolute objectivity' and truth 'for me' (Hegel 1985a: 243–7). There, Hegel is concerned to show that although one's *early experiences of* reflection (and not 'reflection' as such, *pace* Habermas) tend to confuse and weaken one's purchase on things that had been taken for granted, this is not the end of the process. Hegel concedes the danger of learning 'how to make everything totter, and in so doing remain standing as a god above the ruins of the world', but he describes this as the 'final, highest vanity'. The job of philosophy is to recognise the 'absolute identity' of the subjective and the objective, and not at all to allow reflection to permit one to triumph over the other (Hegel 1985a: 247). Habermas' gloss on Hegel, 'the world of the divine was changed in the solitude of subjectivity into something posited by ourselves', is profoundly misleading on this point. Much better would be a reading showing that, for Hegel, the world of the divine is no longer encountered as either taken-for-granted objectivity or an object of 'tottering' decisionism but as an objectivity that needs to be recognised as a truth 'for me', i.e. owned by me as authoritative. Such recognition is precisely the kind of 'faith' that Luther insisted was the sole source of salvation over and against things like 'conviction' and 'sensibility' (Hegel 1985a: 243). Against Habermas, Hegel keeps a firm eye on the response of individual human subjectivity in the face of a prior 'objective' (divine) subjectivity. It is understandable that Habermas emphasises the shift from 'metaphysical' to 'post-metaphysical' thinking: this is quite right, as Hegel rejects the dogmatism of an unmediated appeal to the objective. But Habermas will find little assistance from Hegel in defending the idea that the divine is 'posited by ourselves'. For Hegel it is not posited, but recognised, and there is all the difference in the world between these two verbs.[1]

Similar queries can be raised concerning Hegel's alleged view that, for 'Protestantism', 'the host was simply dough, the relics of the saints mere bones' (Habermas 1987a: 17). Habermas is not exactly wrong, but he is misleading in so far as he makes it sound as though Hegel says that this is Luther's view. In fact, in each of three lecture series on the philosophy of religion, Hegel describes three distinct views of the eucharistic bread and wine: the Roman Catholic, the Lutheran and the Reformed. The Catholic view, according to Hegel, is that 'the divine is to be found in the external'; the Lutheran view is that 'the individual worshiper takes up this consumption inwardly, and the sensible is first spiritualised in the subject'; the Reformed view is that the sacrament is 'merely a lively recollection of the past, devoid of spirit' (Hegel 1985b: 155–6, 236, 337–9). Habermas is clearly referring to the Reformed view and not the Lutheran when he talks about dough and bones. He footnotes Hegel's *Philosophy of History* here, however, and not the *Lectures on the Philosophy of Religion*. Hegel is not talking about Protestantism at all at this point in his narrative, but about the effects in Germany of Cartesian philosophy – this is unhelpfully concealed in the form of Habermas' summary (Hegel 1991: 440). Habermas' account is further misleading, however, in placing this description in a list of 'key historical events': Habermas is, characteristically, trying to summarise a history of *development* from the Reformation through the Enlightenment to the French Revolution. Hegel is interested in history too, but he certainly does not think that the Reformed view

---

[1] See also the editorial introduction to this work by Peter Hodgson: Hegel 1985a: 72–3.

represents a culmination of a rational development: after explaining the Reformed view of the sacraments he makes it clear that he finds it deeply unsatisfactory and regards it as constituting a regression behind Luther's philosophically more sophisticated account: 'Luther [was] fully justified in not yielding [to Reformed accounts of the Eucharist], however much he was assailed for it' (Hegel 1985b: 156).

Habermas' further remarks about Protestantism, preaching and the authority of the subject are also misleading. Habermas too freely improvises on Hegel's theme: 'The independent authority of subjectivity was maintained against belief founded on authority, and the laws of nature were recognised as the only bond connecting phenomena with phenomena' (Hegel 1991: 440). There is nothing explicitly about preaching or tradition here, only the reference to 'authority' which is not spelled out. It is perhaps not accidental that Habermas conveniently ignores Hegel's later clarification that 'in Germany the Enlightenment was conducted in the interest of theology, [whereas] in France it immediately took up a position of hostility to the Church' (Hegel 1991: 444). This view, elaborated at some length in the *Lectures on the Philosophy of Religion*, does not harmonise at all well with Habermas' brisk account of the decline of religion and its replacement by philosophy, and his hasty attribution of this account to Hegel.

Habermas' sketch of the shift brought about in modernity involves two distinct movements. The first is the idea that 'religious life, state, and society as well as science, morality, and art are transformed into just so many embodiments of the principle of subjectivity' (Habermas 1987a: 18); the second is the idea that by the end of the eighteenth century 'science, morality and art were even institutionally differentiated as realms of activity in which questions of truth, of justice, and of taste were autonomously elaborated, that is, each under its own specific aspect of validity' (Habermas 1987a: 19). The first of these claims is attributed to Hegel's *Philosophy of Right*. The second is a way of looking at things that Habermas has learned from Max Weber and Emil Lask. Again, it is important to understand that by quoting Hegel and Lask, Habermas owns their accounts (or his interpretation of them, the reliability of which in the case of Hegel I am contesting) and treats them as authoritative descriptions of historical change. With regard to the first claim, that even 'religious life' is transformed into an embodiment of the 'principle of subjectivity', clearly much hangs on what kind of subjectivity is being talked about. Habermas associates it with 'something posited by ourselves'. Hegel, as is well known, has a more flamboyant account of the subjectivity of absolute spirit. This is his experimental reworking of the doctrine of the Trinity and its relation to revelation: it is an account in which the infinite subjectivity of God is made known to the finite subjectivity of human action via the 'determination of spirit' (Hegel 1975: 51). This spirit is self-conscious, and human action is a participation in it, as sensual in religion and as thinking in philosophy. It is also closely allied, in some of Hegel's writing, with the spirit of a particular nation (Hegel 1975: 53). Many contemporary readings challenge Hegel's confidence about how far 'thinking' can apprehend this infinite subjectivity, the well-known problem of how concepts relate to the absolute (e.g. Bowie 1993: 127–77). Habermas challenges Hegel's account of subjectivity by dissociating subjectivity from national spirit and, instead of adopting a God's-eye view of 'World Spirit', offers an account of spirit in the form of a theory of communicative action (Habermas 1987a: 30). Instead of identifying the universal with an ethical totality, as Hegel did, Habermas associates the universal with certain inherent properties of how people communicate: a 'universal pragmatics' (Habermas 1984b: 1–68). Unlike Hegel's account, which is overtly experimental, Habermas describes his own account as one of 'rational reconstruction' which, while speculative, arises from careful consideration of actual practices of communication (Habermas 1984b: 8–14).

However, we must notice something that has happened rather quietly in this development. Hegel's account of spirit was a development of, and perhaps within, Christian philosophical theology. He explicitly discusses the Trinity in the text mentioned above (Hegel 1975: 51). In the *Lectures on the Philosophy of Religion* he even criticises much contemporary modern theology, including that of Schleiermacher, for failing to understand the importance of the Trinity for philosophical thinking (Hegel 1985b: 126–7). Thus the 'principle of subjectivity' to which Habermas appeals is, very obviously, a product of speculative theology: its job is to describe the relationship between divine and human action, and describe how the divine is revealed in history. It may be true that Hegel over-estimates the power of concepts in this matter (Schelling's critique). It may also be true that Hegel identifies absolute spirit too closely with community spirit (Kierkegaard's critique). Neither of these objections rejects Hegel's speculative attempt to recast the doctrine of the Trinity in modern philosophical terms *as such*. Instead, they try to repair it by emphasising the indirect and difficult relationship between human thinking and divine action. Habermas' attempt to take over the 'principle of subjectivity' and to recast it as a theory of communicative action is thus far more radical than either Schelling or Kierkegaard (or Barth, for that matter). Habermas dissociates subjectivity from the doctrine of the Trinity, and from any account whatsoever of divine action. This has been common in German philosophy since Fichte's account of the absolute ego, which was perhaps the first emphatically to make this disassociation. The odd thing is that Habermas should appeal so directly to Hegel's account of subjectivity in order to place his own. How does Habermas explain Hegel's indebtedness to the doctrine of the Trinity? Habermas ignores it:

Just as in art, so also in religion, reflection has broken in; substantive faith has collapsed either into indifference or into hypocritical sentimentality. Philosophy salvages the *content* of faith from this atheism by destroying the religious *form*. Philosophy has no content other than religion, but inasmuch as it transforms this content into conceptual knowledge, 'nothing is [any longer] justified by faith'. (Habermas 1987a: 36)

Remarkably, this view is attributed to Hegel's *Lectures on the Philosophy of Religion*. The relevant passage interpreted by Habermas is this:

Although among the people, i.e., the lower classes, there is still faith in objective truth, the teaching of this truth is no longer justified in terms of faith, once the time has come when what is demanded is justification by the concept. (Hegel 1985b: 159–60)[2]

At first glance this does look as though it can support the claim that 'Hegel takes his leave of the Christian religion' (Habermas

---

[2] I have used Peter Hodgson's edition of this work rather than the older and less satisfactory one cited by Habermas' otherwise excellent translator.

1987a: 35). But things are not so simple. Hegel knows very well that the word 'faith' is ambiguous and difficult to use clearly: mostly he means by it 'the eternal, substantial nature of spirit that has come to consciousness here, exists for consciousness, [so] that what is truth in and for itself has certainty for me' (Hegel 1985b: 150). In the passage cited by Habermas, however, it means something different, namely received knowledge from some external source such as the clergy. Here Hegel is primarily interested not in faith but in the *teaching* of truth and the failure of *modern* religious traditions to teach it properly. This would have been clearer if Habermas had gone on to cite the conclusion of Hegel's argument:

> The [common] people, in which reason remains constantly under pressure, [this] class in whose cultivation the truth can exist only in the form of representation . . . [has been] abandoned by its [theological] teachers. The latter have helped themselves by means of reflection, and have found their satisfaction in finitude, subjectivity, and precisely thereby in vanity; but the [common] people, who form the substantial nucleus [of the population as a whole], cannot find its satisfaction in such things.
>
> (Hegel 1985b: 160–1; Hodgson's interpolations)

Hegel is not 'taking leave' of religion in the everyday sense, as Habermas claims. Hegel has the quite different goal of showing that people are being badly taught and need not an opposition between representation and concepts but a way of reconciling them *within* philosophy. Hegel is trying to repair philosophical theology, not abandon it. And the form of this repair is precisely a reworked trinitarian account (however flawed that reworking may be, if judged against criteria for orthodox theology).

The significance of this is that Habermas is implausibly optimistic in hoping to persuade his reader that he can appeal to Hegel to support Habermas' own account of subjectivity. Hegel's account of reflection has to be read in a very heavy-handed way if it is to be understood as a force working against 'faith' (in either of Hegel's senses). This does not mean that Hegel could not be called as a witness in Habermas' case for modernity, and even in Habermas' more focused remarks about subjectivity. But in order for this to work, Habermas would need to show why it is better for an account of absolute subjectivity, like Hegel's, to be divorced from its theological (trinitarian) context. This, of course, he cannot do, for the same reason that theologians cannot give a good account of why absolute subjectivity *should* be associated with God (rather than with something else, as in Spinoza's account of *Deus sive natura*). Such associations are *already* narrated in the tradition of philosophy and are not established by it. Thus, if Habermas wants to appeal to Hegel for an account of the decline of metaphysical religion, he has to accept Hegel's theological context. If he wishes to go further, and rescue Hegel's philosophical concepts for non-theological use, he will need to give arguments as to why Hegel's theological associations are problematic. Habermas is good at showing that Hegel's close association between absolute and state is not supported by convincing arguments. But he fails to notice the strong connection between Hegel's trinitarian account, in which the incarnational moment is strongly emphasised, and the insistence that the state is the particular form of the absolute's subjectivity. Hegel's 'emphatic institutionalism' (Henrich) is rightly opposed by Habermas, but instead of pointing out that Hegel is insufficiently trinitarian (i.e. he does not correct his emphatic incarnational theology with a doctrine of God and a doctrine of the spirit), Habermas jumps straight to offering a *completely different* speculative account: 'A different model for the mediation of the universal and the individual is provided by the *higher-level intersubjectivity of an uncoerced formation of will* within a communication community existing under constraints toward cooperation' (Habermas 1987a: 40). The problem is that the bigger this jump, the less point there is in appealing to Hegel in the first place. Habermas does not repair Hegel's account here: he simply substitutes a different one.

This has been a necessary detour into issues in the interpretation of Hegel. Most criticisms of Habermas' reading of Hegel concentrate on the theme of *Sittlichkeit* (as we saw in chapter 2), rather than his rather hasty use of Hegel's theological speculation. For that reason it has been worth spending a little time on some of the problems, even if the surface has only been scratched. I have tried to place some obstacles in the way of Habermas' appropriation of Hegel as a narrator of the decline of religion as such. Our primary interest is in the story of modernity's prehistory: the alleged decline of the 'religious-metaphysical' worldview. The more carefully one reads Hegel, however, the more one sees an attempt at a properly philosophical account of the Trinity, of the Eucharist, of faith and so forth, rather than an abandonment of them. Habermas wants very much to use Hegel as a force of disjunction from the past, and it is understandable why: Hegel is an immensely powerful ally. Yet Hegel's account of the prehistory of modernity does not lead in the direction Habermas wants. Hegel is genuinely theological, albeit disastrously heterodox from an Anglican perspective, while being post-metaphysical. His account of the relationship between religion and philosophy is the relationship between sensuous representation and concepts, and while it is true that for Hegel concepts 'overcome' sensuous representation, it is misleading to say that philosophy thereby overcomes religion.

In summary, Hegel tries to repair the shortcomings of modern philosophical theology, not abandon it. Habermas really does abandon it, while at the same time benefiting from many of its categories, which he takes over in secularised forms. For this reason, Hegel is not suitable for Habermas' purposes. The prehistory of modernity told by Hegel is a history of religious thought in need of repair, not a tale about the overcoming of religious thought. It is thus not surprising that when Habermas does wish to depart from Hegel he has to do so in a radical way and substitute a wholly different approach to the question of how universal and particular are to relate. Hegel's prehistory of modernity is thus not Habermas'. Hegel's primary role, for Habermas' narrative, is to set out the problem of modernity: the problem of discovering that dogmatic appeals to metaphysical truth cannot withstand reflective argumentation. Perhaps Habermas wants to read in Hegel the abandoning, and not just the repair, of philosophical theology. Habermas does need to give an account of the rise of subjectivity in the modern period around 1800, but this only requires a story about the overcoming of a dogmatically presented metaphysical worldview, not the overcoming of religious life and thought as such. Of course, Habermas may equate the two, but as he does not say that he does, his remarks about 'faith' and 'religion' remain something of a puzzle.

'Modernity's Consciousness of Time' does, then, contain a speculative prehistory of religion before modernity, but this account is a strange reading of Hegel. We can now ask our second question: does

Habermas need this account? Bluntly, no. We have already considered the ways in which it is misleading. It is furthermore unnecessary because Habermas does not need to discuss religion in order to chart the rise of subjectivity as a major theme in philosophy. This rise occurs *within* the Christian theological tradition in which Hegel was trained. In either case, we learn very little about the characteristics of a 'religious-metaphysical worldview', and it remains unclear whether the turn to subjectivity in German philosophy is for Habermas intrinsically opposed to Christian theology or itself a development within it. Habermas seems to assume that Christian theology is superseded by idealist philosophy, but he nowhere explicitly argues for this. As a result, the reader remains baffled as to why Habermas invokes religion at all in his scene-setting for the philosophical discourse of modernity. It does not seem to serve any useful function.

Habermas' purpose in 'A Genealogical Analysis of the Cognitive Content of Morality' (Habermas 1998: 3–46) is to show how there can be genuine moral argumentation in a cultural situation where the unified narratives handed down in religious traditions have broken down and are no longer universally acknowledged as authoritative. More specifically, Habermas allies himself with the Kantian tradition which 'is not just concerned with clarifying a practice of moral justification that unfolds *within* the horizon of received norms, but seeks to justify a moral point of view from which such norms can themselves be judged in an impartial fashion' (Habermas 1998: 6–7). This essay contains Habermas' most explicit remarks about religion in his whole corpus, and so is of particular interest to theologians. Habermas opens his discussion with the kind of historical comment that is becoming familiar:

after the breakdown of a universally valid 'catholic' worldview and with the subsequent transition to pluralistic societies, moral commands can no longer be publicly justified from a transcendent God's eye point of view.
(Habermas 1998: 7)

Habermas is going to work with two opposing pairs, both of which appear here: Catholic Europe versus pluralistic societies, and transcendent God's-eye point of view versus 'transcendence from within' (i.e. a moral perspective within the world). These pairs, and the discussion about rational justification that is woven around them, signal that the first part of the essay is going to be about religion. Again, it is important to be clear about the 'predicament in which the members of *any* moral community find themselves today' that Habermas hopes this account will illuminate:

in making the transition to a modern society, pluralistic in its worldviews, [these members] find themselves faced with the dilemma that though they still argue with reasons about moral judgments and beliefs, their substantive background consensus on the underlying moral norms has been shattered . . . their initial impulse is to engage in deliberation and work out a shared *ethical* [*ethisch*] self-understanding on a secular basis. But given the differentiated forms of life characteristic of pluralistic societies, such an effort is doomed to failure . . . Let us assume they nevertheless remain resolved to engage in deliberation and not to fall back on a mere modus vivendi [let alone violence] as a substitute for the threatened moral way of life. (Habermas 1998: 39)

For this to be convincing, Habermas has first to say something about how 'substantive background consensus' works in religious life; only then can he proceed with an alternative, namely 'formal' consensus-formation.

It is a characteristically 'developmental' narrative, starting with the prehistory of modernity and its transition from religion to a rational society. As before, we are interested in the details of Habermas' account of this prehistory in order to discover whether 'religious' and 'metaphysical' are identical. In the case of this essay, the task is slightly easier than in previous chapters, because Habermas is less bashful than usual about using words like 'transcendent' and phrases like 'God's-eye view'. Habermas prepares for his question as follows:

In the secular societies of the West, everyday moral intuitions are still shaped by the normative substance of so to speak decapitated, legally privatised, religious traditions, in particular by the contents of the Hebrew morality of justice in the Old Testament and the Christian ethics of love in the New Testament. These contents are transmitted by processes of socialisation, though often only implicitly and under different titles. Thus a moral philosophy that views its task as one of reconstructing everyday moral consciousness is faced with the challenge of examining how much of this substance can be rationally justified. (Habermas 1998: 7–8)

In short, a morality originally rooted in the interpretation of Christian scripture lives on in a secularised form in contemporary Western society. The question is: how much of it can be defended without appealing to scripture? Habermas here reproduces the same framework from Hegel's *Philosophy of History* as in the essay that opens *The Philosophical Discourse of Modernity*: the question of how an apparently *external* source of authority (the Bible) comes into conflict with a self-consciously *internal* subjectivity (the philosophy of reflection).

The biblically transmitted prophetic doctrines furnished interpretations and reasons that imbued moral norms with the power to generate public agreement; they explained why God's commands are not arbitrary injunctions but can claim validity in a cognitive sense. (Habermas 1998: 8)

Habermas points out that the Western morality rooted in the interpretation of scripture relied not on unmediated appeal to scripture, but upon *doctrines* which fostered assent and provided explanations. Such doctrines made it possible to see scripture not as a purely external authority but as claims that can be asserted and defended in argument. Doctrine was the product and condition of public argumentation. Without doctrine, scripture is just an arbitrary authority that has no debatable meaning. So far, Habermas has much in common with Karl Barth, who insists in *Church Dogmatics II.2* that ethics and dogmatics belong together if they are to be thought through (Barth 1957: 514ff.).

Setting his face against the Aristotelian revival in moral theory, Habermas insists that the task of moral philosophy is not to replace the old doctrines with new ones, but to shift away from substantive declaration to analysis of formal conditions:

Moral philosophy does not itself have to provide the reasons and interpretations that, in secularised societies, take the place of the (at least *publicly*) devalued religious reasons and interpretations; but it would have to identify the kinds of reasons and interpretations that can lend the moral language game sufficient rational force even without the backing of religion. (Habermas 1998: 8)

Habermas makes it clear that the task of moral philosophy is not to compensate for the loss of religious descriptions of the world, even in moral argumentation. Instead, its job is to specify what counts as a good argument or a good interpretation in the light of such loss. What, then, has been lost?

Habermas begins his elaboration of 'religious' moral thought with an account of the relationship between scripture and doctrine:

The bible grounds moral commands in the revealed word of God. These commands are to be obeyed unconditionally because they are backed by the authority of an omnipotent God. But if that were the only source of their authority, their validity would merely have the character of a 'must' (*müssen*), as a reflection of the unlimited power of a sovereign: God can compel obedience. But this voluntaristic interpretation does not yet endow normative validity with any cognitive significance. It first acquires a cognitive meaning when moral commands are interpreted as expressions of the will of an *all-knowing* and completely *just and loving* God. Moral commands do not spring from the free choice of an Almighty but are the expressions of the will of an all-wise Creator and an all-just and loving Redeemer. (Habermas 1998: 8–9)

Habermas differentiates between theologies that accept the arbitrariness of divine commands and those that understand God's commands to be consonant with God's wisdom and love. The latter *interpret* God's commands *as* acts of wisdom and love rather than acts of free but senseless sovereignty. Habermas assumes this kind of interpretation to be a response to the question 'why obey God?'. Habermas seems to assume further that the answer to this cannot be 'because God is God': more is needed to fill out the character of who it is who commands. If God were not considered wise and loving, there would be no *argument* for obeying God; rather, obedience would be a matter of giving in to overwhelming divine force.

Habermas risks a further differentiation. There are, he suggests, two types of possible argument, one rooted in a doctrine of creation, the other in soteriology. There are some difficulties for English-speaking non-theological readers at this point, because Habermas misleadingly uses the word 'ontotheological' to describe the doctrine of creation, and because his translator renders *Schöpfungsmetaphysik* as 'creationist metaphysics'. (Habermas does not think that the doctrine of creation is 'creationist' in the modern sense.) These need clarifying, as Habermas obviously means to associate the doctrine of creation with God's legislative wisdom, natural law and the inherent teleology of things in the world: 'the rational content of moral laws receives ontological confirmation from the rational order of being as a whole' (Habermas 1998: 9). Habermas associates soteriology with the promise of salvation, with divine judgement and redemption; this salvation is contingent upon a person 'leading a moral or lawful life' which God judges at the end of each individual's life 'in accordance with his just deserts'.

[God's] justice ensures that his judgment will be consonant with the unique life history of each individual, while at the same time his goodness allows for human fallibility and for the sinfulness of human nature. Moral commands acquire a rational meaning both from the fact that they point the way to personal salvation and from the fact that they are applied in an impartial manner. (Habermas 1998: 9)

This is bold. Habermas chooses to ignore the complex debates about the relationship of redemption, sin and right action in Christian theology in favour of a simplistic account: God judges each individual according to their actions, after compensating for original sin and the innate human tendency to make mistakes. Charitably, one must probably assume that this is not intended to be a nuanced theological account, but a speculation about what Christians were taught in the Church in pre-Enlightenment times.

Although Habermas differentiates the doctrine of creation from soteriology, he does not separate them; he recognises that the key to understanding Christian accounts of God's commands lies in Christology. Habermas' Christology at this point is distinctly Kantian: 'the path to salvation is not predetermined by a system of rules but by a divinely authorised way of life that we are enjoined to emulate. This is what is meant, for example by an *imitatio Christi*, that is, by following in the footsteps of Christ' (Habermas 1998: 9–10). Despite this apparent reduction of Christ to a good example which people might follow, the main point Habermas wants to make is that 'in religious-metaphysical worldviews, the *just* is still interwoven with specific conceptions of the *good life*'.

To the pairing of creation and soteriology Habermas adds another pair: of community and individuality. Each person has a relationship to God that means both belonging to an elected people in covenant with God and being a unique and unsubstitutable person. This pair of identity-forming relations has an ethical analogue. To me as a member of a community, my fellows are part of an 'us', with whom I am in solidarity. To me as a unique person, the other appears as a similarly unique and unsubstitutable individual, whose otherness I must respect through justice. There is both a common bond and the recognition of difference, which together create the possibility of ethics. 'The Judaeo-Christian tradition regards solidarity and justice as two sides of the same coin: they provide two different perspectives on the same communication structure' (Habermas 1998: 10).

This is all by way of a general sketch of a religious ethics: and it is important to remember that for Habermas it is a problem. If the Jewish and Christian traditions have made the generous bequest of an ethics of solidarity and peaceful recognition of otherness, and if this bequest is meaningful because it is rooted in a relationship to God mediated through a particular community, how much of it can be salvaged for a modern society? Modern society, for Habermas, means 'a pluralism of worldviews' where 'religion and the ethos rooted in it disintegrate as a *public* basis of morality shared by all' (Habermas 1998: 10). How much of Jewish ethics survives if there is no generally accepted acknowledgement of God as creator? What is left of Christian ethics when people abandon talk of God's redemptive agency? For Habermas the answer is all too starkly obvious: 'the metaphysical validation of objectively rational moral laws loses its force, and with it the soteriological connection between their just application and the objectively desirable good of salvation' (Habermas 1998: 10–11).

Scripture, for Habermas, is a source of divine commands. The interpretation of scripture is a source of arguments that make these commands meaningful and make argumentation about them possible. Doctrine, the rational form of such interpretation, enables people to have good reasons for obeying God. It is immediately obvious that Habermas does not consider the narrative form of scripture, or the narrative form that doctrine often takes: both are obviously central, for example, in liturgy. Nonetheless, this does not alter the basic point he is trying to make, namely that scripture and its interpretation are only ever meaningful for some *particular* community, whereas the moral life they made possible has extended historically into a modern pluralistic setting. Similarly, the argumentation that accompanied such moral life was possible because of its appeal to doctrines that were particular to *this* community: is such argumentation possible when transposed into a public sphere populated by many different communities and where there is also 'a displacement of epistemic authority from religious doctrines to the empirical sciences' (Habermas 1998: 11)?

Moral argumentation in premodern theology works because everyone agrees that the world is God's good creation and that its teleology is the salvation of all lives through God's reconciling action (Habermas 1998: 11). To discover whether there can be moral argumentation in a modern setting, one needs a good picture of the current condition.

In this new situation, moral philosophy depends on a 'post-metaphysical level of justification'. This means in the first place that, as regards its method, it must renounce the God's eye viewpoint; as regards its content, it can no longer appeal to the order of creation and sacred history; and, as regards its theoretical approach, it cannot appeal to metaphysical concepts of essences that undercut the logical distinctions between different types of illocutionary utterances. Moral philosophy must justify the cognitive validity of moral judgements and positions without drawing on these resources. (Habermas 1998: 11)

There are three points here: method, content and theory. The three points do not stand or fall together: any one or two might be correct without being ruined by the falsity of the third, and for that reason it is important to keep them separate. For example it might be quite right that, as regards method, philosophical thinking must renounce the God's-eye view, but there could still be appeal to creation. This, for example would be the kind of theology elaborated by Nicholas Lash, Rowan Williams and John Milbank (Lash 1992: *passim*, esp. 79–81; Williams 2000: 1–7; Milbank 1990: *passim*, esp. 1–3). These three British theologians would accept the first point, reject the second, and seek further clarification on the third. It is an easy enough matter to correct Habermas' assumption that premodern theology thought it had ready access to the God's-eye view. It could be argued that one of the effects (if not intentions) of trinitarian theology is precisely to correct any one-sidedly incarnational philosophy – and therefore confidence in human absolute knowledge – by drawing attention to the unknowability of the God who makes himself known in human flesh and language (Lash 1992: 91–9). Or it could be argued that a willingness to submit to God's judgement prevents any doctrinal strategy for 'responding consistently and intelligibly to the world's complexity' from identifying itself with God's point of view (Williams 2000: 5–6) Again, however, Habermas' basic point is sound enough: there is no single doctrine of creation and no single account of salvation history that all members of modern society acknowledge as authoritative. The conclusion he draws from this, that no appeal can therefore be made to them in *public* argumentation, is more debatable. The third I leave to one side.

Habermas lists four implausible (to him) responses to this problem: post-metaphysical moral realism (McDowell), utilitarianism, meta-ethical scepticism and moral functionalism. Post-metaphysical moral realists accept that there can be no simple appeal to a world order and instead resort to some form of inner intuition of values. These are just as hard to justify as the simple appeals to a world order. Utilitarians cannot account for normativity and ignore the meaning *for the individual* of equal respect for everyone. Meta-ethical sceptics cannot explain everyday moral practices, which would disappear if ordinary people did not believe in morality. Moral functionalists promote religion because it has positive effects, but this blatant functionalism undermines the *believability* of religious doctrines (Habermas 1998: 11–12). These are contrasted, naturally, with Habermas' own response. He insists that in order for there to be argumentation, the cognitive dimension of religious ethics needs to be recast even though its basis in doctrine must be abandoned. The cognitive dimension in religious ethics is *descriptive*: it is knowledge of the world *as* God's creation. Habermas believes that some post-metaphysical equivalent is needed under modern conditions: knowledge of the world *as* . . . what? Habermas comes at this via a long series of debates with other moral theorists. He insists that there needs to be a priority of the right over the good, because 'the good' is always culturally specific and cannot therefore be the basis for public argumentation between members of different cultural traditions. By contrast 'the right' can be distilled out as a formal process, and not a collection of substantive descriptive claims about the world: for Habermas it is fruitless to search for a commonly shared conception of the good (Habermas 1998: 28). Rather, the proper task of moral philosophy is to elaborate a 'universal' account in which all participants must make appeal to 'a source of authority beyond their own community' (Habermas 1998: 29). This source is, as Habermas says repeatedly in his work, 'an intuitive familiarity with the general structures of our communicative form of life as such' (Habermas 1998: 30). Clearly this appeal must bear a colossal weight: it is Habermas' substitute for revelation. Unlike other 'deep rooted general knowledge' understood as revelation in the major religious traditions, it is something 'of which we become aware only in cases of clinical deviance'.

Habermas here sets himself some formidable challenges: what learning processes foster reliable 'intuitive familiarity'? How is it tested? What model of 'clinical deviance' is authoritative? And so forth. Again, it is important to note that for Habermas such intuitive familiarity is not 'ontotheological' or 'metaphysical', in his senses. It is not a description of the world. Instead it is a knowledge of generalised (i.e. common to all traditions) processes of communication that can be reconstructed by the moral theorist. Thus the moral theorist's job is not to articulate norms, but to articulate the formal conditions under which norms are debated and decided (Habermas 1998: 33). It is for this reason that Habermas has devoted so much energy to the two tasks of (1) narrating the history of the *generalisation* of processes of communication (his version of 'reason' in history) and (2) reconstructing the formal conditions that are implied in the forms of life that embody these processes. These are the 'theory of communicative action' and 'discourse ethics' respectively.

Habermas confronts the costs of his project directly. The decline of religion has serious 'unwelcome consequences' for moral theory, in Habermas' view, and he sees no good reason to conceal them. First, one's understanding of God's judgement and redemption provided motivations for living a good life. Once the religious foundation of ethics is abandoned, there is a 'motivational deficit' in ethics: 'Because there is no profane substitute for the hope of personal salvation, we lose the strongest motive for obeying moral commands' (Habermas 1998: 35). Second, moral realism relied on appeals to doctrines of creation and natural law, and this made it possible to couch moral judgements in the form of 'descriptive statements'.[3] This is no longer possible, because there is no generally agreed description of the world. Foundationalism was a failed attempt to provide just such a description. This means that moral judgements cannot appeal to 'truth' but only to 'rational accept-ability' (Habermas 1998: 36–7). Here we must leave Habermas' arguments, as they have been thoroughly criticised by his fellow moral philosophers and it is not our task to tread these well-worn paths.[4] Rather, we are interested in the identity Habermas asserts between 'religious' and 'metaphysical' worldviews.

The problem is, precisely, that such identity is merely asserted. Habermas scarcely draws breath as he conflates the doctrine of creation with natural law, and he draws no distinctions between different approaches to the latter. The idea that theories of natural law arise from engagement with scriptural narrative, and as philo-sophical commentary on it, is not explored. Similarly, the irreduc-ibly narrative form of most accounts of soteriology in the Christian tradition is described in a decidedly propositional way: Christians must live a good life because God will judge their individual lives. It is not at all obvious why there would be any Christology at all in this account: the exemplary function of the life of Christ could perfectly well be discharged by prophets and saints without any need to speak of incarnation. The equivalence of 'ontotheological' with 'metaphysical', and the association by Habermas of 'metaphy-sical' with 'doctrine of creation', is not wrong – there is no shortage of historical examples to support such associations – but it is badly one-sided. If there is a history of 'positivity' in Hegel's sense (i.e. doctrines with substantive content that are affirmed), there is also a history of speculative reserve, in which it is acknowledged that God cannot be described adequately in human language. It is not obvious in what sense this tradition of 'negative theology' is 'metaphysical' in Habermas' sense (i.e. a positive description of what the world is

---

[3] Habermas' translator renders 'descriptive Aussagen' as 'assertoric statements'; I have stayed closer to the German so as to bring out Habermas' emphasis on the everydayness of premodern moral judgements.

[4] For one of the most patient and decisive critiques of Habermas' ethical project, which also works through a lot of the prior secondary literature, see Bernstein 1995.

'really like'). It is certainly not 'ontotheological', however this is understood. The two things Habermas ignores, namely the narrative form of much theology on the one hand, and practices of speculative reserve on the other, amount to a serious shortcoming in his account of premodern theology. Habermas is not wrong to associate pre-modern theology with 'metaphysics', in his restricted sense, but he is culpably one-sided in wholly *identifying* them. Trinitarian theology is both 'metaphysical' (in its positive moments) and self-correcting (in its negative aspects); Habermas' exclusive focus on the first makes his account easier and shorter, but buys its simplicity at too high a cost.

Again, however, it must be emphasised that Habermas is not really interested in religion. He is interested in placing the moral problematic of the present in an historical context, while doing justice to its religious origins. This is surely a good idea. The problem is that his account is over-explanatory. His enthusiasm for developmental accounts (of reason, of the decline of religion) is an obstacle to subtle analysis. He does not need to *explain* how religious worldviews came to be publicly devalued: it is enough to observe, more modestly, that there are rival worldviews and that no single one commands universal assent. Habermas wants to draw the further conclusion that *therefore* religious worldviews *as such* are devalued. They may well be, but it is not obvious why it follows from a public awareness that there are multiple narratives. The existence of rival worldviews does not *necessarily* devalue worldviews as such. Habermas has no arguments for such cause and effect, beyond his general remarks about the effects of reflection. And he does not need them. What he does need, given the goals of his project, is arguments for certain philosophical substitutions for theological topoi. For example he wants to replace the cognitive power of unified worldviews with the cognitive power of a unified post-metaphysical worldview rooted in an analysis of the structure of communication. To do this, however, he does not need to show that religious worldviews are devalued. He needs merely to assume that his reader accepts his (weaker but more plausible) claim that the existence of rival worldviews requires some public practice for coordinating ethical debate without relying on the dominance of any single such worldview. In short, his 'philosophical' account of the prehistory of religious thought can be stripped of its strong developmental narrative of the waxing of reason and the waning of religion and still do its principal job: to show that ethical argumentation in the public sphere cannot proceed on the basis of one dominant worldview but must find some other process. This still leaves room for his own project. There may be good reasons for rejecting this project. But whether one applauds or critiques it, it does not require a strong thesis about the decline of religion.

The identification of 'metaphysical' with 'religious' thought is false. The history of speculative reserve in negative theology is a significant precursor to modern post-metaphysical theology, some aspects of which have been briefly mentioned. There is nothing in Habermas' account which renders 'post-metaphysical theology' unintelligible, or any arguments against its consistency. In my view, there are some aspects of post-metaphysical theology that offer some advantages over Habermas' own project, most notably in the handling of scripture and prayer, a topic to which we shall return.

In summary, Habermas uses Christian philosophical tools to perform non-theological tasks. This claim is not very interesting: most European and North American philosophers work with tools inherited from the ancient Greeks via Jewish, Christian and Muslim appropriation. Of substantially greater interest, I hope, is the claim that it is not only the tasks but *their objects* that have a theological status. One, very brief, way of describing theology is as the discipline devoted to testing rival interpretations of scripture and ritual. On this definition, Habermas is obviously not doing theology. At the same time, he is most definitely engaged in a discipline devoted to testing rival interpretations of something. This something he calls (after Husserl) the 'lifeworld'. Habermas is not contributing to debates about scripture but to debates about how the lifeworld is to be interpreted, and how to treat criticisable validity claims that are raised. However, the 'lifeworld' is doing an analogous job for Habermas to the one that scripture does in theology. It contains 'background consensus', 'things taken for granted' and 'basic presuppositions'.[5] The role of this kind of entity in philosophy

---

[5] Here I am working through some issues raised by Peter Ochs in Ochs 1998: 316–25.

was first raised to prominence by F. H. Jacobi in his critique of Kant (Jacobi 1994: 580ff.). Jacobi called it something 'taken-to-be-true' (*Fürwahrhalten*). The significance of its role in philosophy has been much discussed by some recent philosophers.[6] Jacobi and his inter- preters do not notice its similarity to the role of scripture in theology because late-eighteenth- and twentieth-century philosophers are, alike, heirs to the separation of scripture and philosophy which had, in medieval theology, been taken together (Frei 1974). Jacobi's successors Schelling and Hegel were much more interested in ex- perimental developments in the doctrine of the Trinity in their treatment of the role of 'the absolute' than they were in the role of the 'taken-to-be-true'. Hegel did consider the latter, which he called 'the universal' and which he associated with the interpretations of the world held by the community of 'ethical life'. 'Ethical life' has a lot in common with Habermas' 'lifeworld': both do the job that scripture had done previously. Contemporary continental philoso- phy has largely taken up the question of the absolute rather than the question of the 'taken-to-be-true', as Andrew Bowie has shown (Bowie 1993: 55–90; Bowie 1997: 1–27). And because Hegel's switch from scripture to ethical life has been so comprehensively taken up – even by Nietzsche – the big questions in treatments of rationality and morality are concerned with something called 'relativism' rather than the (perhaps equally perplexing) question of the existence of *different scriptures.*

Habermas gets into difficulties because, although he takes over the philosophical tools for interpreting scripture, he does not see the analogy between lifeworld and scripture. Thus, he recognises that there are different lifeworlds and devotes his time to developing criteria for adjudicating their 'rationality'. But lifeworlds are differ- ent from scriptures in one crucial respect. One can (and Habermas infamously does) offer an evolutionary account of the development of lifeworlds; one can (and Habermas does) even narrate the histor- ical transition from 'primitive' to 'modern' lifeworlds in a way that implies that the human race makes progress from one stage to the next. If one tries to do the same with scripture, it is obviously

---

[6] Beiser 1987: 44–91; Bowie 1997: 28–52; Franks 2000: 95–116; Pinkard 2002: 87–104; Henrich 2003: 82–112.

nonsense. Scriptures change, admittedly. They do so, however, remarkably slowly: almost infinitely more slowly than lifeworlds. Moreover, the really significant changes, such as when groups of Jews split off to reinterpret Jewish scripture Christologically, thus bringing a new tradition into being, are certainly not evolutions. They are, precisely, radical reinterpretations. The same is true of the genesis of the Qur'an. They are all related to each other through their shared history, and through their constant (sometimes happy, sometimes unhappy) engagements with each other. But in what sense can one say that there is a linear progression? What 'line' would this be? This is a problem even before one introduces simple but important issues such as traditions which are not reinterpreta-tions of Jewish scripture, or complex issues such as the embedded-ness of scripture in liturgy and the havoc this wreaks on narrowly textual conceptions of textuality.

This does not amount to a defence of theology. It may be true that earlier traditions held together the interpretation of scripture with rabbinic mysticism (Judaism), trinitarian speculation (Chris-tianity) or Sufi mysticism (Islam). It may also be true that trinitar-ian speculation was supplanted by an idealism of the absolute (Schelling and Hegel), which in turn led to the philosophy of *Sein* (Heidegger) or *différance* (Derrida), whereas the interpretation of scripture was replaced by the status of ethical life (Hegel) or the will to power (Nietzsche).[7] Yet it is also unfortunately true that most theologians, at least in the Christian tradition, do not seem to see the need to develop philosophical projects that are viable alternatives to these supplantings and replacements. There are exceptions, such as John Milbank's trinitarian semiotics, although even this seems heavily indebted to the Romantics and their privileging of aesthetics over the interpretation of scripture. Con-temporary theology rarely matches the quality of contemporary philosophical interpretations of Hegel, Schleiermacher, Nietzsche

---

[7] This kind of account is in its infancy, and it is early days for substantiating these claims adequately. On Derrida's debt to idealism see Dews 1987 and Bowie 1990, 1993; on the relationship between scripture and philosophy see Ochs 1998; on the transmutation of Christian doctrine into social philosophy see Milbank 1990.

or Adorno, whose work is probably in most urgent need of theological reinterpretation.[8]

Nevertheless, the theological comparison yields some useful tools. Instead of privileging or rejecting concepts about rationality, it shifts focus to *which scriptures* are being interpreted, as well as the familiar Habermasian questions about how these interpretations are publicly tested. This means that the lifeworld would not need to be treated as if it were scripture (Hegel's error, taken up by Habermas) but could be restored to its rightful, more modest, second-order place: the realm of what I have called 'doctrine', i.e. the arena of revisable and changeable practices of interpreting the world/scripture/ritual. This would take up Habermas' currently problematic notion of language-independent 'world', which he describes as 'freed of all specific content'. Habermas wants to do a perfectly reasonable job here, but this concept is ill-suited to it. He wants to talk about the taken-to-be-true (Jacobi) that validity claims are interpretations *of.* He also wants to say that this is 'identical' and 'shared' and that although it has no concretely interpreted meaning *yet,* it is the agreed basis upon which interpretations are to be based, and about which communities can debate rationally. Much better would be the unity of scripture/nature – the 'two books' of Renaissance thought – that the community has in common, but about whose meaning its members disagree. This has two advantages. First, it identifies something that not only *is* held in common but can relatively easily be *shown to be* held in common. Scriptures are written on scrolls and in books that can be consulted. Even in the complex case of scripture embedded in liturgy, the liturgies can be observed, and there are sometimes written rules for how they are to be conducted. Second, and more importantly, it makes it plain from the outset that there are *different scriptures.* This frees the philosopher from the impossible tasks either of specifying a universal rationality that governs all lifeworlds or of positing allegedly incommensurable forms of life. Both these latter positions result in intolerable aporias, which proponents of each are able to expose in the other. With an account of the unity of scripture/nature, as in the

---

[8] For a sample on Hegel see Milbank 1990: 147–76; Shanks 1991; O'Regan 1995; Williams 1995; Adams, 2000: 286–92; Desmond 2003.

case of Habermas' observations about the reliance upon scripture of Aquinas' account of natural law, one would not be surprised to find structurally similar philosophical methods with radically different social ontologies, and one would have a reasonably sound analytical method for charting the similarities and differences. One can have a Hegelian reading of Torah, and one can have a Rosenzweigian reading of Matthew's Gospel. One can even have a Nietzschean reading of Zoroastrian legend. In each case the philosophical method is distinguishable from the scripture it interprets, and one does not need an overarching account of 'rationality' to explain the points of contact, or a dogmatic belief in incommensurability to explain the radical divergences.

Theologians should not ask Habermas to take up these suggestions. They should be crafting philosophical theologies themselves, and to do this requires relearning the philosophical traditions *as* religious traditions of interpreting texts and practices. The current division of specialisation between dogmatic and philosophical theology in some British universities, for example, seems to me a problem. The separation of theology and biblical studies is even more serious: dogmatic theology and biblical interpretation cannot be undertaken without the use of philosophical tools. Philosophical theology that is undertaken without attention to texts in the tradition falls foul of Habermas' objection that it is no longer theology in any interesting sense. To be a post-metaphysical theologian, in a way that philosophers like Habermas cannot dismiss in advance, requires overcoming divisions of specialisation and reintegrating historical, biblical, dogmatic and philosophical studies. If Habermas had been a theologian, he might have been a good example of this. Such integration, however, is not merely a matter of restructuring university departments: it requires reshaping the apprenticeships of theologians so that neither Barth's dogmatics nor Kant's critical philosophy are an 'option'. This is a tall order, but it seems to me that philosophers like Habermas have no good reason to take contemporary theology seriously until it is pursued seriously.

CHAPTER 9

Habermas in dialogue with theologians

This chapter illustrates some of the issues that arise when theologians try to make use of or engage with Habermas. It is not designed as a comprehensive account of theologians' engagements with him, or of his replies to his theological critics. The theological literature on Habermas is substantial, and although it continues to attract some interest in the English-speaking world, many of the German texts are untranslated.[1] It is unnecessary to review the German literature here, as this has already been expertly and critically undertaken by Hermann Düringer in his thorough evaluation of Habermas' work. Düringer offers commentary on Helmut Peukert, Edmund Arens, Rudolf Siebert, Karl Bauer, Wolfgang Pauly, Wolfhart Pannenberg, Trutz Rendtorff, Henning Luther, Jens-Glebe Möller and Micha Brumlik.[2] Düringer observes dryly that tracing all Habermas' direct and indirect influences on theology would be worth its own study. This is plainly unmanageable, given the extent to which Habermas' work permeates arguments about postmodernism. Düringer limits himself to the commentary given by German theologians on Habermas' work. The concern of this study is, however, not with the interaction between Habermas and theologians, but with his account of theology and with responding

---

[1] The most significant are Schillebeeckx 1974: 102–55; Rendtorff 1975; Tracy 1981; Peukert 1984; Höhn 1985; Siebert 1985; Bauer 1987; Glebe-Möller 1987; Arens 1989; Pauly 1989; Walsh 1989; Lakeland 1990; McFadyen 1990: 175–90; Luther 1991; Browning and Fiorenza 1992; Knapp 1993: 499–683; Schmidt 1994; Arens 1995; Engel 1995; Forrester 1997: 165–92; Junker-Kenny 1998; Campbell 1999; Düringer 1999; Lalonde 1999; Shanks 2000; Eduardo Mendieta, 'Introduction', in Habermas 2002: 1–36. The latter is a republication by Polity Press of essays by Habermas on theological themes, together with an interview with the editor discussing 'God and the World'.
[2] Düringer 1999: 225–304.

to some of the problems he raises concerning argumentation in the public sphere between members of different traditions. Nonetheless, Habermas does have a characteristic response to theological engagements with his work. This is worth rehearsing because I need to show that the criticisms and responses advanced in this study do not fall foul of Habermas' usual replies to theologians.

Two of the most instructive engagements with philosophical theology by Habermas concern the work of Helmut Peukert, a Roman Catholic theologian and former student of Johann Baptist Metz, and Michael Theunissen, holder until 1998 of the chair of theoretical philosophy in the Free University of Berlin. They are the most instructive because both Peukert and Theunissen, in very different ways, attempt to use problems in philosophy as a springboard to make substantive theological claims. These two thinkers are also worth considering because they explicitly embrace a post-metaphysical approach to theology. The meaning of post-metaphysical thinking has been addressed in earlier chapters; it is the acknowledgement that there is no deductive or discursive route from thinking to the grounds of thinking. To think post-metaphysically is not to deny such grounds, but to reject any attempt to explain them through theory.

The salient aspects of Peukert's and Theunissen's claims can be rehearsed. Peukert begins with the aporias present in Habermas' theory of communicative action. For Peukert, the problem is that theories of action with universal intent are intended to embrace the possible participation only of *living* partners in discussion, and thus exclude the dead. In Theunissen's case, the problem is the phenomenon of despair and the challenges it poses for genuine atheism. Peukert's substantive claim is that only theology can provide a theory of action which embraces the dead, because only theology's faith in the resurrection can make sense of their agency. Accordingly, only theology can provide a genuinely universal theory of communicative action (Peukert 1984: 202–10).[3] Theunissen begins

---

[3] Peukert has in fact two aims: (1) to use a theory of communicative action as a method for fundamental theology; (2) to force Habermas' version of communicative action to become theological. He pursues these two aims by exploring themes of freedom, guilt, death and solidarity – the latter derived via Metz from Benjamin's concept of history. This is treated critically in Düringer 1999: 227–42.

with the phenomenon of despair. His concern with this theme arises from his research interests concerning the relationship between psychiatry and theology, and exploring different models of selfhood. Theunissen's substantive claim is that the only way out of despair is for the finite subject to give up on the repeatedly experienced hopelessness of positing itself, and to acknowledge the power of the other in positing it. Because no finite power can adequately secure the subject's selfhood, it is forced to acknowledge the reality of an infinite other, and atheism is rendered impossible (Theunissen 1997: 360–1).

I do not propose to rehearse these arguments in further detail because Habermas' objections are fundamental, and do not consist of exposing mistakes in his colleagues' detailed reasoning. Rather, he identifies a problem that is there right from the start: the principle of proving a positive conclusion from the acknowledgement of problems with negative judgements.

The arguments of Peukert and Theunissen have a method in common. They identify a negative moment, a philosophical lack. Peukert draws attention to the lack of true universality in an allegedly universal theory of communicative action. Theunissen points to the negativity towards finitude that despair presupposes. Both draw positive conclusions: therefore there *must* be a more true universality (Peukert); therefore there *must* be infinite love (Theunissen). Both extend this theologically: therefore a universal theory of communicative action *must* embrace Christian faith (Peukert 1984: 235); therefore a negatively oriented theory of communication *must* embrace the action of the Holy Spirit, which is the medium in which the Father and the Son communicate (Theunissen 1997: 360).

Habermas' responses mirror these similarities, and the structure of his rebuttal is similar in each case. He freely concedes that there are philosophical problems with universality, and he has no hesitation in acknowledging that philosophy is metaphysically inadequate: for Habermas philosophy does not neatly and without remainder comprehend totality. However, he does not agree that, for this reason, there is a need for a theology which makes good philosophy's shortfall. The shortfall is real, and nothing can make it good. Habermas has learned very well from Adorno's critique of Hegel that successes in philosophy where problems in the world are solved in the realm of thinking remain, precisely, solutions in the realm of thinking: so long as one keeps an eye steadily on tackling problems in the world, one should not seek contentment in fantasy solutions. The task is to find an appropriate model for the relation between theory and practice. For Habermas, problems in philosophy are also problems for theology, and he is insistent that theologians should admit this. In a nutshell, the existence of aporias in thought does not prove the existence of resolutions in thought, only a spur towards constant revision of attempts to reconcile thinking with experience.

The experience of problems that are not merely imagined but which intrude into everyday life invites critique of practices and beliefs with a view to the transformation of everyday life. The best that theological arguments can manage here is a demonstration that Christian practices and beliefs do a better job of transforming everyday life, as judged against criteria agreed by participants in the argument. This would be no small contribution to healing problems in the world. Habermas himself readily acknowledges that religious thought does have great potential to bear, transmit and hand down forms of hope that guide practice in this way. In a passage theologians rehearse often, he says:

Philosophy . . . will be able neither to replace nor to repress religion as long as religious language is the bearer of a semantic content that is inspiring and even indispensable, for this content eludes (for the time being?) the explanatory force of philosophical language and continues to resist translation into reasoning discourses. (Habermas 1992a: 51)

Such an affirmation might be a sufficient basis for wishing to send one's child to a religious school, if one wished him or her to learn this inspiring and indispensable content, and so be educated as a hopeful soul. However, it is very far from achieving what Peukert and Theunissen want, namely an assent to religious claims. 'We become aware of the limits of that transcendence from within which is directed to this world. But this does not enable us to ascertain the *countermovement* of a compensating transcendence from beyond' (Habermas 2002: 80). In other words, the inadequacies of our finitude are not evidence of God. Even if they were evidence for something, it is not obvious how one would show that this was God.

Those familiar with debates about the relationship between philosophy and theology may see some analogy between Habermas' disagreements with Peukert and Theunissen and disagreements over how to interpret part of the early *prima pars* of Aquinas' *Summa Theologiae*. The so-called 'five ways' are treatments of motion, causation, necessity, predication and teleology. Each is characterised in turn, a conclusion is reached, and finally the phrase 'quod omnes dicunt Deum' or some variant is used.[4] Any claim which tries to connect reasoning about motion to conclusions about God has a 'problem of transition': it does not have at its disposal an explanation of what binds the two things together. In German philosophy, for example, Schelling might claim that the 'absolute' is 'God'. Yet even his most generous Christian readers can at best concede that while God exists, and while Schelling has good arguments in favour of presupposing that there is the absolute, there is no conceivable way to *show* that they are identical. They might just as well be completely different things, and Schelling's non-Christian readers have no difficulty grasping his arguments without making that particular connection.[5] Aquinas' association between 'first cause' and 'God' is simply that: an association. There is no 'transition' between the one and the other. Considered musically, the first theme is articulated in simultaneous counterpoint with the second theme; there is no attempt to develop the second theme, through musical argument, out of the first. They are 'already' heard together, and all Aquinas does is to draw attention to the fact that one can sound one theme and then the other, having *already* noticed that they can belong together, and so *notice* the possibility of association. The problems start when theologians claim, unlike Aquinas, that one can indeed develop the second theme out of the first. When this happens, problems of transition appear.[6]

---

[4] 'and that is what everyone calls God'. This is the phrase at the end of the third discussion, on necessity.

[5] See Bowie 1993 for an excellent example: Bowie understands Schelling much better than most theologians, and is able to do so without entertaining any theological notions. Frederick Beiser argues further that the absolute actually did not play a central role in German Idealism, including Schelling's, and insists that it is a mistake to emphasise it at the expense of other themes: Beiser 2002: 5.

[6] In this account I have freely reworked themes explored by Cornelius Ernst in his 'Metaphor and Ontology in *Sacra Doctrina*' (Ernst 1979: 74).

Peukert makes claims that bear some resemblance to those of Aquinas in the 'five ways'. Peukert's argument is part of a general attempt to investigate the ways in which theological claims can be verified, against the background of developments in theories of science. Peukert establishes to his own satisfaction that verification in sciences of any kind falls under a theory of communicative action. Practices of verification are best theorised as instances of communicative action. Theology, in his view, must accept the same standards and practices of verification as any other science. His theological claims are advanced on this basis and, interestingly, he begins with the phenomenon of death. The death of the other is placed by Peukert in the context of the presupposition, made in Habermas' theory of communicative action, of an unlimited community of communication. The action of remembering the dead risks reducing the other to something 'simply registered in a proposition' (Peukert 1984: 234), and this causes an asymmetry of relations between the living and the dead. In an echo of Benjamin, via Metz, the dead are part of the community; this asymmetry is intolerable, and calls for a restoration of equal relations between partners. Peukert supplies this by asserting that anticipation of one's own death is, *pace* Kierkegaard and Heidegger, not primarily the anticipation of one's own death, but an experience of solidarity with the other who is already dead. This is a 'reality' which saves the other from annihilation. He then makes his 'five ways' move:

This reality disclosed in communicative action, asserted as the saving reality for others and at the same time as the reality that through this salvation of the other makes possible one's own temporal existence unto death, must be called '*God*'. Within a situation of communicative action, which is ultimately inevitable, the reality of God becomes *identifiable* and *nameable* through the communicative action itself. In this way, the basic situation of the disclosure of the reality of God and its identifiability, and hence at the same time the origin of possible discourse about God, are given. (Peukert 1984: 235)

Just as Aquinas mounts an investigation into causation and, having identified the first cause, says 'and that is what everyone calls God', so Peukert mounts an investigation into solidarity with the dead and, having identified the source of possibility of such solidarity, says 'this reality . . . must be called "God"'. But what about this 'must'? Aquinas just observes that when everyone talks about God, they are talking about the first cause. He does not say that the first cause must be called God. Indeed, one of his more recent interpreters considers that Aquinas himself understands how little the five ways achieve (Kerr 2002: 76). There are problems with the detail of Peukert's argument, such as his rather vague notion of 'relations' with the dead, his exaggerated understanding of asymmetry, the thinness of God's identity, the unwillingness to engage in detail with scriptural texts and the heavy reliance on Heidegger's notion of 'being towards death'. Habermas does not tackle these directly; his objections are – rightly – more basic.

Peukert's argument should read as follows. The dead are excluded from some communities of communication; some theories of communication exclude the dead; some theories exclude the reality of God; God raises the dead to new life; communities oriented to the resurrection include the dead in their communities of communication; theories which include the reality of God can meaningfully include the resurrected dead; theories which do this are more universal than theories which do not.

Instead, Peukert's argument is this. The dead are excluded from some communities of communication; some theories of communication exclude the dead; some theories exclude the reality of God; God raises the dead to new life; communities oriented to the resurrection include the dead in their communities of communication; theories which include the reality of God can meaningfully include the resurrected dead; some theories which exclude the dead claim to be universal; they are mistaken because they exclude the dead; therefore, to be universal, they must include the reality of God.

One can see where the problem lies: Peukert's argument contains an undisclosed premise, namely 'there must be a truly universal theory'. The argument presupposes both the reality of God and the necessity of there being a universal theory. There is more to the problem than merely the presence of an undisclosed premise. There is also a matter of the relationship between wish-fulfilment and reality. Habermas insists that 'the experience of a burning lack is still not a sufficient argument' (Habermas 2002: 80). This repeats a

point made by John Milbank about Peukert's claim: 'one cannot
see the imperative necessity to turn the wish into a postulation'
(Milbank 1990: 239–40).[7] Habermas does not wish to deny the
importance of wishes; indeed, he often goes out of his way to
endorse his theological partners' desire to do justice to experiences
of modernity's negative effects on selfhood, its tendency to obliterate the past and its inability to generate sources of hope out of itself.
One of the striking features of Habermas' rhetoric about the role of
religion in society is this emphasis on hope, which he perhaps
learned from Kant, who gives hope a central place in his *Religion
within the Bounds of Mere Reason*. Nonetheless, Habermas refuses
to encourage attempts, whether by theologians or philosophers, to
conjure positivity out of the failure of negativity. He characterises
Peukert's argument as an attempt 'to force the secular opponent into
a corner by way of an immanent critique such that the opponent can
find a way out of the aporias demonstrated only by conceding the
theologically defended affirmations' (Habermas 2002: 78). His own
alternative to Peukert's attempt to ground faith (even if one charitably denies that Peukert is trying to prove the *necessity* of faith) is
found in his reflections on the debate between Horkheimer and
Benjamin concerning theological perspectives. I rehearse it here not
as refutation of Peukert, but to show how seriously Habermas takes
issues of tragedy:

the posthumously obtained approval of the victims [of history] remains
abstract, because it lacks the force of reconciliation – it cannot later drown
out the protest expressed in their lifetimes. There remains a stain on the
idea of a justice that is bought with the irrevocable injustice perpetrated on
earlier generations. This stain cannot be washed away; it can at most be
forgotten. (Thompson and Held 1982: 246)

Habermas does not advocate amnesia: he seems to practise a
modified stoicism which refuses either to march on cheerfully or
to wallow in self-reproach; he is mindful of the past but refuses to be

---

[7] Habermas' essay was first published, in German, in 1991. I have altered the translation. To
my knowledge, Habermas was not aware of Milbank's argument, but the latter in any case is
a version of a critique of Kant articulated by his contemporary Wizenmann, and which
Kant cites in the *Critique of Practical Reason* (Kant 1996: 255). This point is well brought out
in a discussion of Peukert's argument by Thomas McCarthy (McCarthy 1991: 211).

incapacitated by it. In a more sustained meditation on Horkheimer's residual metaphysical (Habermas calls them 'theological') commitments, Habermas suggests that the true place of solidarity is in 'linguistic subjectivity, communication, and individuating socialisation' and not in an 'underlying essence' or a speculatively entertained 'world-will' (Habermas 1993a: 143). This kind of solidarity does not 'wash away' the past (echoes of Psalm 51:1–2 and Revelation 7:17) or forget it: it does what it can, remembering the dead with a compassion *that is not intended as a substitute for divine justice.* It resolutely refuses to solve the suffering of the past with metaphysical cleverness, and equally refuses to offer any alternative. Again, he has learned well the lesson of Adorno that where one finds resolutions in thinking that are not accompanied by resolutions in the material conditions of human suffering, one finds society's self-deceptions reproduced in philosophy, not sources of hope. It is not just appeals to God as the guarantor of reason (Kant, Hegel) that Habermas opposes; he is just as opposed to appeals to God as the guarantor of the irrational ground of reason (Jacobi, Schopenhauer, Horkheimer): these are, alike, instances of 'the metaphysics that not only philosophers but even theologians themselves must today get along without' (Habermas 1993a: 134). I agree with Habermas. Of course compassion is not enough; but perhaps there is an even bigger problem when philosophers and theologians claim to know what 'enough' might be.

Habermas' rejection of Theunissen's arguments has the same structure, although its tone is more appreciative. This is perhaps, in part, because his essay was a contribution to Theunissen's sixtieth-birthday Festschrift, and returned the kindness of Theunissen's *laudatio* delivered when Habermas received the Adorno prize in 1980 (Theunissen 1981: 41–57). Habermas' engagements with Theunissen are at a higher level than his rejection of Peukert's solidarity argument. He is less concerned with tactics designed to box secular thinkers into a corner, and more with 'the claim that essential contents of the Christian gospel of salvation can be justified under the conditions of post-metaphysical thinking' (Habermas 2002: 111). Theunissen's project is of more interest to Habermas, I think, because it is a test case. Theunissen makes claims that are particular to a tradition; he tries to justify them according to generalised criteria. Habermas is sceptical that it is ever possible to redeem validity claims whose origin lies within a particular tradition in a public sphere where only generalisable criteria can be admitted as valid by participants in argument. Theunissen makes this attempt; Habermas believes that Theunissen gives the best possible version of such an attempt; he is interested in evaluating its strengths and weaknesses.

Habermas is familiar with the theological projects of Johann Baptist Metz and Jürgen Moltmann, and he contrasts Theunissen's methodology with theirs. He is attracted to two aspects of Metz' and Moltmann's thinking. The first is their affirmation of history and memory, which he sees as attempts to reinterpret Christian accounts of time. Moltmann and Metz, for Habermas, try to free Christian theology from association with the models of time found in 'Hellenistic' philosophies, in which the soul strives for an eternity freed from the messy specificities of finite life. Instead, they try to retrieve Christianity's eschatological dimensions, which anticipate the fullness of time, rather than escape into timelessness. In short, mutability does not need to be overcome. The second aspect of Metz' and Moltmann's theology which attracts Habermas is their confrontation with Western Christianity's collusion with forces of social and political domination. Metz' rejection of the identity of Christianity and bourgeois interests and Moltmann's insistence that Christian theology must articulate God's presence not merely in the Church but paradigmatically in the poor seem to Habermas positive developments in a tradition which has, he thinks, often enforced a particular metaphysical account of cosmic hierarchy and order. What distinguishes Theunissen from Metz and Moltmann is 'the claim that he can achieve their common goal with non-theological means' (Habermas 2002: 112). Whereas Metz and Moltmann both root their projects in a renewed political theology (Metz) or redescribed theology of the cross (Moltmann), Theunissen attempts his redemption of Christian claims through a philosophy which is not limited to the Christian tradition.

Habermas finds Theunissen insufficiently theological. Whereas Metz and Moltmann engage in forms of argumentation that lose their persuasive force when divorced from the particularities of their theological tradition, Theunissen appeals to phenomena that are, or appear superficially to be, more general: pessimism and despair.

Theunissen's attempt to 'turn despair against itself' (Habermas 2002: 113) may well arise from a Christian faith in a healed eschaton, but confusingly it is presented as hope that things will get better here and now. Habermas admittedly fails adequately to describe the relationship between faith and hope, but he identifies one of the tasks of theology, namely how to connect eschatology with judgements about ordinary time. Is the constitution of the self that Theunissen outlines something to be achieved in our earthly lives, or is it something that awaits the new creation? For Habermas Theunissen seems to argue for the former, but by using Christian reflections on the latter. More straightforwardly, Habermas has two objections to Theunissen's procedure. One rejects Theunissen's 'negativistic' procedure; the other rejects the ease with which Theunissen magically transforms 'transcendental questions' into 'anthropological facts'.

These both need rehearsing a little. First, the method of negativism. Theunissen's argument has three moves. (1) Humans find themselves in despair. (2) The possibility of selfhood requires the annihilation of despair. (3) Following Kierkegaard (*Sickness Unto Death*) the self understands that its despairing attempts to posit itself are only possible because of a prior dependence on the infinite power of an 'other'. This, Theunissen calls God. The method is negativistic because it arrives at the notion of God through the negation of despair, not through positing God. Although Habermas does not draw attention to it, this bears a family resemblance to Schleiermacher's remarks, in *Glaubenslehre*, about the self's feeling of radical dependence. This notion is in continuity with a long history of Christian reflection, stretching back at least to Scotus, about how infinity and finitude are thinkable by finite subjects. The obvious question to pose to any figure in this tradition is: what connects notions of infinity to notions of God? Habermas does not raise this question. Instead, he mounts an immanent critique, and identifies problems internal to Theunissen's explanation. Habermas points out that calling despair a 'sickness' requires a presupposition of some notion of health. If health is used as a criterion for judging degrees of sickness, then one *already* knows something positive. For this reason, the procedure is not negativistic after all. It may be true that God is not posited at the start; but health certainly is. This argument is not intended to defeat Theunissen's theological strategy;

rather it is designed to ruin Theunissen's strong distinction between normativistic and negativistic approaches. To the extent that Theunissen relies on a prior, positive and normatively laden concept of health, his approach is just as normativistic as Habermas' own.

Second, the mistaken identification of transcendental questions with anthropological facts. Habermas echoes his earlier query about how the eschaton is related to ordinary time. How is something 'world-constituting' like the 'conditions of selfhood' related to something 'within the world' like 'despairingly wanting-to-be-oneself' (Habermas 2002: 121)? Habermas further wonders how Theunissen knows that 'despairingly wanting-to-be-oneself' is part of the human condition: what makes it an anthropological fact? Even if Theunissen can establish that it is, it is possible in principle that someone else might justifiably make the opposing claim that 'hopefully wanting-to-be-oneself' is part of the human condition. Habermas suggests that the problem with Theunissen's transcendentalism is that he fails to appreciate a significant difference between Kant and Kierkegaard. Whereas Kant's transcendentalism starts from the 'fact' of objective experience, which the reader accepts as a fact, and tries to account for it, Kierkegaard starts from 'despairingly wanting-to-be-oneself', which the reader does not necessarily accept as a fact. To the extent that the reader is sceptical about such an existential state, there can be no persuasive investigation into the conditions for that state.

Habermas' arguments against Theunissen can be summarised briefly. The existence of sickness does not guarantee the existence of health, unless one *already* knows about health and uses that normative concept to diagnose sickness. Knowing about health does not necessarily mean that one knows about God. One can add to Habermas' argument: knowing about the 'infinite other' and its constitution of my selfhood does not necessarily mean that I know about God; I only know about the 'infinite other'. Habermas mounts, in the end, an almost Barthian critique of Theunissen:

Theunissen is too much of a philosopher to accept the statement which Dostoyevsky made . . . 'If someone could prove to me that Christ is outside the truth, and if the truth really did exclude Christ, then I should prefer to stay with Christ and not truth.' (Habermas 2002: 123)

Habermas identifies the problems of transition raised by Peukert and Theunissen. He is willing to concede the philosophical claim and entertain the validity of the theological claims. On the philosophical side, universal theories do exclude the dead (Peukert) and the despairing self's self-reliance may indeed deepen its despair (Theunissen). On the theological side, God raises the dead (Peukert) and God is the source of all authentic selfhood (Theunissen). Habermas simply denies that there is any way to make a plausible transition between them. To use my musical analogy, the second theme does not develop out of the first. Peukert and Theunissen may choose to sound them together, and they may even be a good counterpoint to each other (this is more obviously true of Theunissen). But this does not mean that there is any connection between them at any deeper level. For the connection to bear any argumentative weight, there needs to be development and transition from one to the other. This Peukert and Theunissen do not provide; *nor could they possibly do so.*

It is not true that Peukert and Theunissen have potentially good arguments, but use them incompetently. They have arguments which are *in principle* impossible to mount persuasively, and which they in fact deploy as well as possible. Problems of transition cannot be solved by argument. It is crucial to see that the 'argument' of both Peukert and Theunissen relies on there 'already' being a connection. *They do not argue that there is a connection.* How could they? What would this look like? Peukert, for example *presupposes* that God raises the dead. There is no reason to suppose that Peukert is wrong. The problem is that although positing God's existence, together with the actions Peukert attributes to God, does indeed solve the metaphysical problem, this does not make it true. Showing this is easy: one merely has to produce two metaphysical accounts, each of which is as internally consistent as the other, which are incompatible. In the study of religions this is the normal state of affairs.

Theologians are often surprised to learn that Habermas responds to his theological partners in dialogue in this way, just as they are astonished at the breadth of his theological engagements when rehearsing themes in Hegel's philosophy. More importantly, his arguments are persuasive. Habermas has a further two-pronged approach to his theological colleagues which is worth setting out briefly. (1) Habermas exposes all 'liberal' or 'Kantian' approaches, which push for universality, as insufficiently theological: his partners simply fail to make scripture central to their arguments. For Habermas, this renders them uninteresting. This is a 'Lindbeckian' critique. (2) Habermas dismisses all 'conservative' or 'traditioned' approaches as damagingly sectarian, in that the claims made can in principle only be persuasive to members of the same tradition. For Habermas this renders them useless in the public sphere. This is an 'anti-Hauerwasian' critique. Basically, for Habermas, a theologian is either an uninteresting liberal or a useless sectarian.

Habermas comes very close to theologians who criticise attempts by their colleagues to come to premature and dangerous accommodations with trends in social science. Take the following: 'the more that theology opens itself in general to the discourses of the human sciences, the greater the danger that its own status will be lost in the network of alternating takeover attempts' (Habermas 2002: 73). This warning, made in response to theologians who met with Habermas at a Chicago conference in 1988, is not so far removed from the main thesis in Milbank's *Theology and Social Theory*.

Habermas is, however, also very distant from contemporary post-liberal theology. The following is noteworthy: 'I hold that a conversation cannot succeed between a theology and a philosophy which use the language of religious authorship and which meet on the bridge of religious experiences that have become literary expressions' (Habermas 2002: 75). This warning against using words like 'redemption', 'messianism' and 'new creation' as mere metaphors (rather than as claims rooted in scripture) should worry theologians, because it obviously does not occur to Habermas that *all* theological language, especially that rooted in scripture, is properly metaphorical. Perhaps his theological colleagues have not suggested this to him.

Habermas' opinion admittedly reflects some current debates in Christian ethics, but it fails to take account of the more sophisticated approaches which seek to overcome starkly drawn contrasts between 'tradition' and 'publicity'. He does on occasion reflect explicitly on the differences between theology and philosophy in a post-metaphysical context, and his views indicate that he might advance different arguments if he engaged with post-liberal thought.

Five of his claims are particularly interesting. First, he suggests that theology is distinct from religious speech. This distinction resides in its practice of *interpreting* ritual acts in non-ritual language. (He gives the example of baptism and Eucharist: theology interprets their meaning.) Second, he thinks that historically theology presented no danger to faith so long as its interpretative language used the categories of classical metaphysics. Third, he believes that under post-metaphysical conditions, theology reinterprets beliefs in terms of 'profane everyday *praxis*'. Fourth, he claims that this 'public theology' strips religious practices of their religiousness. Fifth, he argues that religious traditions thus lose their identity. These five moves can be summarised: the collapse of metaphysics caused theologians to assimilate to the atheism of university life, and thus betray their tradition (Habermas 2002: 75–6). Again, this is strikingly reminiscent of Lindbeck.

This little narrative is vague as it stands. I propose two immediate refinements. Habermas is making two kinds of claim. His claim about 'what theology is' is grammatical. It is a claim about how to use the word 'theology'. His claim about what 'public theology' does is empirical. It is a claim about what theologians have actually done in recent work.

To the first, grammatical, claim one can pose the obvious question: is it a good account? I think that it is not. Habermas assumes that the task of theology is the interpretation of ritual and something called 'religious language' in terms that are 'metaphysical'. He strongly implies (but admittedly does not outright say) that such interpretation is no longer 'religious'. This is how I understand his claim that theological discourse 'distinguishes itself from the religious by separating itself from ritual practice in the act of explaining it' (Habermas 2002: 75). There is something obviously right about Habermas' account: theologians do indeed try to interpret texts and actions using language other than that found in those texts and actions, and the purpose of such interpretation is to render them thinkable or intelligible or meaningful. The language of baptism, to use one of Habermas' examples, is very ancient, and theological interpretation is necessary. Those who use ancient forms of speech are either baffled by words and concepts no longer in everyday usage (e.g. 'anointing' or 'the devil') or are insufficiently baffled because they assume that they know what is meant by words that are in everyday usage, but which now have a significantly altered range of meanings (e.g. the 'persons' of Father, Son and Spirit). At the same time, Habermas' description is unsatisfactory. Why does he suppose that interpretations are 'distinguished from the religious'? Is it obvious what he means by 'the religious'? Some guesswork is needed here. Perhaps he means that the liturgical declaration 'I baptise you' is distinguished from second-order talk about what 'I baptise you' means. Certainly the first is liturgical, whereas the second is not. But what if the context of second-order talk is, say, catechetical, as when a candidate for baptism receives instruction from a priest, and such instruction begins and ends with prayer? Is this 'distinguished from the religious'? It is certainly 'theological' in Habermas' sense.

To the second, empirical, claim one can pose another obvious question: which theologians is Habermas talking about? His claim is that contemporary theology and contemporary philosophy find themselves in a similar situation: their task is to reconstruct discourses into a formal scheme and then to mediate these 'expert' discourses back into everyday life. The philosopher reconstructs 'common sense' into an expert discourse of philosophy, and then acts as an interpreter in carrying its 'essential contents' back into everyday *praxis*. The theologian reconstructs 'religious discourse' and then presents it in the form of 'public theology'. For Habermas, the philosopher has the easier task because the theologian is caught in a bind. The theologian's source is what he calls a 'syndrome of revelation faith, held together in ritualised *praxis*'. The identity of this 'sacred' source is compromised when public theology tries to recast faith's terms in 'profane' terms. Habermas implies that the more intelligible public theologians are, the less theological (because the less sacred) their subject matter becomes. In more extreme language than Habermas uses, public theology is a dangerous parasite on its own body of texts and practices (Habermas 2002: 76). Again, there is a grammatical component to this claim. Habermas relies heavily on the notion that 'in the past' (but when?) there was a 'distance' between sacred and profane. Habermas seems to believe that 'religious discourse' depends for its identity on this distance. He claims outright that religious discourses 'lose their identity' when the distance between sacred and profane is reduced. His empirical claim is that 'public theology' is devoted to precisely this task of reduction. To evaluate Habermas' claim about the distance between sacred and profane is unmanageably difficult, because he does not acknowledge which theoretical account of sacred and profane he is relying on, or how this account might relate to social life in Europe, or in which period or which geographical region he thinks that such a 'distance' once existed. The best guess of a charitable reader is that Habermas perhaps has in mind Weber's thesis of secularisation. If this is so, then Habermas means that the distance between sacred and profane shrinks as the twin forces of Calvinist notions of predestination and scientific notions of causal determinism undermine earlier religious constructions of the meaningfulness of human life.[8] More alarmingly, Habermas would also mean that 'public theology' is itself an agent of secularisation, even though it relies for its own life upon the sacred that it is profaning. I think that this is a reliable reading of Habermas. The question is, then: who are these dangerous public theologians? Habermas names David Tracy, Helmut Peukert and Jens Glebe-Möller. Even in 1988 these were not representative of theology in the university: they are just the theologians with whom Habermas happens to engage.

Perhaps the biggest problem in Habermas' account of the fate of theology in the contemporary world is his understanding of the three routes typically taken by theology in the twentieth century. These routes are (1) the 'Protestant path', (2) 'enlightened Catholicism' and (3) 'methodical atheism'. The Protestant path means appealing 'to the kerygma and faith as a source of religious insight absolutely independent of reason'. Enlightened Catholicism means relinquishing 'the status of a special discourse' and exposing theological assertions 'to the whole range of scientific discussion'. Methodical atheism means 'a program of demythologisation that is tantamount to an experiment'. In Habermas' main example of such demythologisation, Glebe-Möller's *A Political Dogmatic* (Glebe-Möller 1987; Danish original 1982), sacraments, Christology, ecclesiology and eschatology are recast in a 'theology of liberation based on a theory of communication'. Habermas' critique of this is

---

[8] For a succinct account of Weber's thesis see Owen 1994: 113ff.

characteristically damning: it is an interesting and even convincing attempt to reinterpret Christian themes in ways that are relevant to non-Christians. But, says Habermas, 'I ask myself *who* recognises himself or herself in this interpretation' (Habermas 2002: 77). The attempt is simply not Christian. The 'persuasive' account does not reflect a tradition with which anyone would identify.

The three routes Habermas lays out are disastrously narrow. Even the major figures in the German-speaking traditions, whose work Habermas knows – Barth, Bonhoeffer, von Balthasar, Rahner, Pannenberg, Moltmann (I have deliberately mingled Protestants and Catholics) – are resistant to these categories. How much more resistant would be major figures in the French-speaking and English-speaking traditions. Habermas himself admits that his theological partners in dialogue would not wish to be restricted to any of his three paths, but the alternative he attributes to them is that of 'boxing in' their secular opponents, a strategy I have rehearsed above in the case of Peukert. It is tempting to use Habermas' routes for a quite different purpose, and to suggest that to the extent that any theologian's work conforms to one of these routes, his or her work is of poor quality. The further problem with these three routes is that if one identifies theologically informed studies which place in question such narratives of 'reason', of 'scientific discussion' or of 'demythologisation', the categories become less useful.[9]

We can attempt some summary of Habermas' engagements with theology. The most important point is that Habermas has not engaged with post-liberal theology, even though he himself speaks with a remarkably Lindbeckian voice at times. Habermas shows himself skilful in exposing problems with forms of theology that are eager to accept his terms of debate. He exploits that eagerness as a weapon against his theological partners in dialogue. To the extent that theologians are willing to adopt and rely on a theory of communicative action, they abandon their own Christian tradition. Habermas makes this claim, and I think that it is persuasive. His account of that tradition is, however, problematic, as I have shown in previous chapters. Theologians should not accept Habermas'

---

[9] See Funkenstein 1986; Buckley 1987; Milbank 1990; Toulmin 1990; Lash 1996; Williams 2000.

terms of debate: they should reject his description of Protestant 'independence from reason', Catholic 'exposure to science' or 'methodical atheism', because the descriptions of reason, science and method are all in need of serious repair. I have suggested two strategies: first, reconstructing and repairing Habermas' grammatical claims about theology and, second, probing his empirical claims about theologians and noting that his examples are not adequately representative.

In Habermas' defence he has always insisted that he is not an expert in theology, and he has always acknowledged that he cannot claim to debate with theologians on the same level as with philosophers and social scientists. To hold him to account because of his insufficiently subtle theology is as unreasonable as berating a dogmatic theologian for his inability to rehearse the subtleties of Leibniz' theory of knowledge. This seems to me a fair analogy: Habermas' knowledge of theology is on the same level as most dogmatic theologians' knowledge of Leibniz. They have some idea of the main issues, but they would embarrass themselves if asked to explain these in the light of recent scholarship. In previous chapters I have drawn attention to shortcomings in Habermas' theological understanding on the occasions when he has tried to incorporate it into his own publications. It is fair to be critical of him in these contexts, because he volunteers his claims freely. I do not think that it is fair to mount criticisms of his theology when evaluating his responses to theologians, because he has always felt compelled, rather than delighted, to respond. Habermas does not want to be the kind of haughty German professor who makes utterances from a great height and refuses to take questions. If challenged, he feels a duty to answer. It is vitally important to pay attention to his protestations of ignorance about theology, because he has never sought dialogue with theologians. It is the theologians who have always beaten a path to his door. Why, then, have theologians desired dialogue with him, despite his reticence?

It seems to me that his theological colleagues have rightly grasped that something like Habermas' theory of communicative action is vitally needed. There needs to be some way for members of different traditions to be intelligible to their neighbours, and theologians understand the importance of interpreting their traditions for themselves and for others. The level of argumentation in the public sphere on matters of religious belief and practice is dangerously low, and there needs to be a form of discourse which can raise it. Religious traditions wish to be heard in debates about law, medical ethics, international security, the environmental crisis, education and economic development, and there is thus a need for a public sphere in which claims can be raised, challenged, redeemed and transformed. Who else has produced theory in this area at the same level and in the same detail as Habermas? To find fault with theologians for being willing to recast their traditions as modern and secular when engaging with Habermas is easy enough, and I have argued that there are serious faults to be found. Nonetheless, the need they perceive is real, and it is not just understandable but obvious why they might turn to Habermas.

The problem is the desire for theory. It seems to me true that Habermas has the best available theory of argumentation in the public sphere, and equally true that this theory is unusable. It is not merely that Habermas' theory has problems which need repairing. The problem is that he has a *theory* for argumentation in the public sphere. Argumentation in the public sphere is as resistant to theory as the ground of thought. Thinking has a ground, but there is no way adequately to grasp it in thinking. The same is true of argumentation in the public sphere. Such argumentation does have a ground, if it is to happen at all, but there is no way to establish this ground in argumentation. Argumentation presupposes a ground, and here Habermas is strong. But he has consistently pointed to the existence of '*unavoidable* presuppositions'. Here Habermas is weak. He has not only pointed to their existence; he has tried to grasp them. They cannot be grasped.

Habermas is not content to acknowledge *that* there is a ground of public argumentation; he wants to specify *what* the ground is. If such an enterprise is impossible in principle, then his theory of communicative action can at best persuade partners in dialogue *that* their dialogue has a ground and not *what* it is. Obviously one does not need something as complex as Habermas' theory to demonstrate this. If dialogue is possible, then it has a ground. One does not need to ask if thinking is possible, or grasp its ground, in order to think. In the same way one does not need to ask if argumentation is possible, or grasp its ground, in order to argue. Habermas seems to think that people need to be taught such grounds in order to argue well, but this is obviously not true in the case of thinking. The ability to think is practical knowledge, acquired through apprentice-ship, not grasp of theory. The same is surely true of argumentation. To learn how to argue in the public sphere means being apprenticed in practices which form skilful public arguers. The conditions for successful argumentation are not merely skill in speaking and per-suading, but skill in raising, challenging and redeeming validity claims. Habermas' distinction between strategic and communicative action is undoubtedly useful here. If the public sphere is a strategic sphere, then force is the most efficient language. It seems that many governments lack the imagination to think in any other way than strategically, but this is not so true of their citizens, and certainly not eloquent citizens like Habermas. Yet if the public sphere is truly to be communicative, in Habermas' sense, then its participants need to be skilled in argumentation and not merely persuasion.

Theologians do not need more theory. We need better ac-counts of argument, and better models for apprenticeship in public argumentation. These will be the topics of the final two chapters.

CHAPTER 10

Narrative and argument

The preceding chapters have had texts by Habermas as their focus, and have had interpretation and explanation as their goal. They have thus served to make Habermas' views on religion accessible to philosophers and theologians, and to show some of the difficulties that arise if his theory is conscripted for theological use. Habermas is difficult to read, and theological commentary on his work, as distinct from engagement with it, is not plentiful. The previous chapters have tried to fill this gap by illuminating the plain sense of his texts. This chapter has a different aim, and is intended for a more narrowly theological readership. Philosophers outside the Christian tradition are invited to read this chapter slightly differently, and to approach its material as guests rather than as fellow travellers. Here I want to begin putting the previous discussions to work in an attempt to repair problems in contemporary theology.

Areas of expertise in theological work are increasingly specialised, and it is sometimes difficult to generate high-level discussion between specialisms. English-speaking theologians who read Habermas tend to be experts in Christian ethics; within this group they tend to read Kant, Rawls and MacIntyre. English-speaking theologians who read Barth tend to be experts in Christian dogmatics; within this group they tend to read patristic theology, Anselm, Aquinas, Luther, Calvin and Schleiermacher. Habermas is most interesting when he is introduced into discussions held by both these kinds of theologian, neither of whom tend to read Hegel, Schelling or Heidegger. It is thus quite rare for theologians to have a good discussion of the relative merits of Habermas, Gadamer, Foucault and Derrida. The theologians who read this bibliography tend to be 'postmodern' theologians, and in Britain at least are found on the margins of dogmatics and ethics. This is bad for the health of theology. If one wishes to debate the relation between argument and narrative, as this chapter intends to do, one needs to mix these specialisms up a bit. It is impossible to be an expert in all these areas, but without introducing some cross-breeding into the bibliographies, it is difficult to get the different perspectives to interact usefully. This chapter is thus something of an experiment. It is aimed at loyal readers of Hauerwas and Milbank on the one side and loyal readers of Reinhold Niebuhr and David Tracy on the other. These groups rarely interact in a civilised fashion, and it seems to me worth while to raise the level of debate. For philosophers listening in on this debate, Hauerwas and Milbank have a theological following whose work stresses the inner logics and inner narratives of Christian life and thought, whereas Niebuhr and Tracy are heroes for those who stress the need for theology to be intelligible and effective in the public sphere. The first group see themselves as sophisticated reinterpreters of the tradition, and dismiss the second group as too willing to assimilate to modernity. The second group see themselves as making the tradition accessible and relevant in public discussion, and dismiss the first group as arcane. Habermas is an excellent figure to help foster some interaction between them.

The problems raised for theology by Habermas are not theological. His account of the history of theology is weak, as I have tried to show, and if one wished to repair his work here, the first step would be to be a better historian. Habermas does, however, pose two philosophical problems that cannot be ignored. First, when theologians reflect on the importance of tradition, how well do they do justice to the increasing distance from tradition that participants in worship experience? Second, when theologians reflect on the importance of narrative, do they give a good enough account of the relationship between narrative and argumentation? This chapter responds to these challenges.

The first problem is that of the alleged 'distance from tradition' that members of a tradition, and by implication participants in worship, experience. This was the topic of chapter 3. There are many possible responses to this question, ranging from taking Habermas very literally to outright rejection that there is in fact any such experience of 'distance'. In the latter case, it is open to theologians to argue that participants experience no such distance at all. However one engages Habermas, though, the simplest point of departure is to intervene in the argument between Habermas and Gadamer about the effects of reflection on participants' attitudes to tradition's authority. Habermas and Gadamer agree that 'reason' somehow points beyond the limits of tradition. They could, of course, *both* be wrong about this, but I shall assume that they have good arguments for it. They differ in that Habermas thinks that reflection on tradition makes tradition decisively distant from and therefore less authoritative for its participants, whereas Gadamer believes that there is no way to evade the authority of tradition because one's very thinking is conditioned by it. It is important to notice that, in my characterisation of their differences, they do not contradict each other, but place their emphases differently. One could relatively easily harmonise the bare bones of their accounts and suggest that while there is no way to evade the authority of tradition, participants nevertheless experience its authority as weakened by reflection. Habermas and Gadamer do indeed presuppose that this is the case. The important difference is that Habermas wants to intensify this 'distance' and construct a procedural ethics in the gap that opens up, whereas Gadamer wants to expose the distance as dangerous illusion, and to close the gap by encouraging participants to own their traditions more fully.

Theologians engaging this debate have resources that Habermas and Gadamer tend to overlook. Habermas' focus on 'distance' arises because of modern problems associated with reflection, but it could be seen as a descendant of the ancient insight that no concrete form of life adequately corresponds to the kingdom of God. The distance between the kingdom of God and concrete ecclesial communities requires members of churches to be self-critical: communities stand under eschatological judgement whose criteria they cannot accurately anticipate. Thus, Christians are always 'distant' from the Church, and from its traditions, in so far as they recognise that their actual communities fall short of what the resurrection has made possible. In this account, Habermas' focus on distance can be properly intensified: Christians should distance themselves from their traditions to the extent that their traditions fail to anticipate God's reign. However, this makes distance a different kind of inevitability. For Habermas, the distance is a product of reflection as such. For the kind of Christian I am sketching, the distance is a product of reflecting on the difference between divine promise and human institutions. To the extent that traditions do faithfully anticipate God's reign, at least as far as finite humans can tell, the distance narrows. Reflection produces precisely the kind of self-critical orientation Habermas argues for, but instead of requiring an ethics constructed in the gap between participants and their traditions, it calls for an ethics which constantly submits its concrete institutions to divine judgement and judges ecclesial practices as more or less faithful to God's promise of redemption. Gadamer's encouragement of participants to own their traditions more fully is also transformed here: Christians should own their traditions to the extent that they are faithful to God's promise. It is not a matter of choosing Habermas or Gadamer, but of spelling out what kinds of distance from tradition are appropriate, and of placing the authority of traditions under a greater authority. This is famously the concern of Johannes de Silentio's *Fear and Trembling*, in which Kierkegaard's pseudonymous author tests Hegel's model of *Sittlichkeit* against the account in Genesis 22 of Abraham's binding of Isaac, and whose insights Habermas at times seems to transpose into secular terms (Kierkegaard 1983). In theological terms, the incarnational impulse in ecclesiology that recognises God's presence in the Church, which is Christ's body, needs constantly to be subject to correctives from the other trinitarian points of reference, which stress God's unknowability as creator out of nothing and incomprehensible closeness as giver of life. Trinitarian theology simultaneously embraces tradition and places its concrete claims under judgement (Lash 1992).

This response by no means eliminates the questions posed by Habermas and Gadamer. Habermas would still rightly note that the distance from tradition experienced by Christians is not wholly of this self-critical kind. There is still the experience of reflection which lessens the authority of tradition, whether or not that tradition embodies God's promise of redemption. Describing distance from tradition as an aspect of the corrective pressures arising from trinitarian theology does not directly address the question of the loss of authority that Habermas places under scrutiny. Gadamer too would rightly maintain that even the practice of placing the authority of traditions under God's authority is still undertaken within that same tradition, and that there is no account of God's authority that does not simultaneously authorise the tradition that gives that very account. Describing traditions as placed under divine judgement does not challenge the overarching authority of a tradition, but acknowledges it even more strongly. There are no easy answers to these challenges. People really do feel that the authority of their traditions is lessened because they see their traditions *as traditions* and not merely as how the world is. Once I am aware that my tradition is a way of interpreting the world, rather than thinking that my tradition's account of the world simply *is* the only world there is, I am able to take up 'yes/no' positions vis-à-vis the claims made in my tradition. At the same time, for Gadamer there is no higher authority that can be humanly conceptualised, and the authority of tradition is not replaced by any other authority such as that of reason or individual choice. Nonetheless, even in Gadamer's account a tradition only claims inescapable authority *as a whole* and not in any of its particulars. Because a tradition is never experienced as a whole, but only in its particular effects in particular times and places, at any given time it can be experienced as questionable. It is perhaps possible, with Ricoeur, to seek a second naïveté with respect to tradition or, with MacIntyre, to seek ways of deepening one's membership of a tradition of argumentation. Of perhaps greater importance is to try to work through the tasks imposed by recognising that questions of authority are burdened with contradictions, such as traditions' holistic authority but particular questionableness, or members' distance from traditions while they remain inescapably part of them. Seeing both unexamined membership and absolute homelessness as illusions helps focus attention on the more manageable tasks of placing concrete settlements under judgement, and seeking ways of repairing problems that arise within traditions using tools that are given in those same traditions. With Habermas, Gadamer and MacIntyre, there is also the possibility of learning tools for repair from other traditions, by learning their languages and extending the range of grammars of transformation with which one is familiar.

Seeing tradition *as tradition* is a kind of relativism. The traveller's experience of living, and even flourishing, in another country with unfamiliar languages and customs causes one's own traditions to be questioned, even if this only means explaining to a foreigner how one would prepare and eat a meal in one's own home. Yet one never interprets new languages and cultures from the perspective of those cultures, but by using customs and skills of travel acquired as a member of one's own culture. What Habermas insists on, however, is that once tradition is viewed as tradition, and not as how the world is and must be for everyone, there is no way back. Although one cannot escape the authority of a tradition, the very insight that tradition *is* tradition produces a different orientation to it. The question is: what kind of different orientation?

It is not our purpose to answer this question, but Habermas surely has good arguments about some kind of 'distance' being involved. The problem with Habermas' account is that he seems too quick to make 'tradition as such' a problem. The example of table manners shows that 'problems' are in fact thrown up through encounters with customs that differ in their particulars: whether to sit or kneel; whether to use hands or utensils; whether to eat everything up to show appreciation, or to leave a little to indicate that one has been adequately fed. It is table manners that are thrown into question most immediately, not the tradition that hands down those table manners. Habermas moves very quickly from particulars to generalities in this kind of discussion, and seems to imply that when people encounter different table manners, they experience a crisis of the authority of their tradition, and of any tradition as such. This is very hasty. In my example, people are faced with difficult judgements about how to eat, in order to respond appropriately to hospitality. Habermas is surely right to insist that subsequent, more reflective, reasoning about the difficulty of those judgements makes one conscious that traditions are traditions, and renders their table customs questionable. But it does not necessarily follow that such reflective reasoning renders traditions questionable. To learn from Gadamer a little, reflection makes particulars questionable, but to the extent that such questioning arises within a tradition, and to the extent that one is conscious of this, one could conclude the opposite: it renders the tradition itself even more binding. There is a possible case where this might seem not to be true, where questioning certain particulars could be seen as throwing the whole tradition into question. It is open to members to claim that certain customs are a tradition's *sine qua non*, and to insist that if these customs are abandoned, the tradition is destroyed. Something like this might happen when children from a tradition of arranged marriage find themselves in conflict with their parents over decisions relating to their future spouse. Parents can exert force by asserting that a child's actions render her 'no longer Pakistani'. Nevertheless, in this case things might not be as they seem. Such extreme rhetoric has the effect of making the child more acutely conscious of her Pakistani identity and reinforcing it even, and perhaps especially, if she proceeds against her parents' wishes. Habermas is right that this kind of situation throws the particulars of a tradition into question, but he is too quick to assume that it leads to a questioning of the tradition as such.

A distinction helps repair Habermas' account at this point. He is right that tradition as such is a conundrum for philosophers: even in Gadamer's account, traditions do not validate themselves. Any of their particulars can be placed in question, and yet they command absolute authority as a whole because no thought is not conditioned by a tradition. Habermas is also right, I think, to argue that any tradition's authority is experienced as weakened by members who understand that their tradition is a tradition and not how the world is. These two insights are not the same, however. The philosophical conundrum is not identical to the existential problem. It is not self-evident that travellers at table and betrothed young people worry about the philosophical status of tradition, and it is clear that philosophers like Habermas do not find themselves decisively distant from their traditions. Habermas' thinking belongs in the tradition of German philosophy, for example, however much he has learned from the analytic and pragmatic English-speaking traditions.

'Distance' is not a philosophical problem, and it cannot be expanded (Habermas) or contracted (Gadamer) by philosophical arguments. It is an existential task. Its most intense expressions are found in two quite different groups. There are those who surrender their identity because they see themselves as rootless, and those who violently enforce their identity for themselves and others because they refuse to acknowledge any tradition but their own. Neither group has much use for the kind of philosophy Habermas develops. Both groups have an especially difficult time bringing up children. Anomie and reactionary politics call for different forms of healing, but these different forms are both practical. They share a need to discover the history of their traditions, because such history simultaneously anchors identity and throws its self-satisfactions into question. Habermas is too one-sidedly focused on the latter dimension, and this explains why his friendly critics offer corrections that emphasise the anchoring of identity. What is needed is a better differentiation of the problems, and solutions that are tailored accordingly. Thus philosophical problems about tradition call for a more balanced philosophical treatment which does justice to the relationships between parts and wholes, between traditions as such and the particular contents that are thrown into question. Existential problems about authority call for practices that teach the rootless just which roots they are alienated from, and that expose reactionaries to their own awkward histories of violence and oppression, which might challenge and transform their triumphal self-descriptions.

The challenges Habermas poses to theologians are thus both philosophical and existential. On the philosophical side, it is not enough to argue 'for tradition'. Admittedly, it is important to challenge one-sided accounts which suggest that the authority of tradition is abolished by the individual's exercise of reason. Forms of moral theory that try to abolish tradition or attempt to erase narratives which embody virtues certainly require repair. Habermas nevertheless offers a corrective to the idea that tradition is a good. Members of traditions need resources for placing particulars in question and submitting institutional settlements to judgement. The way Habermas does this is hostile to religious traditions, however, even when he affirms particular aspects they may have, such as narratives of redemption and hope in Judaism and Christianity. It is hostile because he argues for forms of ethical commitment that transcend religious traditions. The philosophical task for theologians is to find a way to affirm their traditions while simultaneously affirming the self-criticism that their particular histories, so often violent and fearful, make necessary. On the existential side, it is not enough to advocate religious practice as a cure for anomie or reactionary politics. There need to be educational practices that combine worship with reflection; to some extent worshippers need to become students of theology too.

In my own Anglican tradition, where I currently worship in the Scottish Episcopal Church, it would be relatively easy to make some preliminary suggestions. There is a need not just for youth groups aimed at 12–18-year-olds, but educational groups for the 18–40 age group introducing the theological tradition and its variants, reflecting on the meaning of baptism and the Eucharist, rehearsing some of the historic debates that situate the Anglican tradition vis-à-vis Catholicism and Protestantism, practising different styles of interpreting scripture, learning how to pray and so forth. Without study groups like this, the only education available to Scottish Anglicans (or English Anglicans living in Scotland) will be sermons or the occasional book recommendation. This is not enough for an age group who need a community which extends beyond Sunday worship, and who are bringing up children who themselves pose difficult theological questions. It is important to get specific like this when addressing Habermas' arguments. Habermas is good at identifying general problems, but his audience is so broad that he makes very general comments about social transformation. His context is the university, where those who undergo tertiary education mostly spend only three or four years. While that is certainly long enough for sociology and philosophy students to grasp his arguments, what churches have to offer is forms of education – within traditions – that extend beyond this formative influence into the generative period where young people try to discern their vocations and have children. My own Anglican tradition tends to focus its educational energies on children, teenagers and university students rather than young parents and those in their first or second jobs. If Habermas is right in saying that members of traditions find those traditions set at a distance from them, the 18–40 age group are crucial, and church resources will need to be put into their continuing education. This is a very brief and sketchy response to Habermas, but something like it is required if theologians are not to be mired in generalisations. Jewish and Muslim philosophers, to name only two non-Christian groups who play an important role in the contemporary Western university, will surely have similar concerns, with different resources to hand, depending on geographical location.

The second problem raised for theologians by Habermas concerns the relationship between narrative and argumentation. Much recent theological writing, not least in Christian ethics, lays heavy emphasis on narrative. Narrative – the stories that make people who they are by describing the world and forming their characters – is associated with schooling in the virtues and with shaping social ecclesial life. This emphasis on narrative is intended to repair at least two perceived problems in previous Christian ethics: the predominance of propositional language in articulating ethical rules (deontological approaches) and an unhealthy preoccupation with extreme scenarios designed to provoke ethical reflection ('what would you do if a murderer held a gun to your child's head?'). These are problems because propositional language – 'lying is wrong except when . . .' – reduces Christian ethics to rules that are too abstracted from the messy particularities of life, and tends to compact the Gospel into ungospel-like statements which seem to have little to do with God made known in Jesus Christ. Dreaming up extreme scenarios prevents the kinds of formation that enable members of churches to learn sound judgement in everyday life and be members of communities which participate in God's reconciliation with the world. The emphasis on narrative is associated, in the Christian tradition, with renewed attention to biblical stories (stories of God's ways with the world), with attempts to understand ethical reflection as an outworking of doctrinal understanding (e.g. Barth's 'ethics is dogmatics'), with an interest in moral theory that emphasises the virtues (e.g. MacIntyre's 'Aristotle versus Nietzsche'), with the formation of Christian character (Hauerwas), with recovery of the narrative nature of doctrine (Frei, Lindbeck), with the exposure of many modern metaphysical commitments as myths of violence (Milbank) and with descriptions which make connections between Christian worship and ethics.

The various approaches to narrative do not, and are not intended to, add up to a system. They signal a basket of concerns which broadly harmonise with each other, while admitting disagreements on details, such as whether Christian ethics needs to be decisively pacifist, whether pneumatology is a central category, whether the non-human natural world is to be given the same dignity as humanity, and so forth.

A focus on narrative generates problems. Does it draw too sharply the line between deontological and virtue-based approaches? Does it adequately address the needs of Christian communities which still have leadership roles in wider society? Does it help with debates within churches about certain propositional statements (e.g. 'homosexuality is condemned in scripture')? Is it too inward-looking, or even sectarian? Does it foster sufficient commitment to non-biblical categories such as democracy, human rights or animal rights? Does it hinder inter-religious dialogue? These problems are not lethal to a focus on narrative; indeed, addressing them keeps a concern with narrative alive and helps it develop. They do, however, seem to have an underlying question. *What is the relationship between narrative and public argumentation?*

The question about the relationship between narrative and argument lies squarely within the set of concerns addressed by Habermas. For Habermas a concern with narrative is, quite properly, a matter for members within a tradition. In Habermas' imagination, however, if narrative is all there is, one has a model of public interaction where various groups, each rehearsing its own narratives, come together and can do little more than wait their turn to recite them. In Habermas' mind the groups would not genuinely interact. They might – at best – listen to each other's narratives, but they cannot genuinely argue, because argument presupposes agreement at a certain level. Narrative is not an agreement-type category. Habermas does not engage Christian ethics directly on this point; indeed, his speculative history of Christian ethics (Habermas 1998: 3–46) shows no awareness of narrative approaches. He does, however, deal with the question of the relationship between narrative and argumentation in an excursus in *The Philosophical Discourse of Modernity* entitled 'On Levelling the Genre Distinction between Philosophy and Literature' (Habermas 1987a: 185–210). Although his concern here is with Derrida, some of the broader themes may provide some tools for handling the issues raised by narrative for Christian ethics.

Habermas wishes to draw attention to the losses incurred when philosophical texts are read as literature, and are subjected to literary criticism rather than philosophical argument. He claims, but does not argue, that there is a clear distinction between 'problem-solving' and 'world-disclosure'. Philosophical argument is oriented to problem-solving: a philosopher inherits a problem along with techniques for analysing and solving problems, and uses these techniques to find appropriate solutions. Poetry is oriented to world-disclosure: art imagines the world in a certain way and makes the world meaningful for people by making associations. This kind of distinction is common in Habermas' work, and is profoundly problematic. He tends to divide the world up into 'spheres' (e.g. science, morality, art) or 'expert systems' (e.g. research, law, art criticism) in order to do justice to what he understands to be the increasing differentiation of areas of modern life.

In Habermas' favour there obviously is this differentiation, as can be seen when scientific research becomes subject to moral debate or legal challenge, or where the moral influence of artistic products is debated: these debates bring to light real confusions within societies whose members think (albeit mistakenly) of scientific research as objective and non-moral, or imagine that the aesthetic genius is not subject to the same social norms as ordinary folk. In such debates on television or on the radio, the person hosting the discussion produces any number of experts in research, experts in ethics, even experts in religion: these forms of expertise are different from each other, and arise from different regimes of apprenticeship.

Against Habermas, however, such differentiations are often very shakily based. It may be true that the formation of laboratory scientists does not include formation in the philosophy of science or moral reasoning, but the alleged objectivity of laboratory research is still an illusion, as Habermas often insists. Social differentiation of roles and forms of expertise are often rooted in social mistakes about objectivity, about the relationship between art and morality, or even about the relationship between scientific research and aesthetic production. Against Habermas there are still ideal types in the public imagination that contradict this differentiation: the violinist-detective; the artist-surgeon; the evil mad genius scientist. These ideal types cross the boundaries of differentiation. It is true that the admiration people feel at such feats of multiple expertise betrays a basic social belief that these areas are indeed decisively differentiated, and that it is rare to find such Renaissance virtuosity. But the boundaries are false: Sherlock Holmes' violin-playing *helps* his detective work; the evil mad genius scientist's laboratory work is *central* to his plans to dominate the world. Problem-solving and world-disclosure are not as decisively separate as Habermas insists, and the spheres of differentiation are obviously blurred when an artist produces a painting inspired by legal cases about *in vitro* fertilisation.

Because of the way Habermas draws up the terms of debate, it seems obvious that narrative is about world-disclosure, and argument is about problem-solving. This is Habermas' position. He wishes to preserve the genre distinction between philosophy and literature, to sharpen the distinction between problem-solving and world-disclosure, and to rescue philosophy from turning into just another medium for world-disclosure, where problem-solving is disastrously abandoned in the ludic vaguenesses of literary criticism. Habermas even constructs a fascinating quasi-Freudian interpretation of the self-consciousness of literary critics in the university. Habermas speculates that in North American universities, literary critics were tormented with the anxiety that their work did not conform to norms of scholarly-scientific respectability. In this charged atmosphere, Derrida was welcomed with open arms because his literary deconstruction overcame the 'metaphysics of presence' and the hegemony of 'logocentrism'. The power of this approach to destroy the scientific pretensions of philosophy freed literary criticism from having to submit to pseudo-scientific standards. By annihilating the distinction between literature and literary criticism, and between literature and philosophy, above all in the hands of Paul de Man, literary critics won for themselves the double crown of academic and literary respectability, even genius (Habermas 1987a: 191–2). Habermas' description of North American literary criticism is misleading, however. He conceals from his readers the German genealogy of literary criticism and its origins precisely in philosophical responses to problems in Kant's work. Andrew Bowie's *From Romanticism to Critical Theory* gives a far better account, explicitly engaging with Habermas, and supported by extensive discussion of the history of German philosophy, of the development of literary criticism in the German tradition, and shows how Derrida's concerns emerge from the heritage of German Romanticism of the late 1700s (Bowie 1997: esp. 182–92). The distinction between 'philosophy' and 'literature' is not so clear even in Habermas' own German tradition (Behler 1993: 299–305).

The task for theologians is to muddy the clear opposition between narrative/world-disclosure and argument/problem-solving. We have already made a start in drawing attention to ideal types, in whom such oppositions are overcome. Another approach is to refuse the choice between maintaining and levelling the genre distinction between literature and philosophy. This is a false choice. To put it simply, there are distinctions between literature and philosophy, world-disclosure and problem-solving, narrative and argument; but these distinctions are not between wholly separate practices, but between different aspects of the use of language by subjects. This needs spelling out a little.

The German philosophical tradition is dogged by a 'which comes first?' question: which is prior, the subject or its language? If the subject is prior, then the problem is to explain how it is that the subject has no thoughts that are not housed in language and in tradition. If language is prior, then the problem is to explain how the subject learns language and is able to use it spontaneously and creatively. Solutions to this problem are many and varied. Habermas, for example, thinks that language and language-use come first, and that subjects are constituted inter-subjectively to express the unity of reason in a diversity of its languages. Habermas' problem, then, is to do justice to spontaneous and creative use of language by the subject, and it is no accident that his theory is largely silent on questions of aesthetics. He relegates aesthetic pro-duction to one of three autonomous value spheres, and is resistant to any attempts to allow it to bleed into the others, above all into the problem-solving sphere of philosophical moral reflection. That bleeding is partly what his arguments against levelling the genre distinction between philosophy and literature are concerned to staunch. I shall not rehearse the arguments for and against Habermas on this point. Instead, I wish to suggest that we can reject the priority question as misconceived. Neither the subject nor language is prior: they are always manifest together in any use of language by the subject. The subject and language both come first, if you like. Following Bowie's exposition of Schleiermacher's herme-neutics in the context of these wider issues, it is sufficient to say two things. All uses of language are conditioned by a language's rules and boundaries (language comes first). All uses of language are uses by a subject who is able spontaneously to apply rules, extend boundaries and learn new languages (the subject comes first). This is a drastic abbreviation of a complex history of debate extending through the work of every major German philosopher (Bowie 1997: 104–37; Bowie 2003). We need its conclusion, however, to help address the question of the relation between narrative and argumentation.

It is clear what has to happen formally: good accounts are needed of the relationships between problem-solving and world-disclosure, between literature and philosophy, between poetry and science, between invention and investigation, between the subject and lan-guage. It is clearly unsatisfactory to leave the matter at this formal level: it is not enough to say that such accounts are needed. Yet specifying things more concretely is notoriously difficult, and involves patient analysis of detailed arguments in the work of many major philosophers. While that is unmanageable in this context, a little more does need to be said. The first step is to make analytical distinctions without over-drawing them to the point of false separa-tions. Problem-solving and world-disclosure are distinct: playing Chopin does not necessarily perform a non-musical problem-solving role, and solving simultaneous equations does not necessarily reveal anything meaningful about the world in which we live. Nonetheless, they are not separate. It is commonplace in musical analysis to talk about thematic musical 'problems' which certain developmental material 'resolves'; and one of the reasons geometry was so spell-binding for Descartes and Spinoza was that it revealed a certain kind of order in the world which was a source of hope in conflict-ridden Europe (Toulmin 1990). Even in Habermas' problem-solving work, which is admittedly and self-consciously non-poetic compared with Heidegger's, there are occasional flashes of world-disclosure, such as his comments about language being in its very nature the form of human intentions to understand one another.

The relationship between narrative and argument needs to be teased out in this kind of context. Biblical stories do not necessarily embody debates, and ham-fisted attempts to make them do so, through practices of raw proof-texting, reduce arguments to conflicts of opinion. Similarly, arguments are not necessarily constructed narratively, and there is no reason why philosophers should not continue to work with formal logic to solve linguistic puzzles. Even so, philosophical arguments can very obviously be constructed narratively. MacIntyre's *After Virtue*, Toulmin's *Cosmopolis*, Taylor's *Sources of the Self* and even Habermas' *Philosophical Discourse of Modernity* all tell a story in order to construct their arguments. Habermas is actually one of the most narrative-minded philosophers in the German tradition, and to read his work is constantly to read stories about the history of German thought and the parts played by individual philosophers. At the same time, when members of Christian communities come together to debate vital issues, what is most urgently needed is biblical stories, not the practice of citing isolated passages to support individual points. The story of Job is often rehearsed when questions of theodicy are raised by a community in a situation of unintelligible suffering. The story of Jesus' ascension is often retold when questions about the presence and absence of the body of Christ are debated. These stories are not always told merely as preliminaries to argument, but can be used as focal points for interpretation while participants reason through the problems set before the community. This is even more obvious when reading Jewish rabbinic literature, in which arguments often seem to be nothing but narrations and renarrations of biblical stories (and Christian theologians can learn a great deal from this practice). It is possible for communities to reason through problems by interpreting scripture together. When this happens, the distinction between narrative and argument is not abolished, but made subservient to a basic, and rightly mixed up, practice of argumentative narrative. The task of the final chapter is to outline an example of this.

How does this help with the problem raised earlier for a focus on narrative? The root problem was not the use of narrative *inside* the community, but the role of such narration when different communities, with different narratives, meet together in the public sphere. Habermas' solution to this problem is to appeal to an authority higher than narrative: he insists there is a reason that transcends the diversity of its voices, and a rational commitment to ethical procedures that transcends the body-and-soul commitments to a tradition's stories and customs. This cannot be acceptable to members of religious traditions, because the highest authority is God, as understood – or, better, precisely as *not* understood – in the particular tradition. Against Habermas, any attempt to transcend this tradition, which simultaneously receives revelation and refuses to 'comprehend' it, is not just an ethical position but the abolition of the Christian tradition. It would acknowledge a higher authority than the one who is revealed as unintelligible yet known in Jesus Christ.

This still leaves the question: how do communities with different narratives meet peacefully in the public sphere in order to argue with, and not merely encounter, each other? Habermas suggests one answer: they should all agree to suspend their narratives in order to find procedures they can all subscribe to. Although Habermas' discussion of the history of philosophy is intensely narrative, in his discourse ethics he tries to purge narrative from his account of ethical problem-solving and lay things out as procedurally and formally as possible (even if, after all, it is still rooted narratively in the tradition of German philosophy).

At the other extreme would be something like the suggestion in John Milbank's earlier work, and given its influence in theology, it is worth considering it in a little detail. In Milbank's *Theology and Social Theory*, encounter between traditions has as its goal a kind of contest, where each participant tries to out-narrate the other, although in the Christian case this is performed with a desire to imitate God's harmoniousness rather than human competitiveness. The themes of contest (Milbank 1990: 1–6, 327–31) and harmony (Milbank 1990: 363, 427ff.) are not easy to reconcile in this account, but it is obvious that Milbank desires to reconcile them. Milbank explicitly eschews argument in favour of renarration and redescription. Here, the work of Alasdair MacIntyre becomes important. Milbank, like Habermas, understands the problems that MacIntyre has when trying genuinely to *argue* against Nietzsche using the tools of narrative: argument requires a stable and agreed account of how things are, together with stable and agreed rules for making judgements. Habermas tries to identify those rules. Milbank takes the other exit:

But *my* case is rather that it [secular reason] is only a *mythos*, and therefore cannot be refuted, but only out-narrated, if we can *persuade* people – for reasons of 'literary taste' – that Christianity offers a much better story. This all sounds much less serious than what MacIntyre has to offer, but I must still press my case. (Milbank 1990: 330)

Milbank and Habermas have the same objection to MacIntyre: there can be no universally persuasive account of 'virtue in general' or 'tradition in general' which is at the same time produced from within a particular tradition:

The curious, although highly interesting paradox of MacIntyre's ethical philosophy, is that the same appeal back to an ethics of virtue invokes at once a metaphysical, and at the same time a historicist dimension ... MacIntyre's realism conflicts with his historicism. (Milbank 1990: 338–9)

Either his metatheoretical claims about stages of increasing reflexivity hold for any tradition whatsoever, in which case they could not have been developed from within the context of a particular research tradition, which contradicts the presupposition on which they rest; or these claims lose their context-transcending meaning and have only local validity, but then MacIntyre becomes entangled in precisely the relativism he tries to avoid. . . (Habermas 1993a: 100–1)

Where Habermas tries to forge a different context-transcending set of tools, which we have examined in previous chapters, Milbank radicalises the priority of narrative:

There is for me no method, no mode of argument that charts us smoothly past the Scylla of foundationalism and the Charybdis of difference. Nor do I find it possible to defend the notion of 'traditioned reason' in general, outside my attachment to a tradition which grounds this idea in the belief in the historical guidance of the Holy Spirit. (Milbank 1990: 327–8)

Habermas and Milbank obviously have very different responses to the primacy of narrative: Habermas tries to leave it behind by developing a procedural ethics, whereas Milbank insists that there is only 'local validity', to use Habermas' phrase. It is nonetheless important to realise that they are both more radical than MacIntyre in their attempts to develop a genuinely post-metaphysical approach to truth-claims. Both argue that it is impossible to make metaphysical claims *and* do justice to the local particularities of traditions. Both thus give up on this kind of metaphysical possibility: they bid decisive farewell to the principle of sufficient reason.

There are, however, problems with both these radical projects. We have rehearsed the principal difficulties with Habermas in previous chapters, and they concern the precariousness of trying to sit between Kant and Hegel on matters relating to ethical life. Milbank has the opposite problem. Argument mutates into 'literary taste'. This is doubtless intended to shock, and it can be read as a tongue-in-cheek overstatement. Milbank says the same thing more straightforwardly, however: 'The task of such theology [like Milbank's] is not apologetic, nor even argument. Rather it is to tell again the Christian *mythos*, pronounce again the Christian *logos*, and call again for Christian *praxis* in a manner that restores their freshness and originality' (Milbank 1990: 381).

The freedom opened up by this renewed telling, pronouncing and calling is fully exploited by Milbank in a most alarming way, and it is difficult to be generous in interpreting the following claims. 'Even Plato and Aristotle were inhibited by such a mythical inheritance: in the end they could only think of goodness and happiness as occupying certain privileged sites of self-presence over against an irredeemably chaotic and conflictual cosmos. They isolated islands of peace, but peace was not seen as coterminous with Being. Only Christianity (and perhaps Judaism) affirms such an ontology, and so fully evades an incipient nihilism' (Milbank 1990: 262). '*Only* Christianity, once it has arrived, really appears ethical at all. . .' (Milbank 1990: 362). '[A] tradition (is Christianity the *only* tradition in this sense?) automatically *consists* in the imagination of a reality in which traditioned processes themselves participate' (Milbank 1990: 430). 'And the absolute Christian vision of ontological peace now provides the only alternative to a nihilistic outlook' (Milbank 1990: 434).[1]

While it is important to note that these claims are taken out of context, things are still difficult *in* context. Charitably, one should note the points at which this kind of speech interrupts itself. Milbank admits that the possibilities inherent in Christian theology

---

[1] All italics in the original.

have only been 'spasmodically realized in Christian history' or have been present only 'intermittently during the Christian centuries' (Milbank 1990: 368, 432). Moreover, he insists on the fact that Christian inattention to political theology brought about forms of politics more violent than those of the distant past. The Church is a house of extreme possibilities: either it 'enacts the vision of paradisal community ... or else it promotes a hellish society beyond any terrors known to antiquity' (Milbank 1990: 433). Nonetheless, one has to view with some anxiety quite how easily this peaceful reteller of the Christian *mythos* permits himself the use of the word 'only'. Perhaps the most worrying claim is the first one, with its at first sight generous 'and perhaps Judaism' qualification. It is worrying precisely because in all the others one can imagine the writer carried away with delight, enthusiastically extolling the virtues of his own particular tradition, ecstatically oblivious to other religious traditions that may have their own languages for dealing with sociological problems thrown up by modernity. In the first claim, however, this charming image is unavailable. With breathtaking boldness Judaism has, indeed, been considered in the balance by the author; it is accorded parenthetically faint praise. Is this the peaceful face of harmonious out-narration?

Difficult questions like this lie behind the discussions in the final chapter about scriptural reasoning. For the moment, they may make us appropriately gloomy (although not pessimistic) about the prospects of a radical narrative approach to truth for a public sphere in which different traditions meet each other. They should also alert us to the real problems that post-metaphysical approaches, like those of Habermas and Milbank, offer in that public sphere. Habermas is so allergic to the word 'only' that it is most unlikely that his readers will ever find him willing to privilege any particular tradition's vision of the good. Milbank, by contrast, is addicted to it, perhaps because when one is being radical about the orthodoxy of one's narrative, one cannot imagine anything else. Neither is much help in its current form. What seems unavailable is any kind of compromise position. The choice they offer the reader is not attractive, but any attempt to negotiate a settlement involving a resolution of tradition in general and tradition in particular will fall foul of the criticism that both these post-metaphysical thinkers make of MacIntyre.

There is a way forward, however. The difficulties with Milbank's use of 'only' are not intrinsic to his position. Moreover, the rhetoric about the theological task being renarration rather than argumentation is itself performed argumentatively. This means that some preliminary repair can be undertaken relatively easily, and the two points can be taken briefly one at a time. First, the use of 'only'. Milbank's insistence that persuasive rhetoric is different from metaphysically grounded argument, and that only persuasive rhetoric is available to a truly postmodern theology, does not require him to make exclusive claims about Christianity. Indeed, the practice of making exclusive comparative claims presupposes the kind of overarching perspective that Milbank usually claims is unavailable. One should therefore interpret Milbank's exclusive claims about Christian theology as a generous invitation to members of other traditions to investigate their own histories to see whether they too might have resources for peaceful social theory. This is a stretch for the reader, but by no means an impossible one. Second, the distinction between rhetoric and argument is, in my view, entirely subsidiary to the more important insight that metaphysical grounding is unavailable to participants in discussion. Milbank elides 'argument' with the principle of sufficient reason (the starkest form of metaphysical grounding); there is no necessity to do so. There does not need to be metaphysical grounding for there to be argument; there simply needs to be agreement at a level more basic than the topic currently being argued about. If one is arguing about whether there should be an international court of justice, one needs to have agreement at a more basic level about the importance of international law, the importance of justice, and the authority of courts. This requirement is infinitely regressive in principle, but in practice it stops once (or if) an appropriate level of agreement has been secured. (The problems with Habermas' discourse ethics are not about this insight, but about the methods he uses to secure the universalism intended to support *how* people arrive at appropriate levels of agreement.) Milbank's discussions of rhetoric should thus be read precisely as *arguments* which work (if they do) because his readers share with him agreement about matters more basic than the issues Milbank is currently investigating.

There is another way of approaching the choice offered by Habermas and Milbank, namely the transcendence of tradition (Habermas) or the refusal to see anything except particular traditions (Milbank). This is to note that many of the interesting questions in philosophy arise because of problems of self-reference. From the liar's paradox ('Right now I am lying to you') to the impossibility of the subject thinking itself thinking (which produces reflections on the 'absolute') there are no easy resolutions to the difficulties encountered when the occupier of a perspective tries to get a firm purchase on that perspective. It is possible that something is true of the attempt to get a perspective on tradition, and that the problems Habermas and Milbank see in MacIntyre's position arise from issues of self-reference transposed to the level of tradition. If this is so, then the claim to have resolved the problem, either by transcending tradition or by digging deep into it, is wrongheaded. The conundrums of self-reference are best approached obliquely, by drawing attention simultaneously to the logical puzzles *and* to the incontrovertible fact that life goes on anyway. The fact that the subject cannot think itself thinking does not mean that it cannot think; nor does it mean that it is not the subject that is thinking about the problem. It means that attempts to ground the subject's thinking through that same thinking fail. That does not mean that thinking is ungrounded; it means that its ground is ungetatable.

It is possible that Habermas is making Hegel's mistake of trying to ground thinking in thinking, but transposing it to the level of tradition. This is difficult to see clearly, but perhaps Habermas tries at times to ground tradition in 'competence to acquire tradition'. At his best, Habermas tries instead to draw attention to those times when 'life goes on anyway', namely the commitments to under-standing and rules for argumentation that people in fact have. At other times, he has implausibly insisted that these commitments are 'inescapable' because of the structure of universal pragmatics. Habermas' expressions of the latter have admittedly become less emphatic, and in more recent work he says only that the 'broadly normative content' that underlies practices of communication 'can only be made plausible through the lack of alternatives to a practice in which communicatively socialised subjects always already find themselves engaged' (Habermas 2001: 99).

It is less obvious what kind of mistake Milbank might be making, if indeed he is making one. His radical embrace of tradition may be wrongheaded because he is dealing with a problem with self-reference; he thinks that he has resolved it, but such problems are intractable at the level of logic. To try the analogy of the subject thinking about thinking, Milbank says in effect 'There is only thinking, after all!' This abandons the problem of the ground of thinking rather than solving it. To say 'There are only particular traditions, after all!' is to abandon the problems of tradition: how it is that members of different traditions can understand each other; how it is that people can learn to be part of a new tradition; how translation is possible, and so forth. One needs also to say, 'There is understanding, after all!'

What Habermas and Milbank need is a way of sticking with the problem rather than trying to solve it. Interestingly, when it comes to questions about the subject thinking about thinking, Habermas and Milbank are well aware of the problems. They do not, however, see an analogy between problems of self-reference at the level of individual subjectivity and problems of self-reference at the level of tradition. The task is to find a way to draw attention to the occasions when life goes on anyway, when people do travel between traditions, *and* to find ways of thinking about them even though they are finally inexplicable. Habermas moves too quickly to an 'explanation', by trying to ground a context-transcending procedural ethic in the presuppositions of those who engage in actual practices of argumentation. Milbank too hastily gives up on it by insisting that, because no adequate theory of the transcendence of tradition is available, all the reader will get is a retelling of the Christian *mythos*.

Habermas presents the bigger obstacle to the Christian theologian. This is because he is the more consistent thinker, and the better one understands his project, the clearer it is that reason and tradition are antagonistic for him, and that he locates rational moral philosophy not in the public sphere of the actual encounter of traditions, but in the ideal zone of commitments to procedures. Habermas is a good critic of MacIntyre's tendency to generalise, but his solution is to maintain traditions (solely?) for their ability to bind identities and command allegiance, while reserving for procedural ethics, emptied of all particular notions of the good, all the authority of reason and genuine agreement. To assent to this is just impossible for Christians, and surely not just Christians.

Milbank aims to aid theology. He has not commanded the audience he deserves among practitioners of 'secular reason', perhaps because he tries to out-narrate it rather than repair it. Nonetheless, he has many (admittedly frustrated) admirers among Jewish philosophers, and it would not be surprising to find appreciation from Muslim philosophers too. This must be puzzling for a writer who not only prosecutes an unreservedly trinitarian philosophy, but even makes bids for Christian superiority and makes derogatory comments about other religious traditions. Nonetheless, it is not hard to see why Jews and Muslims might find his work generative: Milbank helps members of religious traditions move not only beyond MacIntyre but even beyond Lindbeck.[2] Whereas Milbank tries to develop MacIntyre's account of tradition beyond and away from the notion of 'tradition in general', his critique of Lindbeck attempts to give a better account of the relationship between narratives and the rules, reconstructed in philosophical theology like Lindbeck's, for interpreting them. In a nutshell, Milbank shows that Lindbeck's account of rules is not merely an appropriate abstraction from Christian practice, but is inappropriately ahistorical. Milbank argues that the repetition of narratives *and* the rules which guide their interpretation are *both* fully historically embedded in particular times and places. Milbank is not arguing against formal schemas, of course: he makes much use of them himself. Rather, his characteristic refrain is an insistence that even the most rarefied schematic idealisation is only meaningful when understood as an historically located product, and used in historically specifiable ways. In this way, the critique is similar to that of MacIntyre: the arguments of both MacIntyre and Lindbeck are instructive, but they need to be radicalised so that *no part of the account* is exposed to the

---

[2] For Milbank's critique of MacIntyre see Milbank 1990: 326–79, esp. 330–1, 350–1; for Milbank's critique of Lindbeck see Milbank 1990: 382–8. Lindbeck has been influential in some areas of contemporary Jewish philosophy, e.g. Ochs 1998: 308–16.

danger of seeming unhistorically located. This means rejecting 'tradition in general' (MacIntyre) and supposedly ahistorical 'rules' (Lindbeck). This helps to repair the problem Milbank perceives in Lindbeck, namely that the kinds of 'narrative' upon which Lindbeck lays such weight appear more inflexible than the kinds of 'doctrine' they are meant to fill out. Doctrines are speculative for Milbank, and because they are vague, general and approximate, they are appropriately cautious tools for handling the indeterminacies and surprises of the stories Christians tell about God and the world. This is, he argues, a better model than one which polarises historical narratives and trans-historical rules (Milbank 1990: 385–6).

It is here that Milbank is most influential for his fellow Christians, attending to problems in modern theology, and repairing the work of his forebears and contemporaries. And it is no surprise that it is here that Milbank has the most influence on Jewish philosophers who, like Christians, surely have a stake in questions of the relationship between traditions and investigations into truth. It is also in discussions of this kind that Milbank shows himself skilfully willing to stay with the problems, rather than claiming to resolve the difficulties. He understands very well, for example, that the answer to heresies is not simply 'to repeat the narratives in a louder tone' (which is how some readers might mistakenly think to interpret Milbank's remarks about out-narration) but to find rhetorical tools which do justice to the traditions and the narratives about which heresies are mistaken interpretations, without trying to ground these tools, which is futile (Milbank 1990: 383). One can quibble with Milbank about whether 'rhetoric' is the best category for categorising such ungrounded persuasive argument/non-argument, but this kind of approach is clearly the kind of attention to the problem that theology needs.

The problem about how traditions encounter each other in the public sphere still refuses to go away, but already in these debates it is possible to see that the problem can be better specified. Somehow there need to be resources for identifying and repairing mistakes, for 'problem-solving' in Habermas' sense. The problem is not that such resources cannot be grounded in the diverse public sphere, but that *they cannot even be grounded inside the traditions themselves*. Habermas thinks that argumentation is relatively easy within traditions and that the problem is to find procedures for arguing between them. Milbank's work helps theologians to see that the problems are already there inside the Christian tradition (and surely other traditions too). Internal disagreements cannot be settled by appeal to traditional criteria, because these very criteria are themselves always historically located and are vague, general and approximate. One might say that Habermas' problem with argumentation in the public sphere is not obviously different from Milbank's problem with heresy. To put it provocatively, *Habermas isn't troubled enough by tradition.*

Here, some genuine headway with Habermas' initial problem is being made. The problem about how traditions encounter each other might best be tackled at the same time as the problem of how argumentation *within* traditions is possible. Milbank constantly rehearses a pattern where any speculative tools considered must be understood as fully historically located and provisional, where argumentation is not distinct from rhetorical persuasiveness, and where refutation and renarration are identical. To extend Milbank a little, this does not mean forbidding the development of tools or practices that connect (i.e. transcend) traditions, but being constantly mindful that such tools and practices are speculative, historically located, provisional and internal to the tradition in which they arise. It also means being willing to stay with the problem, by which I mean acknowledging that such work cannot ground itself or adequately locate its own perspective: problems of self-reference must remain problems even as one acknowledges that life goes on anyway.

The relationship between narrative and argument is also clarified a little. By taking narratives and the speculative tools used to interpret them *together* and by understanding that they are *both* historically and traditionally located, one arrives at the insight that argument and renarration concern the testing of ungroundable claims. To fill this out adequately, there would clearly need to be a detailed account of the different tests that might be applied to such claims. In this context it will have to be sufficient to suggest that to take a claim seriously is to test it in as many ways as possible. There is no need to advocate some kind of absolute testing, which Habermas seems to do in his 'principle of universalisation' or 'rule of argumentation' which he calls '(U)'. We can consider this briefly with a view to repairing it.

(U) is proposed by Habermas as follows. 'Every valid norm must satisfy the condition that the consequences and side effects its *general* observance can be anticipated to have for the satisfaction of the interests of *each* could be freely accepted by *all* affected (and be preferred to those of known alternative possibilities for regulation)' (Habermas 1993a: 33).

Habermas' critics have argued that this is a bad rule, because only a tiny fraction of our moral problems pass its stringent tests (Finlayson 1999: 46). From the preceding discussion in this chapter, it should be evident that the further problem is that its author has attempted to disguise the fact that it is historically located. Like Kant's categorical imperative, which it is intended to replace, its self-presentation is insufficiently bound to a tradition. Instead of principles like this, one can work just as well with more modest sentences. To illustrate, I have invented an example:

Inherited norms often become problematic for contemporary Christians. When this happens, we should test them by any available means. While there is no reason to suppose in advance that any norm can withstand all possible tests, perhaps the better a norm does in the face of such testing, the stronger its claim is on those Christian communities for whose members those tests are authoritative. When engaging in this kind of enterprise it is important to remember that forms of testing are just as culturally specific as the norms they test, and this needs to be taken into account when trying to resolve debates between Christian communities that differ significantly in the kinds of testing they tend to use. Under such circumstances there is every possibility that testing norms becomes very difficult and painful. Such problems are real and cannot be magicked away by clever theories but must be worked through patiently, with all participants mindful that even our most cherished beliefs stand under divine judgement, and that the first and second commandments are to love God with all one's heart and love one's neighbour as oneself.

This is messy as a 'principle' and is vague about what to do in a crisis. It can obviously be improved upon: one could say a lot more about nearly every sentence in it, *because it constantly invites the reader to be more specific.* It cannot be universalised, because its bottom line is a thoroughly tradition-bound commitment to the 'summary of the law'. Moreover, the very paragraph itself is a criticisable validity claim, and makes no bid to situate all possible validity claims. It also makes questionable theoretical claims, such as that forms of testing are always culturally specific, or that the summary of the law is more important than anything else one might say about conduct during debate. I think that these claims can be defended, but they are certainly questionable. Yet just because it is culturally located, it is not necessarily *only* of use for Christian communities. It could very easily be taken up and modified by members of another tradition. Were this to happen, at a bare minimum the word 'Christian' would disappear, and quite possibly it might inspire a very different form of words. But it might continue to be the latter's original inspiration. It is *this* kind of mutation that is so hard to theorise. What is going on when a member of one tradition learns from culturally specific formulations in another tradition and re-authors them, perhaps radically, for a new situation? This is the well-known theory-resistant question of translation.

Habermas wants to say too much about this, and Milbank too little. Habermas, faced with this kind of evidence, immediately launches a series of researches into discovering, isolating and reconstructing the formal characteristics of the meta-principle, of which the culturally specific claims are supposedly a particular instance. Failing this, Habermas wants at least to identify the universal pragmatics that underlie such processes of re-authorship. Milbank's position on this is to deny the unity of the subject and to suggest that we 'hold inside our heads several subjectivities'. If Milbank moves to America, 'I simply become American *as well as* English, or more American for a time, before reverting' (Milbank 1990: 341). The denial of the unity of the subject and the speculation that identities are additive need to be supported by more detailed investigation than Milbank is able to give them in the context of his arguments about relativism, and I leave them to one side. The question of inter-cultural understanding is obviously a substantial area of scholarship in philosophy and in social anthropology, and it is not possible to rehearse the main arguments here. Some minimal indications need to be made, however. Presumably there *is* some connective tissue that makes re-authorship between traditions possible, otherwise one would have to deny that it happens. Here, it is important to draw attention to the 'life goes on anyway' dimension: learning between traditions does happen. At the same time, there is no reason to suppose in advance that such connective tissue can be specified in a theory. One can even, with Habermas, call it 'Reason', and say that it is the guarantor that underwrites all such connections. But, against Habermas, one must also say that calling it 'Reason' does not add anything to the existing insight that there must be connective tissue, and calling it a guarantor of actual connections does not mean that it will necessarily guarantee potential connections. This is a version of what the German Idealists call the 'absolute', although unlike Schelling and Hegel I do not wish to argue that it is divine. Of course, when Christians meditate on the possibility that there is connective tissue that binds difference together, their thoughts might naturally turn to the Holy Spirit, and to the unpredictability of where that Spirit blows. This does not add any philosophically useful information. It might, however, help them pray.

Another small advance has just been made in our investigation into the ways in which traditions encounter each other in the public sphere, and the roles played by narrative and argument. Members of traditions do learn from members of other traditions, and for this to be possible, there must be some connection between them. However, it is an open question whether this connection can be specified. Furthermore, it is not obvious what use it would be, at least for our question of problems in the public sphere, if one *were* able to specify what it is that connects members of different traditions. It is hard enough to say what binds members *within* a tradition, given the intensity of debate and amplitude of disagreement that most real traditions exemplify. As far as theory goes, at least for our purposes here, it is enough to say that people do belong to traditions, and to observe with delight that members of different traditions do learn from each other, as in the example of Jewish philosophers learning from Milbank's Christian trinitarian social theory. This whole book is another example, in that it has learned many of its lessons from the Jewish American pragmatism of Peter Ochs and attempts to re-author its insights in the language of German philosophy, transposed into English idiom, with attention to its implications for Christian theology.

While this may be enough as far as theory goes, it is certainly not enough *tout court* to observe what actually happens in the world. The practices of learning between traditions contribute to the repair of problems internal to those traditions, and thus participate in the healing of suffering in the world. This is good, and because it is good we should wish not merely to notice what is going on, but to find ways of making more of it happen. This is Habermas' goal too, but his heart is set on formalising matters as much as possible, and he gambles too heavily on the possibility that the dissemination of his procedural ethics will contribute to social transformation. There is good reason to be less sanguine. The question about how different traditions encounter each other in the public sphere is urgent, and what is required is not a theory about how they *should* come together, but discoveries of instances where they *do* come together peacefully and learn from each other. This chapter has attempted to make some headway in some of the theoretical questions surrounding the encounter of traditions, but this is not adequate for the much more untidy business of promoting peaceful argumentation between traditions in specific situations. That will be the concern of the final chapter.

A summary of this chapter's main narrative about argument is needed. Our opening problems were, first, how to do justice to the relationship between membership of tradition and existential distance from tradition and, second, how best to characterise the relationship between narrative and argument. In response to the first question, I argued that one needs to distinguish between philosophical puzzles and existential problems. I suggested that one learns from Gadamer that even one's questions about particular aspects of a tradition are raised in a language formed by that tradition, using criteria derived from that tradition, for subjects whose identity is constituted in that tradition. To the extent that one recognises this, even questioning aspects of one's tradition binds one more closely to it. One learns from Habermas that the discovery that one's tradition is a tradition, and not the way the world just is, causes one to experience a certain kind of 'distance' from the tradition, and a weakening of its unexamined authority. I raised the possibility that this insight might be a distant cousin of the Christian insistence that all aspects of tradition are to be submitted to divine judgement, and that a tradition's authority is always less than that of God. In response to the second question, I suggested that one should preserve distinctions (narrative/argument, world-disclosure/problem-solving) without making separations, and that one can learn from Milbank (who has learned from Gillian Rose, who learned from Hegel) that formulations of rules are just as historically situated as the material from which they are drawn. I argued that it is more important to pay attention to practices than to theorise them, especially in the cases of the formulation of doctrine *inside* a tradition and of learning from other writers *across* traditions. Instead of solving the problems, I have tried to draw attention to the problem of trying to solve them (using the analogy of self-reference), and argue instead for staying with the problem while simultaneously paying attention to cases where life goes on anyway. In sum: the critic of Habermas can do worse than become an amateur social anthropologist as a response to intractable philosophical problems. *Only* an attention to actual practice can do justice to the relationship between narrative and argumentation. We now turn to this.

CHAPTER 11

Scriptural difference and scriptural reasoning

This final chapter will present an alternative to Habermas' theory of communicative action. This might seem an immodest claim, considering the vastness of Habermas' learning and his extraordinary energy in pursuing a systematic account of communicative rationalisation. It is not such a big claim, however, because no attempt will be made to formulate an alternative *theory* to that of Habermas, or to engage in an activity comparable to his. The argument presented here has insistently been away from theory which grounds practice and towards attentiveness to particularities which might be translatable from one context to another. Theological critics of Habermas have admittedly to confront a kind of disappointment with settling for the *fact* of communication between traditions at a formal level rather than an *explanation* of how it is possible. This disappointment is a good disappointment, because any claim that one can achieve satisfaction at the level of theory or explanation must in principle be bogus, if Schelling's arguments against grounding (reviewed in earlier chapters) are convincing. However, at the level of lived life, they should not try simply to live with disappointment. The 'fact of communication' is a fragile matter, beset with many obstacles. Like Habermas, theologians interested in the public sphere should hope to promote more of these 'facts' and to refuse melancholy contentment with current damaged practices.

There are many objections to Habermas' theory, some which criticise details, some which aim at very basic questions. For my purposes, two in particular are fatal to his project. The first is the Hegelian objection to Habermas' Kantianism, as presented in chapter 2. The second is the Schellingian objection to Habermas' Hegelianism, discussed briefly in chapter 5. Habermas situates his theory between Kant and Hegel: the more he edges towards Kant, the more he exposes himself to Hegel's challenges; the more he edges towards Hegel, the more he exposes himself to Schelling's challenges. Hegel's critique of Kant is that any attempts to transcend the context of ethical life can be shown to be bound to that same ethical life if it is to bear on what real people actually hold to be moral. Schelling's critique of Hegel is that attempts to conceptualise the absolute or a philosophy's bids to grasp its own basis theoretically must fail because of the relationship of reflection to its ground. For this reason, Habermas' attempt to situate himself between Kant and Hegel does not seem very promising.

There is another side to Habermas' account that I have tried to describe. Habermas steers his theory remarkably close to certain themes in Christian theology. His theory often simply secularises theological topics. In place of the interpretation of scripture he offers two different kinds of interpretation: the lifeworld as interpretation of 'the world' (in his specialised sense) and reflective communicative action as the interpretation of the lifeworld. In place of revelation, he offers two kinds of knowledge: the 'moment' of communicatively achieved consensus and the 'intuition' that the fact of translation implies a universal reason whose features can be known by rational reconstruction. Given this proximity to theology, it is important to acknowledge that there are fundamental problems for theology which cannot be solved by philosophy. The following examples illustrate some of these well. How does one know that God is revealed in scripture? Which scriptures are more central than others? Which interpretations of scripture are better than others? Are criteria for adjudicating competing interpretations of scripture more authoritative than scripture itself? How do we learn that scripture is authoritative, and is that learning mechanism more authoritative than scripture itself? This list can obviously be extended almost infinitely. The reply that questioning cannot get behind tradition, so to speak, is true but only suggests that these questions cannot be profitably pursued to a definite end point; it does not mean that they are trivial questions. The problem for Habermas is that having secularised his theological topics he then has to relearn the problems associated with them – from scratch. Any attempt to secularise theology must deal with the most

sophisticated and subtle forms of that theology. Habermas' secular-
ising work deals largely with simplistic and sometimes downright
bad theology, as I have tried to show especially in chapter 9. The
effort required to secularise theology is vast, and in a world where
religious traditions need to encounter each other *as religious* it seems
a needless expenditure of precious energy.

A surprisingly large proportion of Habermas' work is devoted to
charting the decline of religious thinking; it is a decline of which he
approves; religion's only saving graces are its language of hope and
redemption, which, *as yet,* philosophy has not been able to appropriate, and its ability to supply its members with substantive ethical
commitments which can then be coordinated via discourse ethics. It
has been necessary to go through this material in detail in order to
find out how emphatically Habermas insists on a process of rationalisation away from European religion. My reading of Habermas
has tried to separate his interest in processes of rationalisation from
the question of whether rationalisation leads members of modern
European societies away from religion. One can claim that many
members of modern societies are indeed led away from religious
practices. But it is not clear that the reason for this, if it is true, is
rationalisation. Instead, I have tried to indicate that some of Habermas' rational markers, such as differentiation of world from worldviews, are just as much a development within religious traditions as a
development away from them. The occasional invocation of post-
liberal theologies has been intended to give examples of theologies
that share many concerns with Habermas. In the case of Rowan
Williams this is the concern to wean philosophy away from the
God's-eye view. In the case of John Milbank it is the desire to
elaborate a philosophy based on the presupposition that reality is
fundamentally peaceful and the puzzle is violence/distortion, rather
than the contrary view that reality is fundamentally violent and the
puzzle is love/healing. Williams and Habermas are equally committed to methods of training that constantly guard against seeking to capture the God's-eye view. Milbank and Habermas are
equally insistent on the priority of peace, and they both mount critiques of Hobbes' 'state of nature', Nietzsche's 'will to power' and
Heidegger's 'being towards death', and for similar reasons. Along
these axes Habermas is much closer to Williams and Milbank than

he is to thinkers like Rorty and Lyotard, even though he would find arguments with Williams and Milbank harder to understand because they use such different philosophical languages. Habermas can understand his arguments with Rorty better than those he might have with Williams because of the philosophical approach shared by Habermas and Rorty, even though he would reach certain kinds of agreement more rapidly with Williams because of their shared concerns about the relationship between the God's-eye view and argumentation. My task was to find out how serious Habermas' objections to religious philosophy are, and whether they pose a strong challenge to an essentially religious project like scriptural reasoning, which will be discussed below. I judged that these objections are not serious. This is not because Habermas argues badly, but because he hardly argues at all: his eye is on rationalisation, not the decline of religion. Thus I do not think that his theory of communicative action ruins scriptural reasoning in advance.

My root objection to Habermas is not subtle. He rightly claims that the plurality of worldviews does not simply produce a lovely rainbow of differences but throws up profound challenges to how argumentation in the public sphere is to proceed. He also wishes to point his readers in the direction of an approach that might coordinate different traditions in the public sphere in a way that fosters non-violent argumentation and what he calls 'symmetrical relations' between participants in dialogue.[1] He does so against a background assumption that reality is peaceful and that distortions are distortions of a prior state that is itself not distorted. The force of the better argument is, for Habermas, more basic than coercion, which he insists is parasitic on communicative action. My objection is that if Habermas is content to reproduce this basically Augustinian account of reality, an 'ontology of peace' (Milbank), why does he not also reproduce an account that works with, rather than against, the assumption that different traditions take different texts to be

---

[1] If the focus of this chapter were critique, it would be worth spending some time exploring the limitations of Habermas' overemphasis on symmetry. As Eikelman and Salvatore point out, this model of the public sphere 'unrestricted by considerations of status or authority' is an obstacle to charting different kinds of publicity in modern cultures, including Islamic ones (Eikelman and Salvatore 2002: 106).

'scripture' and interpret them in ways that are sometimes in concord and sometimes in conflict? Taking religious discourses seriously, which means taking their approaches to scripture seriously, may be a condition for good-quality argument in the public sphere, not an obstacle to it.

Habermas assumes that religion is metaphysical. This is not untrue: even the most cursory ethnography of contemporary Jewish, Christian and Muslim life and thought would yield examples of metaphysical thinking almost immediately. But this point merely establishes that the metaphysicality of religion *happens* to be the case in certain common circumstances. There is no reason to assert an intrinsic relation and to think that religion is *by definition* metaphysical. Even the most basic understanding of the history of Christian theology yields examples of anti-metaphysical thought, such as the tradition of so-called 'negative theology', or the self-correcting patterns of thinking embedded in the doctrine of the Trinity. Religion is metaphysical and it is anti-metaphysical. One would not need to scour the daily newspapers too hard to discover immediately that modern everyday thought is both precritical and critical (in the Kantian sense), depending on the writer and the anticipated readership. Different levels of sophistication jostle side-by-side with each other. This is perhaps a trivial point, but Habermas seems oblivious to it in theology: he assumes that religious thinking is metaphysical, and those contemporary post-metaphysical theologies with which he is familiar (considered in chapter 9) are not a fair representation of contemporary theology.

In order to offer an alternative it is important to confront two formidable obstacles. The first is the challenge by Habermas that any account of reasoning must be able to show that there is some point in attempting genuine argumentation in the public sphere, and not simply reduce argumentation to the clash of competing worldviews. There are accounts which accept such a reduction, and Habermas considers them nihilistic and irresponsible. I agree with Habermas: either there really can be argumentation, in which case one should try to give an account (not necessarily an explanation) of the reasonings that support it, or there cannot, in which case one must – intolerably – give up on public debate. The second is the challenge to Habermas by his Hegelian and Schellingian critics, who insist that there is no criterion for judgement that is not indissolubly bound to a particular form of ethical life and that there cannot be a theory of the bases of philosophy.

Any good alternative to Habermas must therefore promote genuine argumentation in the public sphere, must accept that theory does not ground or transcend ethical life, and must acknowledge that the bases that give rise to argumentation cannot themselves be theorised. My impression of the secondary literature on Habermas is that most critics have a relatively easy time arguing the Hegelian and Schellingian critiques, but struggle badly to achieve a good account of argumentation. There is a tendency in many of his critics to oppose narrative and argument to each other and to privilege the former. To the three conditions already named, I therefore add a fourth: that any good alternative to Habermas must do justice to the complex interrelationship between narrative and argument, and to the parallel connection between world-disclosure and problem-solving. We have probed some of these issues, especially the latter, in chapter 10.

Instead of offering an account of how these four conditions might be related theoretically, and speculating about the kind of practice that might meet those conditions, I propose willingly to accept that action precedes reflection, and 'rely on the uncontrollable reality of the fact that we are always already engaged in interpretation and understanding' (Bowie 1993: 188). In other words, we need an already-existing practice over which its participants neither have nor seek control, and which can serve as an example on which to reflect.

'Scriptural reasoning' is the relatively recent name given to the practice, by members of different traditions, of reading and interpreting scripture together.[2] The reading of scripture has historically been overwhelmingly intra-traditional: members of *one* tradition meet together to read and interpret sacred texts. This has been, and still is, the focal practice of reading scripture for members of

---

[2] For a descriptions of this project, which is well supported by online resources, see the website for The Society of Scriptural Reasoning. At the time of writing it is hosted by the University of Virginia: *http://etext.lib.virginia.edu/journals/jsrforum*. My description of scriptural reasoning is not normative, but is an attempt at description arising from participation.

religious traditions, and this is true also for those who do scriptural reasoning. Scriptural reasoning is thus not a focal practice for its participants, but an extension of that practice in a way that is not necessarily warranted by the theologies of the participants' traditions, and may – on certain interpretations – even be forbidden by them. At the moment the traditions engaged in scriptural reasoning are various different kinds of Islam, Christianity and Judaism, although it is in principle extendable to others. Scriptural reasoning thus means, for its participants, acknowledging that their particular traditions do not encourage their joint reading of scripture, but doing it anyway.

What actually goes on? To answer this adequately, we would need an attentive ethnography of a variety of occasions and practices. Such an account is lacking, and we must make do with my own inadequate sketch. This is not the familiar self-deprecating posture of academic false modesty: my account really is inadequate, and a better one is needed. It seems to me so important to describe, however, that even a defective account is better than none.[3] At events of scriptural reasoning, participants meet in small groups in which at least two traditions are represented. (Scriptural reasoning cannot be done by one person alone under any circumstances, or by two or more if they belong to the same tradition.) The Jewish word for this small-group study, sometimes adopted by Christians and Muslims, is *chevruta*, meaning a group of friends. The normal practice, although others are possible, is to select texts in advance from the Tanakh, the Qur'an and the New Testament, which participants are encouraged to read beforehand, and then to read and interpret them together. Texts from at least two traditions are chosen. (Scriptural reasoning cannot be done by reading a text from just one tradition.) There is no fixed rule about how to select texts for study: sometimes a theme will be chosen, and members of different traditions select texts that seem appropriate. There is no prescribed outcome for scriptural reasoning study, or any prescribed process for how the sessions are to be conducted. In practice, it is common for more experienced participants to show newcomers by

---

[3] For essays on scriptural reasoning see Ford and Pecknold (forthcoming).

example. There are rules for scriptural reasoning, written by Peter Ochs and commented upon by many participants, available on the scriptural reasoning website, noted above. These are not rules in the sense of a society's or club's rules, which are its constitution, or rules in the sense of the Rule of St Benedict, which lay down how the practice must be done. Rather they are a response to the desire to describe the practice (and some of the history) of scriptural reasoning in an orderly way. There is also an unpublished 'handbook of scriptural reasoning', written by Steven Kepnes.

Scriptural reasoning is a practice which, while theorisable to an extent, cannot theorise its own bases. The different scriptures – Qur'an, New Testament, Tanakh – are not chosen because there are good reasons for choosing them, but because it is obvious for Muslims, Christians and Jews to read these texts. No further justification is offered for reading these texts rather than, say, Greek plays or ancient Egyptian poetry. Members of the traditions might speculate about how it was that certain texts came to be canonical, or about how a certain form came to be taken to be the authoritative version of the text, but this would have no bearing on the treatment of the texts as scripture, i.e. as holy books authoritatively teaching about God and the world.

The principal conditions for participation seem to be membership of one of the traditions and the desire to understand members of other traditions' interpretations of their own scripture, and their interpretations of one's own scripture. This does not rule out those who deny that they have affiliation with a tradition, but such people seem to be treated as honoured guests rather than as participants. Christians, Muslims and Jews freely interpret each other's scriptures, and it is not uncommon to find that a participant from one tradition knows the details of a text from another tradition, and the history of its interpretation in that other tradition, better than a participant who is actually from that other tradition. It is not merely about knowing texts, however. The process of 'reasoning' is not just the teasing out of interpretative issues, but also the making explicit of 'deep reasonings'.[4] By deep reasonings, I mean the written record

---

[4] The sentiment is Jeffrey Stout's (Stout 2004: 1–15); the phrasing is Chad Pecknold's (Pecknold forthcoming).

of arguments from the past, perhaps including minority positions that did not win the day, but which have been preserved. Philosophers in the Anglo-American traditions are in the habit of distinguishing between (a) definitions, axioms and presuppositions, (b) logics and rules for reasoning and (c) actual chains of reasoning, argumentation and conclusions. This is immensely useful. The religious traditions do not encounter each other with different initial (a)s and shared procedural (b)s, but with long histories of (c)s, where communal identities are expressed at a profound level. It is not just the exposure of (a)s that needs to happen in argumentation; it is the rehearsal of (c)s *as expressions of identity.* An example of such a specific chain of reasoning in the Christian tradition might be the documents relating to the Council of Nicaea in AD 325. The Nicene Creed preserves the settlement of that council; the surviving documents – which can be studied – form part of the deep reasonings that led to its formulation and permit, to an extent, the rehearsal of the debates for and against Arius. Scriptural reasoning is a practice of 'publicising' deep reasonings, so that others may learn to understand them and discover why particular trains of reasoning, and not just particular assumptions, are attractive or problematic. *Scriptural reasoning makes deep reasonings public.* It sees them not as particularistic obstacles to debate, but as conditions for conversation, friendship and mutual understanding. Without deep reasonings, there are no religious traditions to speak of. Depth is not obscurity, however: the acknowledgement of depth is a recognition that it takes time to plumb. Scriptural reasoning models the discovery that making deep reasoning public is not only risky – because one makes oneself vulnerable when revealing what one loves – but time-consuming. It is a non-hasty practice, and is thus a kind of beacon in our 'time-poor' world.

This is a very brief and minimal description of what scriptural reasoning is: scriptural texts from at least two traditions being read by members of at least two traditions. It is minimal because scriptural reasoning is resistant to this kind of descriptive attempt, namely a member of only one of the traditions trying to give an overview of it. Each of the three Abrahamic traditions has its own rules for interpreting scripture (and internal disagreement about these rules), and even if there is overlap between them, it is not the overlap that makes scriptural reasoning possible. The significant point of contact is a shared desire to study scriptural texts. The most striking thing about the context of scriptural reasoning is not consensus but friendship. To use the word *chevruta* to describe the meeting of Muslims, Jews and Christians is itself surprising, and the actual friendships that are formed through such study do not lessen that surprise. Consensus can be measured and managed, and to that extent is an appropriate object of a theory like Habermas'. Friendship is altogether more confusing, and even the most sophisticated philosophical accounts of it somehow repeat the absurdity of the hopeless lover who tries to persuade the other to love him by using arguments. Abstract description of friendship is nearly as pointless as thirstily trying to make sense of water. Friendship is nonetheless the true ground of scriptural reasoning, and who can give a good overview of that? The traditions have different understandings of friendship with God, with members of one's own family, with members of one's own tradition, and with strangers. Somehow, the recognition that each worships the one true God moves scriptural reasoning beyond an interaction determined by conventions for showing strangers hospitality. Showing strangers hospitality is a significant enough miracle. Yet scriptural reasoning does not quite reproduce this context: when members of three traditions meet together to study shared scripture, who is the guest and who is the host? In a way that is difficult to be clear about, the participants in scriptural reasoning all find themselves invited, not by each other, but by an agency that is not theirs to command or shape. There is an 'other' to the three traditions, and that seems in an obscure way to make friendships possible.

What does all this have to do with Habermas and argumentation in the public sphere? First, scriptural reasoning is hard to categorise in Habermas' terms. It is traditional, in that it is conducted by members of traditions, who read texts that are authoritative for those members. It is also not traditional, in that members of tradition A read texts that are authoritative for members of tradition B in a way that acknowledges the sacredness of the text without necessarily acknowledging its authority for members of tradition A. It is hard to know what Habermas would make of this 'religious' disassociation of sacredness and authority. Indeed, it is hard to know what scriptural reasoners make of this approach to sacredness. Second, it coordinates discussion (I do not yet say argument) between members of different traditions without requiring a commitment to a universal that transcends those traditions. It is not even true that each of the traditions encourages the practice of scriptural reasoning, so there is no element that is common to each of the traditions. What brings members of the different traditions together is obscure, and may be different in each case.

We can now ask whether scriptural reasoning thus fulfils the conditions listed above. (1) Does it attempt to transcend the limits of ethical life? In one sense, no. Participants engage in scriptural reasoning only as members of a particular tradition, only speak from out of this tradition, and acknowledge no authority above that of their own tradition other than the authority of God. In another sense, yes. Participants acknowledge that God is not circumscribed by their tradition, but is the non-circumscribable possibility of its very existence. God transcends ethical life, but the human practices of scriptural reasoning do not. (2) Does it attempt to theorise its own basis? No. The basis of scriptural reason seems defiantly obscure, and the theology of any one of the traditions is not sufficient to describe it. It is true that all three Abrahamic traditions are committed to hospitality, but their accounts of why hospitality is good are different, and in any case there is something more than hospitality going on in scriptural reasoning. (3) Does it do justice to the relationship between world-disclosure and problem-solving? Yes. Scripture is read as world-disclosive, indeed revelatory, and as a resource for problem-solving *at the same time*. The most obvious problem is the damaged relationships between members of the traditions of Islam, Judaism and Christianity, and scriptural reasoning is an attempt to repair that damage. The narrative form of scripture and the narrative form of scriptural reason are aspects of a profound problem-solving practice. (4) Does it promote genuine argumentation in public discourse, rather than the mere juxtaposition of different narratives? This question is not so quickly answered. I think the answer is yes, in so far as there is not just shared discourse, but genuine argumentation. The criteria for argumentation understood and used by participants in scriptural reasoning are not easy to be sure of. The criteria for argumentation which one can try to reconstruct from displays of 'deep reasonings' are different for each of the traditions, and there is disagreement within those traditions. At the same time there are other criteria for argumentation which are not necessarily from within any one of the three traditions, yet which are the basis for judgement: many of the participants are trained in modern universities which promote the kind of argumentation that Habermas claims is a feature of any argumentation. It is not straightforward to determine if it makes sense to ask whether scriptural reasoners' skill in argumentation is learned within their tradition, or outside it in the university. Most participants would affirm that universities are *shared* space rather than *neutral* space, although the differences between these are not easy to be clear about. Perhaps the more important distinction is between *shared* space and *contested* space. The difference matters: where both sides acknowledge that the other claims to belong there, in the first case (shared space) one accepts that claim and in the second case (contested space) one rejects it. The idea of *neutral* space seems to imply that anyone or no-one belongs there.

The practice of scriptural reasoning is difficult to adjudicate with respect to Habermas' requirement that it promote argumentation rather than merely juxtapose narratives. This is because it seems to call into question the strong contrast between argumentation and narrative that Habermas characteristically makes. The scriptures are narrative; the interpretations are narrative; the doctrinal or legal norms that arise from interpretation are often narrative. Yet at every stage of reading there is argumentation. Reading the plain sense generates arguments almost at once about what words and sentences mean – especially when the scriptures are read in their original languages and translations side-by-side. Interpreting the text more freely than in the plain sense throws up arguments about the legitimacy of the interpretation according to certain criteria, conventions and histories of interpretation. Engaging with doctrinal or legal norms means reviewing the history of argumentation that gave rise to the doctrines or laws. The narrative and the argumentative seem to be taken together. Members of the same tradition often argue with each other, and in a complementary way it is not uncommon for the lines to be drawn diagonally across traditions: Christians, Muslims and Jews who believe that one's interpretation should stay close to the plain sense will often find common cause and argue against their colleagues who are prepared to permit very broad latitude in interpretation. Philosophers listening in on this discussion will, incidentally, be intrigued to learn that it is highly irregular for any participant to defend his or her claims as 'a matter of faith'. They are nearly always supported by reference to texts instead. I am unsure of the precise import of this fact. It seems worth mentioning given that many philosophers suspect that religious people use their religious faith as a rhetorical means for blocking requests for reasons. Scriptural reasoning does not display this phenomenon.

Habermas' scheme makes it difficult to account for these practices of argumentation. He might say that there is some implied common philosophical method that makes such coordination possible, and in any particular argument he would be right. The most transparent arguments are between members of the same tradition who share a philosophical method; the most obscure arguments are between participants from different traditions who use different philosophical methods, and the latter can sometimes be far more significant as points of contact, or as obstacles, than which traditions they belong to. Arguments between members of different traditions who use the same philosophical methods (e.g. pragmatism, transcendental idealism, phenomenology) are far easier to map than arguments between members of the same tradition who use different philosophical methods. Yet although it is easier to map arguments between those who share a philosophical method, it remains the case that the members of the same tradition are in some sense closer to each other than members of different traditions. I do not know how to specify further this 'some sense'. At this stage, I can do no better than indicate that members of different traditions who share a philosophical language have arguments that are easier to follow than members of the same tradition who use different philosophical methods, but at the same time those who share a tradition have more in common than those who share a philosophical method. In this sense Habermas is closer to Williams and Milbank in the way that members of the same tradition are close to each other, even though his arguments with Lyotard or Rorty are easier for him and his readers to follow, because of their shared philosophical methods.

In chapter 4 we considered Habermas' distinction between 'normatively ascribed' and 'communicatively achieved' agreement. It was explained as the difference between (a) claims which appeal to *already accepted* background assumptions, and which invite a 'yes' response, and for which (in my interpretation) a 'no' would be intolerable and (b) claims which invite a 'yes or no' response and which are genuinely open to contradiction. For Habermas a communicatively achieved 'yes' is hard won, and therefore binds those who agree on it together in some socially significant way. This is an interesting idea because it raises the hope that the critical impulse that is almost always associated with loss of solidarity in a lifeworld is, for Habermas, also a potential source of being bound together, thus repairing what is often called the 'motivational deficit' in Kantian moral theories. I agree that Habermas has a point in differentiating between a 'yes' that is hard won and a 'yes' that is secured in advance. But it is far from obvious that this is directly related to social solidarity. Those who achieve a hard-won 'yes' may indeed be bound *to the decision* for the simple reason that it was so costly. But is it really clear that they would be bound *to each other* thereby? Possibly; but Habermas offers no good arguments for this, and so his claim cannot be evaluated further. Scriptural reasoning offers an alternative, and in some ways bleaker, scenario. There is genuine argumentation between participants, and it is by definition across different traditions. Most kinds of 'yes' that arise are certainly hard won in Habermas' sense. But are they 'normatively ascribed' or 'communicatively achieved'? Here scriptural reasoning is an anomaly for Habermas. By 'normatively ascribed', Habermas refers to assumptions *within one tradition* that secure agreement. By 'communicatively achieved', he means the generation of agreement *across traditions* without appeal to norms held to be true in only one tradition. But participants in scriptural reasoning acknowledge *only* the norms of their own tradition, and subject them to no higher authority except that of God.

Argument in scriptural reasoning can generate agreement across traditions, although agreement is not its goal: its goal is study rather than agreement. What, then, is the generation of agreement *across traditions* while appealing to assumptions *within one tradition*? Do participants in scriptural reasoning suspend their commitments to their tradition? They do not. Do they acknowledge the authority of the other tradition for themselves? They do not. Do they acknowledge the authority of the other tradition for the other? They do. This latter stance is by no means unintelligible for Habermas, but it is not one that he considers much. Habermas' characteristic move is to emphasise the transcending mechanisms inherent in things like translation, rather than focusing upon the aspects of a tradition which orient its members towards strangers. Scriptural reasoning does the reverse. Its members have almost no interest in 'shared' or 'common' assumptions, beyond the commitment to study together. Or, if they do show interest, it is a kind of delight in discovering such shared or common life; it is certainly not such sharing that makes study and argumentation possible. Instead, it is the desire for friendship with God, which is understood differently in each tradition, which illuminates desires for friendship across traditions, and which again is understood differently in each tradition, that brings people together for study.

Acknowledging the authority of the other tradition for the other is not 'rational assent' or an intellectual position vis-à-vis that tradition, but a gesture of friendship. It has something to do with hospitality, but as I have already indicated, in scriptural reasoning it is very difficult confidently to assign the roles of guest and host. It is vital to acknowledge that this is bleaker than Habermas' theory. The commitment to friendship, with God and stranger, is not 'communicatively achieved': it is already there. It is hard to imagine scriptural reasoning between participants who do not already share this commitment. Again, this commitment is understood differently in the three traditions and so cannot be counted, in a simple way, as common ground. In Habermas' theory, participants *become bound* by the process of argumentation. In scriptural reasoning they are *already bound* by their own traditions. Participants do form friendships, even very deep ones, with each other, but probably not because 'communicative action is a switching station for the energies of social solidarity' (Habermas 1987b: 57). Habermas' theory offers the *generation* of solidarity *across traditions*, if it is true. Scriptural reasoning does not. Neither does it rely on 'overlapping consensus': it relies wholly on *already existing* commitments *within one tradition*. The possibility of friendship in this environment is not theorisable, except in a vaguely Augustinian sense that people who love the same things are like each other. But notice that even this is a *Christian* observation, because it acknowledges Augustine as an authority, and Augustine's account of the unifying power of love is rooted in a Christian account of the relationship between God's love and human action.

There is, arguably, one aspect of scriptural reasoning that has something of a 'transcending' quality, in Habermas' sense. This is the fact that none of the three traditions encourages or even licenses *chevruta* study with members of the other two traditions. Participants come together as members of their own 'houses' of Islam, Judaism and Christianity. But they study in an imaginary 'tent of meeting' that belongs to God, and not to any of the houses.[5] The desire to enter this tent is intelligible *within* any one tradition, because it is a desire for God, and if God is to be found in this tent, then that is where I should be. But it also tugs in the opposite direction: it denies, somehow, the sufficiency of any one tradition. Now, this needs saying with some care: it cannot possibly mean (for me) that Christianity is in some sense insufficient, and Islam is more sufficient. If I were to express this belief, my Muslim colleagues would be the first to say that they cannot do scriptural reasoning with me, because I have forfeited the very difference between us that makes such study possible. Rather, it means acknowledging that God is great: greater than language, greater than traditions, greater than scripture. Here there can be no theory in a strong sense, because God's greatness cannot be circumscribed, and its extent cannot be charted. There is thus a transcendence of tradition, but this is identical with God's transcendence, and not with any human project – and certainly not with any appeal to 'reason', whether unified in its diverse voices (Habermas) or in any other way. Again, each tradition understands God's greatness differently; but each of these understandings seems to attract people into this tent of meeting. No theory is needed beyond that. And even if someone were clever enough to construct a good theory, it could never substitute for the *already learned* commitments within any one tradition.

---

[5] These terms come from an unpublished essay by David Ford, Daniel Hardy and Peter Ochs.

We have come a little way: argumentation and narrative are closer together in scriptural reasoning than Habermas believes them to be in university debate, and there is genuine argumentation in scriptural reasoning even though there is no commitment to some neutral or universal criterion that transcends the traditions. To return to a theme raised in chapter 4, disagreements between members of different traditions are not always experienced as 'intolerable', although disagreements between members of the same tradition can produce stresses when voiced in the company of strangers. The fact of tolerable disagreement, within and across traditions, ruins Habermas' easy distinction between sacred and modern forms of thinking. Nonetheless, we are still some way off from an account that can show how something like scriptural reason illuminates argumentation in the public sphere at the level of drafting and passing legislation. On this question, some reserve is essential. Scriptural reasoning actually happens: it is a practice that interested guests could find out about, witness and describe. Theoretical reflections come second. In the case of something big like the public sphere, scriptural reasoning has not been tried out much. As I indicated in chapter 1, we should equivocate about whether there can be an inter-religious public sphere in Habermas' sense, given that the public sphere is itself a tradition-specific concept. There are two problems with it. First, although it is a Christian institution by virtue of arising in Christian Europe, it has not been properly theorised within contemporary Christian theology; this is one of the tasks for Christian theology identified in chapter 10. Second, analogous terms need to be theorised within Judaism and Islam and other religious traditions. There is no public sphere in the Middle East; perhaps it displays a 'Muslim street' (Eikelman and Salvatore 2002). There is ample room here for scholarship within and across traditions. That said, scriptural reasoning has made little impact in the public sphere: there have been no instances, as yet, of committees drawing up recommendations for legislative bodies on the basis of discussions rooted in cross-traditional *chevruta*. There is no good purpose to speculating about what its outcomes might be. For the moment we must rest content with sowing the thought that it might be a good idea to find out how well it works. Someone should try it out. If the problem of argumentation in the public sphere is as serious as Habermas says it is, then a potential resource like scriptural reasoning – which offers not just the possibility but the actual practice of coordinating different traditions in argumentation – is too good an opportunity to pass over.

CONCLUSION

These remarks about scriptural reasoning are very sketchy, and it is perhaps rather naïve to ask them to bear the weight of this attempt at repair of Habermas' theory. I have claimed, rather than argued, that scriptural reasoning conforms rather well to a Hegelian account of ethical life rather than a Kantian account of morality, and to a Schellingian account of untheorisable thinking rather than a Hegelian account of the absolute. There is much work to be done here, and the task has been outlined here only in a very preliminary fashion. It is worth adding that none of this discussion amounts to a renewed apologetics. I am not sure that it could even be used to promote the superiority of theology over certain secular forms of reasoning. It seems to me that theology is only superior to other forms of thinking in those cases where it actually addresses what Peter Ochs, following Peirce, calls *real* as opposed to *imagined* doubts (Ochs 1998: 60). I doubt that theology can be shown *a priori* to be superior to rival forms of thinking, except in the rather minimal sense that it might under certain conditions be more consistent: only in situations where it is tested and performs well can really interesting claims of superiority be made. This is a rather unfashionable thought in theology these days. The Christian theological mood is confident and combative, and 'the secular' can be sure of a regular drubbing at the hands of skilled philosophical theologians. Yet a thought borrowed from Karl Marx suggests itself here. The theologians have only refuted the secular, in various ways; the point is to change it. Claims to superiority do not invariably serve this purpose well.

Scriptural reasoning is a fragile practice that can be tested and which offers the possibility of challenging and changing certain arenas that are seen as secular. Habermas is not going to be persuaded, at least not by this study, that he should take religion seriously as a modern post-metaphysical possibility. At best he might concede that I have exposed certain weaknesses in his arguments, and at worst he might suggest that my energies are misplaced and would have been better directed at developing the Hegelian and Schellingian critiques further. However, I think that he would be genuinely willing to learn from something like scriptural reasoning. Habermas is the kind of thinker who might readily concede not only the force of the better argument, but the force of the better practice. It is almost certain that he would give a more subtle description of scriptural reasoning than I am able to do, even though he could never do scriptural reasoning: he is formidably good at mapping processes of argumentation. Scriptural reasoning seems to me to be a better practice for coordinating different traditions in genuine argumentation than his own project of discourse ethics. It does so, however, in a very limited context: the interpretation of scripture in *chevruta* study, in predominantly academic contexts. This is, however, changing. Scriptural reasoning is being tried out in all sorts of contexts, and some of its practitioners hope that leaders from different religious communities might find themselves engaging in it in future. This really would be a powerful challenge to the secular, whose principal appeal is precisely its claim to reduce conflict rooted in religious difference through the promotion of neutral criteria for executive, legislative and judicial practices. Showing that the religions are better at healing their conflicts than the secular alternatives would not be just a rhetorical triumph. It would be to have changed something for the better.

The crucial feature of scriptural reasoning – and, in principle, any practice that discharges similar tasks – is that it does not require participants to bracket or suspend or conceal their traditional identities for the purpose of conversation and argumentation. Instead, it provides a context in which participants *learn each other's languages.* At one level this might mean something as basic as learning a few important words in Hebrew, Greek or Arabic. Obviously more encouraging is the possibility of learning the thicker languages of the traditions, not with the goal of inhabiting them but in order to hear the deep reasonings in what others are saying. What Stephen Toulmin calls the project of 'Cosmopolis' (Toulmin 1990) was the goal of discovering or fashioning a universal language that everyone might learn. Such a language would provide a culturally neutral means of communication which would abolish the messy entanglements that arise between actual historical languages. The problem with the cosmopolitan project was not that such a language was never found – one might argue that the new imperialism of spoken English or the dominance of computer languages like C or Java come close to universality – but that it fails *a priori* to house the thick things in life like kinship rules, eating practices, poetry, folk songs and the languages of elusive desire. The joy of learning another language is the discovery of all these things, expressed in fascinatingly unfamiliar ways. Particular languages house histories of wisdom. If members of two different traditions are to understand each other, they can certainly converse in a third language that is native to neither. That will work. But if they wish to understand each other's histories of wisdom, they must learn the other's language. Our children are taught in school that learning other languages is useful because they will be able to close a sale more rapidly if they speak the target language. Again, that will work. But we need to teach them that learning other languages is vital if there are to be friendships within which one learns each other's histories of wisdom, and which foster genuine argumentation in the public sphere. We might also acknowledge the inherent beauty of learning languages: it is a good with its own integrity.

This study has not proven that scriptural reasoning changes things for the better: only actual situations in which it is tested can do that. Instead, I have tried to take Habermas' fundamental problem with the greatest seriousness and to ask, with him, how members of different traditions can genuinely argue in the public sphere. My response has been to look, at some length, at his belief that religious thought has been, and should be, gradually left behind and to suggest, all too briefly, that there might be at least one form of religious practice which fosters genuine argument between members of different traditions. This is not yet argument in the public sphere, but it is perhaps good enough as a prototype, and time will tell whether it is extendable to a degree that will actually promote political change. It is a practice that encourages the learning of the other's language, and without more practices like these, the public sphere will be forced to host argumentation either in imperially dominant languages or in 'third languages' that are not common to any two participants. *Scriptural reasoning is exercised in multiple languages.* This is not the multiplicity of simultaneous translation, as at UN meetings where delegates are isolated from each other by headphones and the staccato chatter of information. It is the evocation of worlds and histories whose marks are left in ancient languages, leaving their traces in turn on participants who are always in the middle of learning to read and hear them. Processes of understanding are inseparable from processes of forming relationships. As Schleiermacher once observed: to understand the other you do not need to share a common language; the only formal requirement is the *desire* to understand the other. Scriptural reasoning schools desires, at the same time as skills, of understanding. The plural public sphere needs schools like this.

Habermas does not think that religious practice is much help beyond being the guardian of a powerful language of hope and healing. This is because he associates religious thought with the metaphysical, with the mythical and with the unreflective. I have placed obstacles in the way of these associations. More importantly, I have tried to outline a religious practice that paradigmatically cannot be called metaphysical, mythical or unreflective. Some Christian theologians have recently been trying to show how the Eucharist is a model for certain kinds of philosophical discourse, not least the articulation of a politics that is radically alternative to the tradition of Hobbes (Pickstock 1997; Milbank 2003). It remains to be seen whether it will feed into non-theological philosophy in the way Hegel's account of Spirit – a manifestly theological topos – shaped subsequent secular thinking. It might. I have looked not at the Eucharist, but at the practice of reading scripture. Like the Eucharist, it is a practice that models a type of philosophical discourse, including peaceful political implications, and it is a radical alternative to the tradition of Kant exemplified by Habermas. Unlike the Eucharist it is not particular to only one tradition, and can be shared. It does not teach a language, but models a practice of learning languages. Just as in combative theologies that meditate on the Eucharist, in the case of scriptural reasoning too it remains to be seen how well it will influence a realm that is disastrously dominated by the view that religion is not just the problem historically but is inevitably and always the problem in public discussion. The advantage of scriptural reasoning is that it not only challenges certain secular assumptions, but obviously brings together members of different traditions in a way that should be quite unintelligible if an account like Habermas' is correct. Scriptural reasoning is very likely not going to cause mass conversions to any of the Abrahamic traditions. But there are millions who are already members of these traditions and who do not yet know how to argue peaceably with each other. Scriptural reasoning is aimed at them. It might not be the solution to every problem.

But secular approaches to religion are not working. It's time to try something new.

References

Adams, Nicholas (2000) 'Eschatology Sacred and Profane: The Effects of Philosophy on Theology in Pannenberg, Rahner and Moltmann', *International Journal of Systematic Theology*, vol. 2, no. 2, pp. 283–306

Alexy, Robert (1978) *Theorie der juristischen Argumentation: die Theorie des rationalen Diskurses als Theorie der juristischen Begründung*, Frankfurt: Suhrkamp

Ameriks, Karl (ed.) (2000) *The Cambridge Companion to German Idealism*, Cambridge: Cambridge University Press

Arens, Edmund (ed.) (1989) *Habermas und die Theologie: Beiträge zur theologischen Rezeption, Diskussion und Kritik der Theorie kommunikativen Handelns*, Düsseldorf: Patmos

  (1995) *Christopraxis: A Theology of Action*, Minneapolis: Fortress

Barth, Karl (1957) *Church Dogmatics II.2*, ed. G. W. Bromiley and T. F. Torrance, Edinburgh: T.&T. Clark

Bauckham, Richard (1987) *Moltmann: Messianic Theology in the Making*, Basingstoke: Marshall Pickering

Bauer, Karl (1987) *Der Denkweg von Jürgen Habermas zur Theorie des kommunikativen Handelns: Grundlagen einer neuen Fundamentaltheologie?*, Regensburg: Roderer

Behler, Ernst (1993) *German Romantic Literary Theory*, Cambridge: Cambridge University Press

Beiser, Frederick (1987) *The Fate of Reason: German Philosophy from Kant to Fichte*, London: Harvard University Press

  (2002) *German Idealism: The Struggle against Subjectivism 1781–1801*, London: Harvard University Press

Bendersky, Joseph W. (1983) *Carl Schmitt: Theorist for the Reich*, Princeton: Princeton University Press

Benhabib, Seyla (1986) *Critique, Norm and Utopia*, New York: Columbia University Press

Bernstein, J. M. (1995) *Recovering Ethical Life*, London: Routledge, 1995

Bernstein, Richard (1978) *The Restructuring of Social and Political Theory*, Cambridge: Cambridge University Press

(ed.) (1985) *Habermas and Modernity*, Cambridge: Polity

Bloch, Ernst (1959–) *Gesamtausgabe*, Frankfurt-on-Main: Suhrkamp Verlag

Bowie, Andrew (1990) *Aesthetics and Subjectivity from Kant to Nietzsche*, Manchester: Manchester University Press

(1993) *Schelling and Modern European Philosophy*, London: Routledge

(1997) *From Romanticism to Critical Theory: The Philosophy of German Literary Theory*, London: Routledge

(2003) *Introduction to German Philosophy from Kant to Habermas*, Cambridge: Polity

Browning, Don and Fiorenza, Francis Schlüssler (eds.) (1992) *Habermas, Modernity and Public Theology*, New York: Crossroad

Buckley, Michael (1987) *At the Origins of Modern Atheism*, New Haven: Yale University Press

Calhoun, Craig (ed.) (1992) *Habermas and the Public Sphere*, London: MIT

Campbell, Margaret (1999) *Critical Theory and Liberation Theology: A Comparison of the Initial Work of Jürgen Habermas and Gustavo Gutiérrez*, New York: Peter Lang

Dallmayr, Fred (1991) *Lifeworld, Modernity and Critique: Paths between Heidegger and the Frankfurt School*, Cambridge: Polity

Desmond, William (2003) *Hegel's God: A Counterfeit Double?*, Aldershot: Ashgate

Dews, Peter (1987) *Logics of Disintegration: Post-structuralist Thought and the Claims of Critical Theory*, London: Verso

(ed.) (1999) *Habermas: A Critical Reader*, Oxford: Blackwell

Dryzek, John (1990) *Discursive Democracy: Politics, Policy and Political Science*, Cambridge: Cambridge University Press

Düringer, Hermann (1999) *Universale Vernunft und partikularer Glaube: eine theologische Auswertung des Werkes von Jürgen Habermas*, Leuven: Peeters

Durkheim, Emile (1995) *The Elementary Forms of Religious Life*, tr. Karen Fields, London: Free Press

Eikelman, Dale and Salvatore, Armando (2002) 'The Public Sphere and Muslim Identities', *Arch. Europ. Sociol.*, vol. 43, no. 1, pp. 92–115

Engel, Ulrich (1995) 'Konsens und Wahrheit: Reflexionen im Anschluß an Jürgen Habermas: Der Dominikanerorden als praktisch verfaßte Kommunikationsgemeinschaft', in Thomas Eggensperger and Ulrich Engel (eds.) *Wahrheit: Recherchen zwischen Hochscholastik und Postmoderne*, Mainz: Matthias-Grünewald, pp. 130–48

Ernst, Cornelius (1979) *Multiple Echo*, ed. F. Kerr and T. Radcliffe, London: DLT

Fergusson, David (2004) *Church, State and Civil Society*, Cambridge: Cambridge University Press

Finlayson, Gordon (1999) 'Does Hegel's Critique of Kant's Moral Theory Apply to Discourse Ethics?', in Peter Dews (ed.) *Habermas: A Critical Reader*, Oxford: Blackwell, pp. 29–52

Ford, David and Pecknold, Chad (forthcoming) *The Promise of Scriptural Reasoning*, Oxford: Blackwell

Forrester, Duncan (1997) *Christian Justice and Public Policy*, Cambridge: Cambridge University Press

Franks, Paul (2000) 'All or Nothing: Systematicity and Nihilism in Jacobi, Reinhold, and Maimon', in Karl Ameriks (ed.) *The Cambridge Companion to German Idealism*, Cambridge: Cambridge University Press, pp. 95–116

Frei, Hans (1974) *The Eclipse of Biblical Narrative: A Study in Eighteenth and Nineteenth Century Hermeneutics*, New Haven: Yale University Press

Funkenstein, Amos (1986) *Theology and the Scientific Imagination*, Princeton: Princeton University Press

Gadamer, Hans-Georg (1989) *Truth and Method*, 2nd edn, tr. J. Weinsheimer and D. Marshalls, New York: Continuum

Geuss, Raymond (1981) *The Idea of a Critical Theory: Habermas and the Frankfurt School*, Cambridge: Cambridge University Press

Glebe-Möller, Jens (1987) *A Political Dogmatic*, Philadelphia: Fortress

Godelier, Maurice (1977) 'Myth and History: Reflections on the Foundations of the Primitive Mind', in *Perspectives in Marxist Anthropology*, Cambridge: Cambridge University Press, pp. 204–20

Habermas, Jürgen (1962) *Strukturwandel der Öffentlichkeit*, Neuwied: Luchterhand

  (1970) 'Towards a Theory of Communicative Competence', *Inquiry*, vol. 13, pp. 360–75

  (1971) 'Vorbereitende Bemerkungen zu einer Theorie der kommunikativen Kompetenz', in Jürgen Habermas and Niklas Luhmann (eds.) *Theorie der Gesellschaft oder Sozialtechnologie*, Frankfurt: Suhrkamp, pp. 101–41

  (1973) 'Wahrheitstheorien', in H. Fahrenbach (ed.) *Wirklichkeit und Reflexion: Walter Schulz zum 60. Geburtstag*, Pfüllingen: Neske

  (1983) *Philosophical-Political Profiles*, tr. F. Lawrence, Cambridge: Polity

  (1984a) *Theory of Communicative Action I: Reason and the Rationalization of Society*, tr. T. McCarthy, Cambridge: Polity

  (1984b) *Communication and the Evolution of Society*, tr. T. McCarthy, Cambridge: Polity

(1987a) *The Philosophical Discourse of Modernity*, tr. F. Lawrence, Cambridge: Polity

(1987b) *The Theory of Communicative Action II: The Critique of Functionalist Reason*, tr. T. McCarthy, Cambridge: Polity

(1987c) *Knowledge and Human Interests*, tr. J. Shapiro, Cambridge: Polity

(1988a) *On the Logic of the Social Sciences*, tr. S. Weber Nicholsen and J. Stark, Cambridge: Polity

(1988b) *Theory and Practice*, tr. J. Viertel, Cambridge: Polity

(1989a) *The Structural Transformation of the Public Sphere*, tr. T. Burger, Cambridge: Polity

(1989b) *The New Conservatism*, ed. and tr. S. Weber Nicholsen, Cambridge: Cambridge University Press

(1990) *Moral Consciousness and Communicative Action*, tr. C. Lenhardt and S. Weber Nicholsen, Cambridge: Polity

(1992a) *Postmetaphysical Thinking: Philosophical Essays*, tr. W. M. Hohengarten, Cambridge, Polity

(1992b) 'Work and Weltanschauung: The Heidegger Controversy from a German Perspective', in H. Dreyfus and H. Hall (eds.) *Heidegger: A Critical Reader*, Oxford: Blackwell, pp. 186–208

(1993a) *Justification and Application*, tr. C. Cronin, Cambridge: Polity

(1993b) *Theorie und Praxis*, 6th edn, Frankfurt: Suhrkamp

(1997) *Vom sinnlichen Eindruck zum symbolischen Ausdruck*, Frankfurt: Suhrkamp

(1998) *The Inclusion of the Other: Studies in Political Theory*, tr. C. Cronin, Cambridge, Mass.: MIT

(2001) *The Liberating Power of Symbols: Philosophical Essays*, tr. Peter Dews, Cambridge: Polity

(2002) *Religion and Rationality: Essays on Reason, God, and Modernity*, ed. E. Mendieta, Cambridge: Polity

(2003a) *The Future of Human Nature*, tr. W. Rehg, M. Pensky and H. Beister, Cambridge: Polity

(2003b) *Truth and Justification*, tr. B. Fultner, Cambridge: Polity

Hahn, Lewis Edwin (ed.) (2000) *Perspectives on Habermas*, Chicago: Open Court, 2000

Hannay, Alastair and Marino, Gordon (eds.) (1998) *The Cambridge Companion to Kierkegaard*, Cambridge: Cambridge University Press

Harrington, Austin (2001) *Hermeneutic Dialogue and Social Science: A Critique of Gadamer and Habermas*, London: Routledge

Hegel, G. W. F. (1969) *Hegel's Science of Logic*, tr. A. V. Miller, London: George Allen & Unwin

(1975) *Lectures on the Philosophy of World History: Introduction*, tr. H. Nisbet, Cambridge: Cambridge University Press

(1985a) *Lectures on the Philosophy of Religion, Vol. 1: Introduction and The Concept of Religion*, ed. P. Hodgson, London: University of California Press

(1985b) *Lectures on the Philosophy of Religion, Vol. III: The Consummate Religion*, ed. P. Hodgson, London: University of California Press

(1991) *The Philosophy of History*, tr. J. Sibree, New York: Prometheus Books

(1999) *Wissenschaft der Logik: Das Sein (1812)*, ed. F. Hogemann and W. Jaeschke, Hamburg: Meiner

Held, David (1980) *Introduction to Critical Theory: Horkheimer to Habermas*, London: Hutchinson

Henrich, Dieter (2003) *Between Kant and Hegel*, ed. David Pacini, London: Harvard University Press

Hobbes, Thomas (1996) *Leviathan*, ed. R. Tuck, Cambridge: Cambridge University Press

Höhn, Hans-Joachim (1985) *Kirche und kommunicatives Handeln: Studien zur Theologie und Praxis der Kirche in der Auseinandersetzung mit den Sozialtheorien Niklas Luhmanns und Jürgen Habermas*, Frankfurt: Joseph Knecht

Horkheimer, Max (1982) 'The End of Reason', in *The Essential Frankfurt School Reader*, ed. Andrew Arato and Eike Gebhardt, New York: Continuum, pp. 26–48

How, Alan (1995) *The Habermas–Gadamer Debate and the Nature of the Social*, Aldershot: Avebury

Ingram, David (1987) *Habermas and the Dialectic of Reason*, New Haven: Yale University Press

Jacobi, F. H. (1994) *The Main Philosophical Writings and the Novel Allwill*, tr. G di Giovanni, London: McGill-Queen's University Press

Junker-Kenny, Maureen (1998) *Argumentationsethik und christliches Handeln*, Stuttgart: Kohlhammer

Kant, Immanuel (1996) *Practical Philosophy*, tr. and ed. Mary Gregor, Cambridge: Cambridge University Press, 1996

Kerr, Fergus (2002) *After Aquinas: Versions of Thomism*, Oxford: Blackwell

Kierkegaard, Søren (1983) *Fear and Trembling; Repetition*, tr. H. Hong and E. Hong, Princeton: Princeton University Press

Knapp, Markus (1993) *Gottes Herrschaft als Zukunft der Welt: biblische, theologiegeschichtliche und systematische Studien zur Grundlegung einer Reich-Gottes-Theologie in Auseinandersetzung mit Jürgen Habermas' Theorie des kommunikativen Handelns*, Würzburg: Echter

Kodalle, Klaus-Michael (1973) *Politik als Macht und Mythos: Carl Schmitts 'Politische Theologie'*, Stuttgart: Kohlhammer

Kortian, Garbis (1980) *Metacritique*, tr. J. Raffan, Cambridge: Cambridge University Press

Lakeland, Paul (1990) *Theology and Critical Theory: The Discourse of the Church*, Nashville: Abingdon

Lalonde, Marc (1999) *Critical Theology and the Challenge of Jürgen Habermas*, New York: Peter Lang

Lash, Nicholas (1992) *Believing Three Ways in One God*, London: SCM
(1996) *The Beginning and the End of 'Religion'*, Cambridge: Cambridge University Press

Luther, Henning (1991) '"Ich ist ein Anderer". Die Bedeutung von Subjekt-theorien (Habermas, Levinas) für die Praktische Theologie', in Dietrich Zilleßen, Stefan Alkier, Ralf Koerrenz and Harald Schroeter (eds.) *Praktisch-theologische Hermeneutik*, Rheinbach-Merzbach: CMZ, pp. 233–54

McCarthy, Thomas (1982) *The Critical Theory of Jürgen Habermas*, rev. edn, Cambridge, Mass.: MIT
(1991) *Ideals and Illusion: On Reconstruction and Deconstruction in Contemporary Critical Theory*, Cambridge, Mass.: MIT

McCormick, John P. (1997) *Carl Schmitt's Critique of Liberalism*, Cambridge: Cambridge University Press

McFadyen, Alistair (1990) *The Call to Personhood: A Christian Theory of the Individual in Social Relationships*, Cambridge: Cambridge University Press

Magnus, Bernd and Higgins, Kathleen (1996) *The Cambridge Companion to Nietzsche*, Cambridge: Cambridge University Press

Marsh, James (1993) 'The Religious Significance of Habermas', *Faith and Philosophy*, vol. 10, pp. 521–38

Matik, Marko (1983) *Jürgen Moltmanns Theologie in Auseinandersetzung mit Ernst Bloch*, Frankfurt-on-Main: Peter Lang

Matustík, Martin (1993) *Postnational Identity: Critical Theory and Existential Philosophy in Habermas, Kierkegaard, and Havel*, London: Guilford Press

Mead, George Herbert (1934) *Mind, Self and Society from the Standpoint of a Social Behaviorist*, ed. C. W. Morris, Chicago: Chicago University Press

Milbank, John (1990) *Theology and Social Theory*, Oxford: Blackwell
(1997) *The Word Made Strange,* Oxford: Blackwell
(2003) *Being Reconciled: Ontology and Pardon*, London: Routledge

Moltmann, Jürgen (1964) *Theologie der Hoffnung*, Munich: Chr. Kaiser
(1975) *The Experiment Hope*, tr. M. D. Meeks, Philadelphia: Fortress
(1976) *Im Gespräch mit Ernst Bloch: Eine theologische Wegbegleitung*, Munich: Chr. Kaiser
(1996) *The Coming of God: Christian Eschatology*, tr. M. Kohl, London: SCM Press

Morse, Christopher (1979) *The Logic of Promise in Moltmann's Theology*, Philadelphia: Fortress Press

Ochs, Peter (1998) *Peirce, Pragmatism and the Logic of Scripture*, Cambridge: Cambridge University Press

O'Donovan, Oliver (1996) *The Desire of the Nations: Rediscovering the Roots of Political Theology*, Cambridge: Cambridge University Press

Ophir, Adi (1989) 'The Ideal Speech Situation', in Y. Yovel (ed.) *Kant's Practical Philosophy Reconsidered*, Dordrecht: Kluwer

O'Regan, Cyril (1995) *The Heterodox Hegel*, Albany: SUNY

Outhwaite, William (1994) *Habermas: A Critical Introduction*, Cambridge: Polity

Owen, David (1994) *Maturity and Modernity: Nietzsche, Weber, Foucault and the Ambivalence of Reason*, London: Routledge

Pannenberg, Wolfhart (1969) *Theology and the Kingdom of God*, Philadelphia: Westminster Press.

Pauly, Wolfgang (1989) *Wahrheit und Konsens: Die Erkenntnistheorie von Jürgen Habermas und ihre theologische Relevanz*, Frankfurt: Lang

Pecknold, Chad (forthcoming) 'Democracy and the Politics of the Word: Stout and Hauerwas on Democracy and Scripture', *Scottish Journal of Theology*

Peukert, Helmut (1984) *Science, Action and Fundamental Theology*, tr. J. Bohman, Cambridge, Mass.: MIT

Pickstock, Catherine (1997) *After Writing*, Oxford: Blackwell

Pinkard, Terry (2002) *German Philosophy 1760–1860: The Legacy of Idealism*, Cambridge: Cambridge University Press

Pippin, Robert (1989) *Hegel's Idealism*, Cambridge: Cambridge University Press

  (1997) *Idealism as Modernism: Hegelian Variations*, Cambridge: Cambridge University Press

Quash, Ben (2005) *Theology and the Drama of History*, Cambridge: Cambridge University Press

Rendtorff, Trutz (1975) *Gesellschaft ohne Religion? Theologische Aspekte einer sozialtheoretischen Kontroverse (Luhmann/Habermas)*, Munich: Piper

Ricoeur, Paul (1973) 'Ethics and Culture: Habermas and Gadamer in Dialogue', *Philosophy Today*, vol. 17, pp. 153–65

  (1982) 'Toward a Hermeneutic of the Idea of Revelation', in L. Mudge (ed.) *Essays on Biblical Interpretation*, London: SPCK, pp. 73–118

Roberts, Julian (1992) *The Logic of Reflection: German Philosophy in the Twentieth Century*, London: Yale University Press

Roderick, Rick (1986) *Habermas and the Foundations of Critical Theory*, London: Macmillan

Rose, Gillian (1981) *Hegel Contra Sociology*, London: Athlone

Rothberg, Donald Jay (1986) 'Rationality and Religion in Habermas' Recent Work: Some Remarks between Critical Theory and the

Phenomenology of Religion', *Philosophy and Social Criticism*, vol. II, pp. 221–43

Schillebeeckx, Edward (1974) *The Understanding of Faith: Interpretation and Criticism*, London: Sheed and Ward

Schleiermacher, F. D. E. (1998) *Hermeneutics and Criticism*, tr. and ed. Andrew Bowie, Cambridge: Cambridge University Press

Schmidt, Thomas (1994) 'Immanente Transzendenz und der Sinn des Unbedingten: Zur Bestimmung des Verhältnisses von Religion und Philosophie bei Jürgen Habermas', in Linus Hauser and Eckhard Nordhofen (eds.) *Im Netz der Begriffe: religions-philosophische Analysen*, Altenberge: Oros, pp. 78–96

Schmitt, Carl (1985) *Political Theology: Four Chapters on the Concept of Sovereignty*, tr. G. Schwab, London: MIT

Schnädelbach, Herbert (1991) 'Remarks about Rationality and Language', in *The Communicative Ethics Controversy*, ed. S. Benhabib and F. Dallmayr, Cambridge, Mass.: MIT, pp. 270–92

Schwab, George (1989) *The Challenge of the Exception*, London: Greenwood

Shanks, Andrew (1991) *Hegel's Political Theology*, Cambridge: Cambridge University Press

(2000) *God and Modernity: A New and Better Way to Do Theology*, London: Routledge

Siebert, Rudolf (1985) *The Critical Theory of Religion*, Berlin: Mouton

Silverman, Hugh (ed.) (1991) *Gadamer and Hermeneutics: Science, Culture, Literature*, London: Routledge

Skinner, Quentin (1982) 'Habermas' Reformation', *New York Review of Books*, 7 October, pp. 35–8

Stout, Jeffrey (2004) *Democracy and Tradition*, Princeton: Princeton University Press

Teigas, Demetrius (1995) *Knowledge and Hermeneutic Understanding: The Habermas–Gadamer Debate and the Nature of the Social*, Lewisburg: Bucknell University Press

Theunissen, Michael (1970) *Hegels Lehre vom absoluten Geist als theologisch-politischer Traktat*, Berlin: de Gruyter

(1981) *Kritische Theorie der Gesellschaft*, Berlin: de Gruyter

(1997) *Negative Theologie der Zeit*, Frankfurt: Suhrkamp

Thompson, John B. (1981) *Critical Hermeneutics*, Cambridge: Cambridge University Press

(1990) *Ideology and Modern Culture: Critical Social Theory in the Era of Mass Communication*, Cambridge: Polity

Thompson, John B. and Held, David (eds.) (1982) *Habermas: Critical Debates*, Cambridge, Mass.: MIT

Toulmin, Stephen (1990) *Cosmopolis*, Chicago: Chicago University Press

Tracy, David (1981) *The Analogical Imagination: Christian Theology and the Culture of Pluralism*, New York: Crossroad

Vico, Giovanni Battista (1948) *The New Science*, tr. T. Bergin and M. Fisch, Ithaca: Cornell University Press

Walsh, Thomas (1989) 'Religion, Politics and Life Worlds: Jürgen Habermas and Richard John Neuhaus', in Jeffrey Hadden and Anson Shupe (eds.) *Secularization and Fundamentalism Reconsidered*, New York: Paragon House, pp. 91–106

Weber, Max (1964) *Religion of China*, tr. and ed. H. Gerth, New York: Free Press

Welker, Michael (1995) *Kirche im Pluralismus*, Gütersloh: Chr. Kaiser

Wellmer, Albrecht (1991) 'Ethics and Dialogue: Elements of Moral Judgement in Kant and Discourse Ethics', in *The Persistence of Modernity: Essays in Aesthetics, Ethics and Postmodernism*, tr. D. Midgley, Cambridge: Polity, pp. 113–231

White, Stephen K. (1988) *The Recent Work of Jürgen Habermas: Reason, Justice and Modernity*, Cambridge: Cambridge University Press

(ed.) (1995) *The Cambridge Companion to Habermas*, Cambridge: Cambridge University Press

Williams, Rowan (1995) 'Between Politics and Metaphysics: Reflections in the Wake of Gillian Rose', *Modern Theology*, vol. 11, no. 1, pp. 3ff.

(2000) *On Christian Theology*, Oxford: Blackwell

Index